FROM HERE TO THERE AND BACK AGAIN

An Autobiography

By

A. John Smither

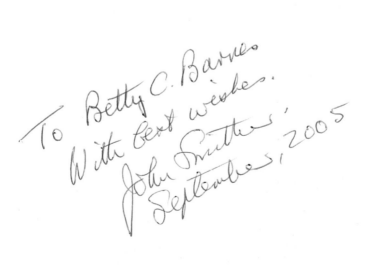

To Betty C. Barnes
With best wishes.
John Smither
September, 2005

ISBN: 1-4107-4218-0 (e-book)
ISBN: 1-4107-4217-2 (Paperback)

Library of Congress Control Number: 2003092384

This book is printed on acid free paper.

Printed in the United States of America
Bloomington, IN

1stBooks - rev. 05/10/03

CONTENTS

WITH LOVE

To my children, David, Nancy, James and Vivian, my grandchildren, David, Jessica, Timothy, Andrew, Benjamin, Kristin and Rebecca and my great-grandsons, Alijah and Cameron, whose curiosity concerning my childhood in England was the inspiration for this literary effort. And to Sally, my dearest wife and best friend, without whose support and encouragement I might not have found the time nor mustered the energy to finish what I started.

PREFACE

Blessed by chance and circumstance to be born in the United States of America in 1927, my life changed dramatically a year later when my parents, with my older sister and I in tow, left their home in Cleveland, Ohio, ostensibly on a short visit to see their families in England, and never returned.

As a result, I lived for seventeen years in England as a "dual-national" before claiming my American citizenship by enlisting in the U.S. Army during World War II. Discharged in the United States in November 1946, I've lived in the land of my birth ever since.

Not unexpectedly, over the years many people, including my own children and grandchildren, have asked the obvious questions: "Where did you get that funny accent?" and, "If you were born here, why did you live in England?" and "What was it like in London during the war?"

In 1999, my oldest granddaughter Jessica, while attending the Bradford, PA campus of the University of Pittsburgh, wrote asking whether she could interview me for a journalism class project on my childhood recollections of England. I agreed to do this and prepared myself for the session by making notes on events that I thought would be of particular interest, but for some reason, Jessica never followed up on her request.

Some months later, as I was about to discard the notes I'd made, my wife suggested, as she had done so often before, that I take the time to write down what it was like to be a child in England during the Great Depression and to live in London through World War II, when England's capital was a "front-line" city, under constant attack from the air for more than five years.

So, what began as notes for a granddaughter's interview blossomed into an autobiography which I've limited somewhat, as follows. Recognizing it was the unusual circumstances of my being born in the United States and growing up in England that prompted this effort, I made the decision to cover only the first 21 years of my life in detail, and merely summarize the highlights of my business career and community activities, and those personal events that helped shape my life during the ensuing 55 years.

Limited as it is in that regard, I hope this autobiography will be read and enjoyed by my family and friends, and perhaps even treasured by future members of the Smither clan, for its value as a window through which they may catch a glimpse into the early life and times, of one of their dear departed.

With my parents long deceased, and having never kept a personal journal, I had to rely solely on my own memory, augmented as respects my childhood years, with input from my two sisters. Their comments on the draft copies I periodically sent them were a great help, although occasionally we found our respective recollections of certain events to be at odds. When that happened, my sisters always graciously agreed that my memories should prevail over theirs.

I further decided that when writing about the tumultuous years leading up to and including World War II, I would weave into the tapestry of my own mundane life experiences, those history making events that were occurring throughout the world at the same time. In so doing, I had an important purpose in mind.

No event in recent history has had a greater impact on Mother Earth's family of nations than the Second World War. Yet despite America's enormous contribution to the Allied cause, without which Germany and Japan would not have been defeated, this important and significant chapter in our country's history, rarely gets addressed or taught in our schools or universities.

Consequently, post-war generations have little or no knowledge of the events of that time, or of the incredible sacrifices made by so many in an honorable crusade to bring peace to the world, and to restore freedom to those millions who had been cruelly enslaved.

Hopefully, my present family members and those of generations yet to come, as they read this book, will gain at least a passing knowledge of the major events associated with the 20th Century's bloodiest and most costly conflict, and a greater appreciation of the many blessings inherent in their American birthright.

CHAPTER 1

English Roots, An American Birthright

I was born on Thursday, April 14, 1927, in Garfield Heights, a suburb of Cleveland, Ohio. Many years later, on a subsequent birthday, a friend presented me with a replica of the April 14, 1927 front page of the New York Herald Tribune. Major headlines focused on the war in China between Nationalist and Communist rebel forces and the feat of two citizen aviators, who, flying out of an airport on Long Island, had set a new American record for sustained flight without refueling. But alas, there was no mention of the first male Smither born that day in the USA!

My father, Benjamin Edward Smither (Ben), was born in July, 1896, and had emigrated from England in 1920. My mother, Esther Matilda Pickett (Hett), who was born in December, 1898, followed my father to the States in 1922. Both were "Cockneys" having been born and raised in Walthamstow, a working-class neighborhood in East London, and were in their teens when they first met.

Dad had an older brother Albert and five younger siblings, Samuel, Hettie, Leonard, Reginald and Herbert. Two other sisters (twins) died at birth. Mom had five older siblings, Walter, Ernest, Ann, May and Lillian.

The only story I remember hearing from Dad about his childhood, concerned an elementary school episode when, as a punishment for a behavior infraction, his male teacher locked him in the classroom closet for an extended period then sent him home before the school-day had ended. His mother, after hearing his tearful account of the incident, put on one of her husband's caps, fastened it securely to her hair with an oversized hatpin, and marched her son back to school and into his classroom. There, before an expectant audience of small boys, she confronted the teacher who had closeted her son.

Obviously, this man had never met my grandmother! He readily admitted to what he'd done and rather arrogantly added that "he'd do it again" if he thought it necessary. At that time, my diminutive grandmother grabbed the teacher by his nose in a vice-like grip, dragged him into the closet and locked the door, to the cheers of the assembled class.

In 1910, in keeping with the working-class customs of the day, Dad's formal education ended on his fourteenth birthday, when he was apprenticed to a local furniture factory where his father, Benjamin Joseph Smither, worked as a wood-machinist and his grandfather, Samuel Smither, was a master cabinet-maker.

Dad's brother Albert had a rich tenor voice and loved to sing. Dad, absent any formal training but with an obvious ear for music, had somehow learned to play the piano. Many Saturday nights during 1913-14, they performed as a team at local vaudeville music halls, where they were popular enough to secure frequent and return bookings. Dad was also a fair soccer player, good enough to play regularly in a local semi-professional team.

On June 28, 1914, in the Bosnian town of Sarajevo, then located within the Austria-Hungarian Empire, the heir apparent to the Empire's throne, Archduke Ferdinand, and his wife Sophie were assassinated by Serbian nationalists, a tragic event which, within six weeks, led to the beginning of World War I. For England, the war began on August 3, 1914, when its ultimatum calling for Germany to withdraw its armies from its borders with France and Belgium went unanswered.

Responding immediately with patriotic fervor but little or no conception of the ghastly slaughter that lay ahead, thousands of young men, including my father and his brother Albert, volunteered to serve in the British Army. Dad entered the Essex Regiment and was assigned to a Signal Corps company. During my childhood, I can't ever recall hearing anything about my Uncle Albert's military service, except that he was killed sometime between March, 1915 and January, 1916, in Britain's ill-fated Gallipoli invasion of Turkey (an ally of Germany) a campaign that cost over 250,000 British, Australian and New Zealand casualties.

My Dad, while miraculously surviving four years in the bloody trenches of France and Belgium, did not emerge entirely unscathed. At the war's end, he was one of only seventeen men left from those who were part of his original regiment at the time of his enlistment.

He had been hospitalized from direct exposure to three separate poison-gas attacks, from superficial shrapnel wounds to his face and for treatment of the symptoms of battle-fatigue, or "shell shock" as it was then known.

Additionally, during his service, he'd become addicted to alcohol, this condition no doubt directly connected to his long exposure to the horrors of trench warfare. On a temporary basis at least, alcohol managed to blot out all that Dad had seen and experienced. As a result, he became (in his own words) a "fall-down-drunk" whenever away from his Army unit.

The only photo I have of my father in uniform was taken while on leave in London. Posing with my mother, in celebration of their engagement, he'd been drinking to excess as usual, and moments after the photo was taken, he fell off his chair and passed out!

If what I know about my father and his family before he left England for the States is somewhat sparse, I must confess that I know even less about my mother's family or her early years.

My maternal grandmother died in 1929, so I have absolutely no memories of her. I can only recall meeting my maternal grandfather twice before he died some four or five years later. I am not sure what his regular occupation was, except at some point he supposedly worked as a servant at Buckingham Palace.

Two of my mother's sisters, Aunt May and Aunt Lillian, I never met. Both had children out of wedlock during World War I and, tragically, both died in their thirties. Mom's unmarried sister Ann, elected to raise May's daughter Ivy. Lillian's son Harold was placed in an orphanage outside of London.

I never met my Uncle Walter either. He had emigrated to Canada after the Great War and died there in an automobile accident. Mom's other brother Ernie, who I can only remember meeting once, lived in Manchester, Lancashire, where he toiled as a "turf accountant", or "bookie" as he would have been known in the USA.

Mom, like Dad, left school at fourteen to work in a local factory. She began dating my father at sixteen and when she was eighteen, (halfway through World War I) they became engaged, no doubt expecting that theirs would be a post-war marriage, at the completion of Dad's Army service.

However, following his discharge in early 1919 and after trying unsuccessfully to find employment, Dad decided that he wanted to get married and, with his bride, seek a new life in the USA. That plan didn't sit well with Mom's parents, who weren't thrilled at the prospect of their youngest daughter finding herself married to a man with an alcohol problem, still without gainful employment, and living 3000 miles away from the family circle.

Dad was adamant about leaving England, but a compromise was reached. The marriage would be postponed. Dad would book passage to America as soon as possible and, after securing work and a place to live, my mother would follow. Her leaving England was conditioned on Dad's promise to her parents that he'd meet her ship when it docked in New York and that they would proceed to get married on the spot. I suspect that my parents, in agreeing to that arrangement, never anticipated an extended separation or how long it would be before they would see each other again.

My father left England in early 1920, one of the thousands of legal immigrants from Europe who flocked to the USA during the decade following the end of World War I. All came by ship and most, like Dad, traveled "steerage." (The 1998 movie *Titanic* gave the world a realistic glimpse of "steerage" accommodations.)

All immigrants arriving in New York passed through Ellis Island, where they were subject to a routine interview and passport check to confirm that their entry was indeed legitimate. This was then followed by a physical exam to ensure that they did not constitute a public health risk. Those individuals whose entry, for whatever reason, was declared not legal, were returned to their country of origin.

Those who did not pass their physicals, depending upon the seriousness of their health problems, were either denied entry and returned, or kept in isolation until declared fit by a physician. When Dad's ship docked, he was suffering from vaccine fever and as a result, was detained a few days on Ellis Island before being allowed to take the ferry into New York City. Upon his release, he promptly bought a train ticket to Cleveland, Ohio.

Dad's decision to make Cleveland his home came out of a chance wartime meeting in France a few months before the 1918 armistice. While on patrol as a Signal Corps lineman, he came upon a piano, abandoned but relatively undamaged, amid the wreckage of a house. Dad never could resist a "silent" piano and despite the bizarre circumstances, this was to be no exception.

Apparently, his impromptu musical interlude caught the ear of a passing US Army physician from Cleveland, Ohio. During that brief encounter, the Yank urged Dad to look him up if he was ever in the States, a casual invitation he clearly always remembered.

Upon his arrival in Cleveland Dad contacted his physician acquaintance, who not only remembered him, but took the time to assist him in finding lodgings suitable for a working-class bachelor. He also helped Dad get his first job as a "soda-jerk" in a local drugstore. Ironically, the store owner pharmacist was an immigrant from Germany, who always referred to Dad as the "Englishman" and who apparently took a vicarious delight in having him subject to his orders and direction so soon after Germany's defeat in the Great War.

Dad also worked as a "pressman" in an automobile tire factory and, for a number of years, was able to parlay his musical talent into a part-time career. Seated at a piano in the front of a movie theater, he would play whatever "mood" music he thought appropriate to the silent plot being projected onto the screen before him. Unfortunately, that career ended in 1927, when "The Jazz Singer", the world's first "talking" movie hit the screens and revolutionized the movie industry forever.

In 1922, some two years after Dad left England, my mother finally set sail for America. True to his earlier promise made to her parents, Dad journeyed from Cleveland to New York City to meet her and the two were finally reunited as Mom got off the Ellis Island Ferry. From there they went directly to a Registrar's Office to secure the necessary marriage license, following which they located the nearest Salvation Army Chapel. There, during a simple ceremony, the Commandant/Pastor pronounced them husband and wife, just in time for them to "honeymoon" on the first train back to Cleveland.

5

On September 23, 1923, Dad and Mom had their first child, a girl who, while christened "Margaret Victoria", was always called "Peg" by family and friends alike. Her birth was particularly significant in its positive impact on Dad, who until then still had a weakness for alcohol. At Peg's birth, Mom made him promise to stop drinking, and about that same time, Dad, who had grown up without any religious affiliation, became interested in the Christian Science Church, which was founded in the United States in 1866 by Mary Baker Eddy.

I don't know what it was about the Christian Science religion, but it clearly transformed Dad. He became a teetotaler and as long as I can remember, he made the reading of the Bible and Eddy's "Key to the Scriptures" a lifelong daily commitment.

Lacking much in the way of anecdotal information, it is difficult to record how my parents individually adjusted to life in their newly adopted country. From what I remember hearing as a child, I suspect that Mom was probably not as happy here as Dad. However, I'm sure they appreciated the comfortable and convenient household amenities that they enjoyed, having come from homes in London that lacked baths, hot running water, central heating or inside toilets. Typical of Mom's generation, her world as a housewife and mother was essentially limited to contact with neighbors, and while it is unlikely that she had any complaints in this regard, I suspect that she secretly pined for her family and friends in England.

Dad, on the other hand, developed a genuine love and affinity for the U.S. and all things American. Basic to these feelings was his discovery that American society was essentially "classless," unlike that which he had known in his native country.

In England, given his limited education, family background and accent, he would have been forever categorized as "lower class" and thus destined for medial or bottom-level jobs and positions, regardless of his personal ambition or talents and skills.

Growing up, I can only remember hearing Dad say positive things about America, and "opportunity" was the word he often used to describe what he admired most about this country. Clearly, he truly believed in the so-called "American Dream," that all citizens, regardless of their backgrounds, are guaranteed the personal freedom and equal opportunity to succeed (or fail) with constitutional protections, unique in all the world.

In 1926, Mom became pregnant for the second time and, as was recorded earlier herein, I entered this world on April 14, 1927, at 1:30am. Birth certificates in those days apparently contained no vital statistics such as baby's weight or length. My certificate indicates only that I was "white" and born "alive." The latter statistic, now that I think about it, was probably the only one that was vital and really mattered!

It is my understanding that my first given name "Albert" was chosen by my father, in remembrance of his older brother who was killed in action during the Great War. From the day I entered this world, I have been called "John" by everyone except my paternal grandfather who, for reasons of his own, always referred to me as "Jack" a moniker which I hated.

At that moment in history, the USA boasted a population of 119 million and an average annual income of $1,554. A three-bedroom house cost $4,825 and a new Ford cost $495. Gas sold for 21 cents a gallon, milk cost 28 cents a quart and bread 9 cents a loaf.

Unfortunately, my days in the land of my birth (at least the first time around) were to be numbered! My maternal grandmother in England was terminally ill, and later that year Mom convinced Dad that the family should return to England for a visit with her mother, before it was too late.

I expect that Dad agreed to her request reluctantly and with some trepidation. He and Mom had been taking the necessary steps to become naturalized citizens, but that process had not yet been finalized. I am sure he worried that if they left their adopted country without the benefit of American citizenship, reentry on British passports might be a problem, because by then, the previous "open-door" immigration policy had been greatly curtailed by new laws and ethnic quotas.

Nevertheless, early in April, 1928, my family left Cleveland on a train for New York City. Peg was four and a half years old and I was a week shy of my first birthday! The train coach was full and I've been told that during the overnight trip, lacking a cradle, Dad placed me in the overhead luggage rack to sleep.

From the train, we went directly to the docks and boarded the "Mauritania" our home for the next five days. This famous vessel, which at the time held the trans-Atlantic speed record, was a sister ship to the ill-fated "Lusitania" which was torpedoed in the Atlantic by a German U-boat on May 7, 1915, with a loss of 1,198 lives, including 128 Americans, a pivotal event which had fanned American sentiment in favor of entering the Great War.

During the uneventful passage to England, I celebrated my first birthday. Needless to say, I have no memories of that event nor of any part of the journey. My sister Peg, however, vaguely remembers that while sea-sickness confined our mother to the cabin for most of the voyage, Dad was unfazed by the Atlantic swells, spending most of his time "tickling the ivories" in the tourist class lounge, where he became an instant popular entertainer.

The Mauretania's home port was Southampton, and from there we went by train to London, where Mom and Dad were reunited with their respective families in Walthamstow. Neither of my grandparents had space enough in their homes to accommodate our foursome, so Dad rented rooms in a house in Chingford, a developing suburb north of Walthamstow.

The house was small, and we shared it with another couple. Not knowing for sure how long we would be in England, Dad had chosen to leave the States without making arrangements for our return. He probably figured he could cover the costs of a short visit and still have enough cash to get us back to Cleveland.

Fate however, had other plans. A month passed and Dad's mother-in-law, whose death was once thought to be imminent, was still hanging on. To complicate matters, soon thereafter, Mom learned that she was unexpectedly pregnant with her third child.

Out of these unforeseen circumstances and financial necessity, our short visit took on long term consequences. When his limited financial resources were depleted, Dad had no choice but to find work and resign himself to postponing the family's return to America indefinitely and perhaps forever.

Metropolitan London, where I would live for the next seventeen years, covered an area of 632 square miles and housed a population of more than 7 million people. For governing purposes, it was divided into 32 boroughs, each with its own neighborhood sub-divisions, consisting of multiple blocks of two, three or four-story look-alike row homes.

Most neighborhoods were illuminated by old-fashioned gas-lamps. I presume these were equipped with pilot lights as twice daily, at dusk and at dawn, an army of men called "gaslighters" would roam the streets, each carrying a long pole with which they reached up into the lamps to turn the flow of gas on and off.

It was a city where mail was delivered to homes and businesses at least twice a day and where, as I remember, neighborhood bars (pubs) and fish-and-chip shops were more numerous than churches.

London also boasted a very substantial cat population. Catering to their feline appetites were push-cart vendors who went door-to-door, peddling slices of cooked horse meat on little wooden skewers. They heralded their neighborhood presence by yelling "cats-meat man" at the top of their lungs.

Little did anyone know at that time, that during World War II when beef, pork and lamb was tightly rationed, horse meat would be sold in butcher shops for human consumption and purchased by many English families, including my own.

Some other neighborhood sights and sounds, still remembered. The "junk" man, pushing his cart and announcing his presence and interest in whatever household items were being discarded, by yelling "rag and bone man." I still wonder about the origin of that strange identifying cry. Did these guys really take old "bones" and if they did, just where were these bones coming from?

On Sundays, other push-cart vendors walked the streets hawking fresh shrimp, cockles, mussels, whelks and live eels. Stewed eel was a working-class delicacy, and I remember once visiting my grandmother's house and being horrified at finding her kitchen sink crawling with what I thought were black snakes. There was a pot of water boiling on the stove, and as I watched, Grandma reached into the sink with one hand and pulled out a squirming eel. With a cleaver in the other hand, she hacked the eel into five or six pieces that continued to twitch spasmodically as she dropped them into the boiling water.

There were also the street musicians, pavement artists and magicians, who showcased their diverse talents to the crowds lined up outside London's many cinemas and theaters, waiting to be admitted. These itinerant entertainers would pass their hats around before the doors opened, thus eking out a bare living from whatever coins were thrown their way.

Few English families owned automobiles, but fortunately, London boasted a public transportation system second to none. A citizen could choose between its "double-deck" red buses or trams (trolleys), the "Tube" (subway) trains or the local steam-trains and travel anywhere in the Greater London area, from morning until late evening, without waiting long for the next available means of transport. Nevertheless, for the working-class majority, walking or using a bicycle were the most common methods used to get from one location to another.

Someone (I can't remember who) once described England as a "nation of shopkeepers." While that was probably not intended as a compliment, it did in fact reflect the everyday reality of English shopping habits at a time when the "one-stop" super-market had not yet been conceived, much less implemented.

Shopping for the family meant visiting many separate stores. The butcher's for meat, the baker's for bread, the green-grocer's for vegetables, the dairy for milk and eggs, the fishmonger's for fresh fish, the tobacconist's for cigarettes, the "off-license" store for bottled beer or alcohol, the chemist for prescriptions and patent medicines and the "sweet-shop" for candy.

Almost all homes lacked refrigerators or even ice-boxes, so perishable foods could not be purchased far in advance of their consumption. For most English mothers, walking each day to and from the various shops was a time consuming, albeit healthy, daily grind for which there was no alternative.

Many stores would provide home delivery service (at an additional cost) of the basic necessities, bread, milk, vegetables and coal. Most delivery vehicles were horse-drawn, which meant that each day every street received multiple new deposits of horse dung, around which pedestrians, cyclists and other traffic moved with special care and concentration! To combat this, each borough employed street-cleaners, usually elderly men, who swept the streets clean and put the accumulated debris in their little carts, which actually were nothing more than large trashcans on wheels.

Unfortunately for these hardworking municipal servants, the street manure they were charged with sweeping up, was nick-named "horse-buns" by young boys like me, who, on the way home from school would pick up the nearest "buns" and use them as ammunition. I'm sure our running battles with friend and foe alike made the clean-up process more difficult.

In retrospect, I find it somewhat embarrassing to remember what a grubby little creature I must have been, except that everything I was doing at the time was part and parcel of growing up in London as a typical boy from a working class family.

Children attending school in England were reminded often of their country's fortunate geographic location, in the absence of which England's historic leadership role in the world's family of nations might have been drastically altered. The latitude of the British Isles matches that of Northern Maine and Canada's Maritime Provinces, locations noted for their snowy winters and frigid temperatures. The unique factor that spares the United Kingdom from those conditions is the balmy influence of the Gulf Stream.

This warm current has historically followed a course up the eastern coast of the US, from the Gulf of Mexico north to the Grand Banks before tacking due east across the Atlantic. It has thus provided Great Britain with a reasonably benign climate, without which England might otherwise have become nothing more than an inhospitable European landmark for six months of the year.

London's weather can be described as "moderate" most of the time. During the years that I lived there, while rain was omnipresent year round, extreme summer or winter temperature variations were unusual. For it to snow any measurable depth was rare indeed. I can't recall this happening more than a few times, and even then all traces were gone within 48 hours.

On the other hand, fog was a much more frequent and often deadly winter visitor to London. Hollywood movie plots set in London almost always depict the city's streets aswirl in a damp mist, similar to that routinely experienced in our country's coastal regions. A true London fog, however, was more akin to an impenetrable toxic air inversion, and when it occurred, it would blanket the entire Greater London area, often lasting for two or three days before completely dispersing.

The major cause of this unique weather phenomenon was smoke from the multiple coal-burning fireplaces, the only source of heat in most London homes. During the long winter days, thousands of fireplace chimneys, factory smoke stacks and hundreds of steam locomotives, discharged countless particles of soot into the atmosphere to mix with the carbon monoxide released from like numbers of automobiles, commercial trucks and buses.

On damp windless days this witch's brew of airborne toxic wastes and gases would descend to ground level as an odiferous and noxious fog, so thick as to halt all surface traffic and leave pedestrians literally lost in their own neighborhoods. It would reach peak density in the late afternoon or evening, stranding at work all those who relied on surface transportation to get them home.

Those who could use the Underground train system were more fortunate, provided they could locate the entrance to their particular station, and then find their way home above ground after exiting the train at their usual destination. After many hours in this toxic environment, Londoners would arrive home looking like coal-miners after an eight hour shift, faces black with soot, runny eyes and noses and congested lungs. The elderly and anyone with pulmonary problems were seriously at risk, and every fog incident took its own deadly toll.

Not until after World War II did Britain's government finally react to what was clearly a serious health related crisis, by enacting legislation that required all coal-burning fireplaces to be replaced by gas or electric heaters. After this became law, London's legendary "pea-soupers" faded into history.

That it was perpetually damp and raw during the winter months is indelibly etched into my childhood memories. We kids would arrive home cold and wet from walking to and from school to a flat in which only the kitchen was heated by a small fireplace. My whole family would congregate around that fireplace, alternating positions so that all of us would eventually get warm and dry.

As was the British custom, I didn't get my first pair of long pants until I turned thirteen. Before then, I wore shorts year-round, regardless of the weather, and my sisters wore short skirts and ankle socks. Our faces, hands and legs were open to the elements, and as a result, we all suffered from chilblains, an inflamed soreness and swelling of the skin caused by frequent exposure to cold and damp conditions.

This painful malady was exacerbated by the very process we used to ease the discomfort, the sudden heating in front of an open fire of those body parts already sore and inflamed. Thus, we inadvertently prolonged, rather than eased, these painful symptoms.

To add to wintertime discomfort, most English bedrooms were not heated. An American visitor, after spending a winter in England, purportedly remarked that whereas in the States, people would undress to go to bed, the English out of necessity would pile on more clothes, and that's about how I remember it.

Hot water bottles were a must, but our family of five only owned two, so some of us had to make do with bricks heated in the fireplace, wrapped in flannel and then placed in our beds. How cold and damp were our bedrooms in the winter? I recall that my bed sheets would actually steam when the hot brick was placed between them! Not exactly a healthy or cozy environment.

CHAPTER 2

Earliest Childhood Memories

On January 19, 1929, my sister Mary Elizabeth was born. At this point, the small house which we shared with another couple was now occupied by seven people, so in 1930, Dad moved us back to Walthamstow into a small rented row-home on the street where his parents lived. It had five tiny rooms and a "scullery" used for storage, and its owner (an elderly man) lived in one of the second floor rooms. My sister Peg still remembers that each morning unannounced, he would traipse through the kitchen on his way to the outside toilet to empty his overnight chamber pot!

Typical of the other houses on the block, our house had one sink with a cold water faucet, no hot running water and no bath. When hot water was needed, it had to be heated in a kettle on the stove. While municipal bath-houses were located throughout London's East End, each visit cost money, so most patrons were adults, and if they had children, they were bathed at home at the sink.

The house had no refrigerator or ice-box, one outside toilet, a gas stove and gas lights. There was no central heating. Each room had a tiny fireplace made to burn coal or "coke," a cheaper but less efficient fuel obtained during the processing of coal to produce "coal gas" used in household cooking and lighting.

In those days in England, "credit" was extended only to the upper or middle classes. Those deemed "lower class" could only make purchases with cash. For example, gas was metered to each house on a "pay-as-you-use" basis. The house meter was equipped to take coins, so that when gas was needed for cooking or lighting, it had to be paid for in advance. When the gas used exceeded the value of the coins inserted, it would automatically shut off until such time as additional coins were fed into the meter.

I imagine my parents, that first year back in England, would have grown quite nostalgic for the simple household comforts and conveniences they'd once enjoyed while living in the USA. However, something was about to happen in America which would have global impact, affecting my Dad's future just as surely as if he had not returned to England.

On October 29, 1929, Wall Street collapsed. In just one day, the value of companies listed on the New York Stock Exchange lost about 9 billion dollars. The event touched most of America when five thousand banks failed and the savings accounts of 9 million citizens were wiped out. The consequences of this catastrophic event caused trade and manufacturing to decline and unemployment to rise worldwide.

From 1930 to 1931, the number of unemployed in England tripled from one million to 3 million, and during the next five or six years, Dad was to find himself in and out of those unhappy and desperate ranks, on a regular and frequent basis.

In comparing life in England to that in the United States during the Great Depression, one needs to factor in the disparate geography of the two countries. America's land mass (3.6 million square miles) is forty-two times the size of England, Scotland and Wales combined. The very size and regional diversity of climate and commerce in the United States acted as a source of hope to many unemployed breadwinners who, having failed to secure work where they lived, could pack all their belongings and seek employment in one of the other forty-seven states.

By comparison, England's farthest western city (Penzance) is less than 400 miles from London, and its border with Scotland is about the same distance to the north. Unemployment was universal throughout Great Britain, so pulling up stakes was not really a viable option, even for those who had been out-of-work for an extended period.

Additionally, given England's rigid, class-driven society, a job could exist but go unfilled until someone with the "right" accent applied. All things considered, I suspect that the unemployed in America might have had it easier than those living in England.

In 1931, at the age of four, I contracted scarlet fever, an acute contagious febrile disease caused by hemolytic streptococci. It is characterized by inflammation of the nose, throat and mouth, generalized toxemia and a red rash. More than seventy years have passed, and I can still recall the onset of that dreaded disease, which in those days, prior to the discovery of penicillin, claimed the lives of thousands of infants and young children.

I distinctly remember being in bed, wet with fever and thrashing around in a highly confused state, when a doctor arrived and diagnosed my condition. He promptly summoned an ambulance and, as was required by law, placed the house under quarantine. I was admitted to the local hospital and placed in its isolation ward, for how long I do not know. I remember seeing my parents only once, and then at a distance as they waved to me through the window of the isolation ward door.

Given the grim child mortality statistics associated with scarlet fever, it was clearly a miracle that my two sisters were not stricken and that I survived its deadly contagion. Not that I emerged unscathed however. Apparently, it left me with a speech impediment (more about that later), and as part of my recovery, I had to learn to walk again, often losing my balance in the process and sometimes with painful consequences.

This condition dogged me for several years, as my sister Peg remembers only too well. When I would fall at school, she would be summoned from her classroom to escort me home, bloodied but unbowed! To add to my physical ailments, I was diagnosed at age seven as being near-sighted and in need of eyeglasses.

In general, following my recovery from scarlet fever, my overall health mirrored that of my childhood contemporaries. Whooping cough was a condition from which few escaped, and my sisters and I each endured multiple bouts. Fortunately, we were spared the ravages of diphtheria, which was a much more deadly and life-threatening contagion.

In those days, tonsils and adenoids were viewed by many in the medical profession as unnecessary appendages and were routinely removed from children if they became infected. For repeated ear infections, the mastoidectomy, a surgical procedure that left a deep incision behind the affected ear, was the treatment of choice. This provided an unmistakable means of identifying those adults who, as children, had grown up in the Thirties.

While my sisters and I suffered through many sore throats and painful earaches, more often than not, our father would involve a Christian Science practitioner on our behalf rather than seek treatment by a physician. Consequently, we emerged from our childhood with all of our ENT parts intact.

I recall too that like most other kids whose lives at home and school were lacking the rudimentary facilities necessary to their daily personal hygiene, I was plagued by pin-worm infestations at a time when there was apparently no medication available to rid the body of this intestinal parasite.

Typically, Dad called in his Christian Science practitioner in an attempt to cure my condition, but without success. A friend then recommended that each night before going to bed and first thing in the morning before breakfast I ingest a raw carrot! All that did was to leave me with a lifetime dislike for raw carrots.

The remedy followed by most parents was to administer a laxative at bedtime and keep the child home from school for a day, the better part of which he or she would spend in the lavatory. I don't recall how often I endured that never effective "cure" but given my somewhat puny physical condition, it was no doubt detrimental, and perhaps even debilitating, to my overall health.

Finally, I remember getting the mumps and suffering for most of a week through the painful symptoms of that acute, contagious disease and the gross swelling of my salivary glands. Dad seemed to find my bloated appearance quite amusing. He'd repeatedly put his bowler-hat on my head and point out to my mother how much I resembled her brother Ernie, who, given his substantial income as a bookie, probably ate much better than we did, and as a result, he had the distinction of being our only overweight relative.

In April of 1932 after I reached five years of age, English law required that my education begin. I've retained only three memories of my first and second years in school. Upon returning home my first day, I confessed to my mother that I'd seen the "cane." Apparently, my father had warned me in advance, that if I misbehaved in school, I'd be whipped with a cane.

No doubt terrified at that prospect, I arrived at school anxious to locate that weapon of punishment. Not knowing what to look for, I had innocently concluded that the long, hooked pole standing conspicuously in one corner of the classroom (which was used to open and close the windows) was the object that the teachers used on children who misbehaved!

Then there was the "locomotive" incident. My father bought me a paper model locomotive. To assemble it, one had to insert and glue the "tabs" on each cut-out piece into the correspondingly numbered "slots." As simple as this sounds, I apparently sought the help of my teen-aged uncle, Bert, who lived several doors away. It was he who actually assembled and finished the kit. When I showed off the finished model in school, I led everyone, including my teacher, to believe that I'd done everything myself.

Unfortunately, my father picked that particular day to walk by the school while my class was in the playground. Seeing my teacher, Dad asked how I was doing and when she commented how well I'd done on the locomotive model, the proverbial cat was out of the bag! Dad made me explain my deception to my teacher on the spot, and the next day she made me do the same to my classmates, thus providing me with a memorable introduction to one of life's most enduring maxims, that "the truth will out."

It was during those early school years that I discovered my speech impediment. In class, whenever I was required to sound off or answer a question, I found myself "tongue-tied," literally unable to mouth certain words, those that began with "problem" letters, without great difficulty.

For example, each morning my homeroom teacher would conduct roll-call. When my name was called I was expected to answer "Present," a simple enough task for every kid in the class, except me! I'd sit red-faced in my seat, trying desperately to spit out the "P" word, usually without success. The teacher would glare and ask sarcastically, "Well, Smither, are you here or not?" guaranteeing that

18

the class would turn my direction and laugh, adding to my stress, discomfort and personal embarrassment.

Clearly, I was a "stutterer," except that I was apparently too proud or stubborn to actually "stutter" in the conventional fashion. I'd get blue in the face trying to mouth the words that began with certain letters, but I never actually stammered. King George VI, father of England's present Queen, suffered from the same impediment. When broadcasting his annual Christmas message to his world-wide subjects, he'd often get stuck in mid-sentence for seconds at a time, as he manfully struggled to mouth certain words. Over the radio, he could be heard taking one deep breath after another until finally, with great effort, he was able to continue. I remember listening and suffering along with him, but, at the same time, I was somewhat comforted in knowing that the sovereign head of the British Empire shared my affliction.

The school principal regularly sent me home with notes for my parents recommending that they seek formal treatment. Dad would ask me if I stuttered, and I'd always deny it. This was not altogether a lie, because at home this wasn't a problem. Now, in my seventies, having never been treated, I'm still afflicted with the same problem, which over many years of public speaking, I've learned to adapt and to keep secret, at least until now!

During the Depression years, many children in London's East End, were mal-nourished, their growth stunted by rickets and serious childhood ailments which, due to their parents' impoverished state, were not always seen or treated by a doctor. To address this problem, public health authorities routinely conducted physical exams in the schools, and sometime early in 1934, I apparently failed to pass my annual physical.

Actually, other than being underweight, a legacy from my bout with scarlet fever, I doubt that there was anything seriously wrong with me that "three squares a day" might not have cured, but the school health authorities recommended that I be sent to a children's convalescent home for six weeks. The home in question was funded by a private charity, and with my stay not costing my parents anything, they probably readily agreed, and at the tender age of six, my bag was packed and I was shipped out!

The convalescent home for boys was located in Poole, outside of Bournemouth, a resort town on England's southern coast. Built at the turn of the century, it included in its impressive roster of wealthy patrons, members of Britain's Royal Family. Many children in its care, unlike me, were truly sick with congenital heart defects ("blue-babies" as they were then called), asthma, physical handicaps and other problems for which today they would receive psychological and medical treatment.

While I expect the home's staff had been selected on the basis that they were all God-fearing Christians, children in those days had few, if any, rights, so the treatment some received and endured, without the benefit of parental contact or support, was at times quite cruel. I remember in particular those kids who were there because of chronic bed-wetting. Like me, most were under seven years of age, away from their parents probably for the first time, with an embarrassing problem for which they needed sympathetic counsel and therapy.

Instead, each morning those who'd wet their beds over night were lined up outside their quarters, most of them in tears and clutching their wet bed sheets, on display for the rest of us as we marched to the dining room. Those poor kids were then taken to the laundry, given tubs and soap, and forced to wash their soiled linens by hand before getting breakfast.

We were served three meals a day, which for most of us meant eating more and better than we were ever used to. Food waste was not tolerated, so while we ate, members of the kitchen staff would patrol the dining area to make sure all plates were thoroughly cleaned. I think this is where I learned to eat almost anything that was put before me without complaint.

I remember when I first ran afoul of the "food-police" and the consequences. On or about the third day, a white boiled fish was served for breakfast. I assume that it was fresh because I don't recall its ingestion caused any casualties, but it had a very strong odor. When I tried to eat it my gag reflexes kicked in, and what had been in my mouth was suddenly on the floor!

In any event, the kitchen staff took umbrage at my reaction and kept me at the table after the other kids had left. They forced me to clean off my plate, which I was finally able to do, despite tears and much gagging. Luckily, all meals were subject to a rigid, unchanging weekly sequence. After a while we all figured out what to expect next, so on the days when that smelly fish was on the menu, I'd surreptitiously divide my helping between the less finicky of my breakfast companions, which was no small feat when accomplished under the eagle-eyes of our warden-like care-givers.

Another incident, one which in today's world is hard to imagine, stemmed from my having been raised in the religion of my father, a Christian Scientist. As a relatively new religion with American roots, Christian Science was not well known in England at that time, where the Anglican Church reigned as the State religion. Upon my arrival at the convalescent home, I was asked my father's religion so that proper arrangements could be made for my Sunday worship. I remember that the lady who asked me the question burst into laughter at my answer, and she had to confer with an associate to find out what a "Christian Scientist" was.

Fortunately for me I guess, Bournemouth was home to a Christian Science Church and arrangements were made from someone from its congregation to pick me up to take me to and from the service. The woman charged each Sunday with making sure I was ready for church would always say something disparaging about Christian Science, which obviously she viewed more as a cult than a religion. Not that her opinion really mattered, because I was driven to church in a CAR! No one in my family or of my acquaintance in London owned a car. I was so thrilled to ride in one for the first time, that the home could have arranged to have me dropped off at a synagogue, I couldn't have cared less!

I survived my "boot-camp" convalescence and returned home, probably in better physical shape than when I'd left. I'd learned to make my own bed, endure the discomfort of having my head shampooed once a week with kerosene (then the anti-lice treatment of choice), to eat just about all food put before me, to ignore religious bigotry and to celebrate my seventh birthday away from my family. After six long weeks, however, I was glad to get home.

During the Great Depression years, my father, like millions of others with families to support, took any job that came his way. My sister Peg remembers Dad working briefly for his brother Sam, but she doesn't recall in what capacity. We both remember that to keep himself off the "dole," he worked for a time going door-to-door, selling tea and other household items.

Earning barely enough each week to provide a family of five with its necessities, and sometimes not even able to do that, must have wounded my father's self-esteem and taxed his patience to the limit. My mother, who had to run the household on whatever allowance Dad gave her, suffered too. She struggled daily to stretch the limited food supply, so that there was always something on the table for her husband and children, even if that meant personally not eating. Recalling how painfully thin Mom was, I suspect that her "going without" occurred quite often.

Certainly, the stress and frustration faced by my parents, stemming from Dad's inability, despite his best efforts, to earn enough to support his family, prompted many arguments between them. These, we kids witnessed and sadly learned to live with.

In 1935, my father was offered employment by the Mutual Property, Life & General Insurance Company as a "debit man," the term given to those on its sales force, who went door-to-door in London's poorest neighborhoods, selling life and accident insurance for just pennies a day. Benefits under these policies were minimal so as to keep premiums affordable.

This made the coverage little more than "burial" indemnity insurance. It was purchased mostly by housewives on the lives of their employed husbands. Premium was payable weekly, and if not paid on the specific day it was due, the coverage would lapse.

Dad's job responsibilities were two-fold. First, he had to convince housewives, most with very limited budgets, to purchase his policies. Every successful sale meant that he then had another policy-holder to re-visit once a week to collect premium as due. At the same time, he was expected to spend as much time canvassing for new business as was necessary to meet his company imposed sales quota, which quota then increased proportionately to his success in securing new business.

In other words, the more successful he was as a salesman, the more onerous and time consuming became his collection duties. This left him with less and less time to make new sales, truly a classic Catch 22 situation.

Etched in my memory is the fact that after Dad got this job, I learned to hate Thursdays! He was required to report to his company's home office every Friday morning and turn in all his paper work and cash receipts for the week. The paper and cash were expected to balance out to the last penny, so on Thursday evenings, Dad sat at the kitchen table and with Mom's assistance, he'd attempt to correlate his total cash receipts for the week against his new and in force business premium.

From the company's standpoint, a policy automatically lapsed if the premium was not paid when due. Non-payment resulting from a policyholder's decision to cancel was one thing, but Dad was basically soft-hearted and he'd agonize over what to do about those who weren't around when he went to collect their premiums, and those who couldn't come up with the full amount due, who'd beg Dad not to let their policies lapse, promising to pay whatever they owed in full the following week.

Dad could keep a policy in effect only by turning in the requisite premium when due. There was no "grace" period, so if he wanted to oblige those policyholders who didn't want their coverage to lapse but who couldn't pay on time, he would pay their premiums out of his own pocket, gambling that he would eventually collect what he was owed. Whenever he opted to do this, Mom's household allowance suffered accordingly, and this would spark loud and bitter exchanges. This is why I grew to hate Thursdays.

As Dad's sales territory expanded, the miles he logged on the job increased proportionately, to the point where, on many days, he walked as much as ten miles. Twenty years earlier, during his Army service, he was diagnosed with varicose legs, so even before he became a debit agent, his veins were causing him much discomfort. This painful condition was greatly exacerbated by the demands of his new job. Why Dad refused to use a bicycle on his route is beyond my comprehension.

He was also plagued on a recurring basis by severe and debilitating headaches, which were usually accompanied by nausea and vomiting. Dad referred to these unpleasant episodes as "bilious attacks," and his only recourse was to lie down until they passed. He was convinced that these attacks were somehow related to his three wartime exposures to poison gas.

Given how little was known then about the long-term consequences of exposure to the various poison gases used for the first time against humans during the Great War, Dad's conviction may very well have been on target. However, he never sought medical treatment and, over time, the episodes became less frequent.

Dad's new job with the insurance company required that we move from Walthamstow to the Borough of Hornsey in North London, into a neighborhood called Stroud Green. Here, we rented a three-room flat on the third floor of a row house, where we were to live for the next four years. The house was owned by a brother and sister by the name of Garner, who occupied the first floor. Our second floor neighbor was an unmarried elderly woman named Miss Battersby.

As a family of five, living in three rooms continued to be a hardship, although our new quarters did represent a "step-up" as we now had access to a bathroom and an indoor toilet, facilities which we were required to share with Miss Battersby. However, we still lacked a hot-water faucet, refrigerator or ice box, wash-machine, dryer or telephone. Our flat was lit by gas and its only source of heat was a small fireplace in one of the rooms.

We did own a radio, however, and this was powered by a "wet" battery called an "accumulator" by the British, which needed to be recharged frequently. Because many old homes and flats like ours were not yet wired for electricity, this method of powering a radio was widespread, and in every neighborhood there was a store which exclusively provided battery charging services. Radio owners needed to have at least two accumulators, one at home in use and the other at the store being re-charged.

This was a somewhat costly process, so radio-time for us was limited on Monday to Friday to the BBC evening news, and on weekends, to an hour or so of something more entertaining.

Unfortunately, the only way my Dad knew for sure that our radio's accumulator needed a re-charge was when the sound faded in the middle of a broadcast. I recall this happened often and usually when we were all sitting in a circle, enjoying the Saturday evening variety show.

Miss Battersby, who lived below us on the second floor, turned out to be an ideal neighbor. I can't recall how or where she was employed, but having no family of her own, she took a great interest in my sisters and I and demonstrated this with many kind and thoughtful gestures.

For example, she would often invite us to visit with her in the evenings. I can see her still, sitting in her rocking chair listening to her radio reading from a book on a music-stand beside her and at the same time, her fingers "flying" as she knitted one sweater or scarf after another, always with a box of Cadbury's chocolates at her side.

I recall too that one Saturday, she took me to London's Covent Garden Theater to see "Swan Lake," as performed by the world renowned Sadlers Wells Ballet. Being only eight or nine at the time, the performance was probably wasted on me, but I remember how exciting it was to ride for the first time into the West End on an Underground train and to walk with Miss B. through the teeming crowds of London's legendary theater district.

Another of her thoughtful gestures occurred around the time that my sister Peg turned thirteen. Miss B. approached my parents and convinced them to let Peg begin sleeping in her flat on a sofa bed, pointing out that this arrangement would afford my sister some much-needed privacy while making things a little less crowded for the rest of our family.

From then on, Dad and Mom slept on a fold-out sofa in the living-room, while my sister Mary and I slept in the flat's only bedroom, Mary on a narrow cot and I on a folding bed-chair. While these living conditions may seem primitive, during the Depression they were more the rule than the exception for the majority of working-class families.

From time to time, we children would pester our parents to get us a cat, but pets were not permitted under our rental agreement. This was probably a blessing, given the fact that we were a family of five, practically living on top of one another, in three small rooms. Any cat adopted by us would have become claustrophobic, in short order! Fortunately, our landlady owned an enormous tom-cat named Tim, whom we were allowed to stroke and pet as often as we wanted.

Caged pets were allowed, so Dad bought us a canary, a cheery handful of yellow feathers, whom we named "Dickie." He would chirp and trill all day until bedtime, when his cage would be covered with a cloth. Sadly, Dickie's life ended abruptly one Sunday evening as we congregated around the fireplace, listening to the radio.

Somehow, the bird got out of his cage and flew haphazardly around the room, eluding all efforts to re-cage him, for more than an hour. Then suddenly, before our horrified eyes, he flew directly into the glowing fireplace coals, where he perished instantly. My sisters blamed each other for the circumstances leading up to his escape from the cage. When their tears and recriminations finally ended, our parents vetoed our pleas for another canary.

There was another event (this one humorous rather than tragic) concerning my Dad, I've never forgotten. Given his natural talent as a pianist, he was always frustrated by the fact that he could never afford a piano. Needless to say, he was thrilled when one of his debit insurance customers offered to give him a harmonium (a small reed organ) if he'd pay to have it picked up and transported to our flat.

It was delivered while Dad was at work, and when he arrived home that day, we were all sitting around waiting breathlessly to hear its first notes. Dad, without even removing his hat or coat, sat down on the organ stool and began pumping away as hard as he could on the foot pedals. These were linked to the bellows which forced air into the reeds, and with Dad's talented fingers on the keyboard, music should have been forthcoming.

Unfortunately, this particular harmonium, over many years of disuse and neglect, had become home to a family of mice! In the course of doing what mice do best, they had gnawed holes in the bellows and nibbled away at the instrument's other vital parts.

After a few wheezes and discordant notes more akin to the wails of a bagpipe, and too structurally damaged to survive Dad's furious pumping, the organ gave one last gasp and collapsed into a sorry pile of rodent-ravaged pieces. Out of the wreckage darted several terrified mice, to the laughter of my mother and the screams of my sisters.

Considering his genuine disappointment, Dad took this sudden demise of his precious organ remarkably well. He cleaned up the mess, burned most of the pieces in the fireplace and before going to bed, put out several mousetraps. By the next morning, the organ and its erstwhile furry inhabitants were history!

CHAPTER 3

English School-Days Remembered

In 1935, when we moved to Stroud Green, Peg was twelve years old, I had just turned eight and Mary was six. We were all required to enroll at the local school, located about 8 blocks away.

Built at the turn of the century, Stroud Green School was typically Victorian in appearance. It was a four-storey, somewhat grim looking structure. It boasted two playgrounds reflecting English society's position at that time, that while boys and girls could study together in the same classrooms, it was better to separate them from each other during their time at play!

The school had a gym in which daily physical training exercises were conducted. There was a workshop where boys were taught rudimentary carpentry and metal work; a room equipped with a stove, sink and sewing machines where girls were taught the basics of housekeeping; and a "bare-bones" laboratory where basic science subjects were taught and simple experiments were conducted.

Unlike American schools, where students routinely move from one classroom to another for their various periods, children in England generally remained in their homerooms for all of the major subjects. Teachers were the ones required to move from classroom to classroom, a process no doubt aimed at controlling students' behavior by keeping their social contacts and interaction during school hours to a minimum.

Ethnically, England's population at that time was almost 100% WASP (White/Anglo-Saxon/Protestant). Since 1534, the country's official religion had been the Church of England. There was no recognized or required "separation" of Church and State, so Stroud Green School, like all of its counterparts in England, began each day with a short religious service of Anglican hymns and prayers.

Student attendance at these religious sessions was compulsory, although Catholic and Jewish children could be excused if this was requested in writing by their parents. My recollection is that this didn't occur often, probably because such a request singled out the son or daughter as being "different." Given the unfortunate tendency of children to pick on those of their peers so labeled, most non-Protestant children preferred to remain anonymous in this regard, and attended the daily religious services without comment or complaint.

Student uniforms were mandated. At Stroud Green School, boys were required to wear white shirts, ties and green blazers and caps, both emblazoned with the initials SGS in red. Shorts and knee socks were part of the uniform and worn all year, fair weather or foul. (Long pants on a boy usually signaled that he had reached his thirteenth birthday.) Girls were required to wear white blouses with ties, blazers, short skirts and ankle socks and a round, wide-brimmed hat sporting a green and red band.

Now a word about classroom decorum. What was then perceived as acceptable student behavior by my teachers and administrators, no doubt reflected society's general view that "children should be seen but not heard" or "should not speak unless spoken to." Disciplinary action with respect to any student infraction of the established rules of conduct was strictly enforced, with punishment swift and sure.

Along with the traditional "I will not talk in class" remedy, which an offending student would be required to write one hundred or more times on the blackboard, cheating was subject to a more subtle form of punishment. Most schools recognized an "honor system," which paradoxically for England, was expected to apply to all children, not just those from the "upper-class" families.

Caught cheating on an exam, a student faced being "sent to Coventry," which meant enduring an indefinite period of ostracism and exclusion by his or her peers. While I still don't know the ancient origins of that punishment, or why it was so named, I remember it was practiced in my school and served as an effective peer deterrent to cheating in the classroom.

Corporal punishment was another permitted option. Most teachers, male and female alike, carried wooden rulers that they were not averse to using on the knuckles of any hapless student in order to get his or her undivided attention. And if the ruler wasn't handy, a school book might be pressed into service, as I learned one day during religious studies.

Mr. Barlow, the teacher, was walking up and down the aisles between the desks reading aloud from the *King James Bible*, Matthew 5, verses 1 to 12. Just as he came up behind me and drew level with my desk, I made the mistake of whispering to the boy next to me. Without breaking stride or his reading cadence, "Blessed are the meek..." he slammed the Bible down on my head and continued his reading, "...for they shall inherit the Earth." Believe me when I say that I can still recite some of the Beatitudes from memory!

Rulers and books aside however, the cane was clearly the disciplinary tool of choice. Students knew that it could and would be used on the spot, without debate or appeal, that their parents had faced this when they were children, and as a result, most parents accepted corporal punishment as a school prerogative. Accordingly, most boys when caned, were reluctant to mention this when they got home, because many times such a confession would trigger parental wrath rather than sympathy.

A school's supply of canes was usually kept in a closet in the principal's office, and all teachers were free to use one whenever they deemed appropriate. The boy to be disciplined was sent to the principal's office to personally select a cane and bring it back to the classroom where his punishment was administered in full view of his classmates.

Being required to choose one's own cane added a subtle dimension to the punishment, and most boys quickly learned from experience, that a thin cane would cut while a thick one would bruise. No doubt the schools viewed letting a student choose between being "cut" or "bruised" as a lesson in democracy!

Over a ten year period, I was caned only three times, which probably meant that I was a model student. Twice my hands were caned (two strokes on each) for "clowning in class," and once, at age fourteen, I was required to bend over while my teacher administered six strokes to my backside. As he put it, I was being punished for conduct "unbecoming of a gentleman." This is how he described my act of leaving the boys' playground and entering the girls' lavatory area to retrieve a soccer ball which the girls had commandeered in fun after the ball had accidentally landed in their playground during recess.

However cruel and inappropriate this form of punishment may seem today, it was clearly very effective in keeping England's schools free from student violence and intimidation. I never witnessed a teacher verbally or physically abused, and no child who wanted to learn ever had to face classroom disruption.

When I compare that environment to the common and random acts of violence, including murder, faced by teachers and students today in our country, and England and other parts of the free world, I wonder if kids might not be better off if being caned was the only hazard they had to worry about while attending school.

Incidentally, there's a reason for my constant reference to boys rather then to children in this commentary. It is because I can't recall ever seeing a girl caned, despite how frequently this punishment was administered, even for minor infractions. It's hard for me to believe however, that the behavior of all young females was always so exemplary, as to never earn them the privilege afforded their male classmates, namely getting to visit the cane-closet and making that important selection.

I suspect for the British, this form of discipline, which was usually administered by a male teacher, if performed on a female would have been viewed as "conduct unbecoming of a gentleman," so it just wasn't done. This prompts me to ask a rhetorical question. If caning was still permitted in our schools, would militant feminists lobby the courts for the constitutional right of females to be punished on an equal basis as males? At the risk of being branded a sexist cynic, a well-worn English phrase comes immediately to mind, "Not bloody likely!"

It was a Stroud Green School where I acquired the nick-name "Kippers," which followed me all my years as a student. As anyone who's visited England knows, the "kippered," or smoked herring is considered a breakfast delicacy, that is if one doesn't mind the arduous task of separating the herring's miniscule flesh content from its multitude of bones!

As I mentioned previously, I emerged from my bout with scarlet fever somewhat of a runt, underweight and all bones, hence the "Kippers" moniker. I also wore glasses and had been labeled at the school as a stutterer. These afflictions guaranteed that I'd be singled out by certain of my classmates for the usual personal, unflattering comments and the occasional physical intimidation.

Fortunately, what saved me most of the time from the class bully-boys was my quick, ever present and usually self-deprecating sense of humor. I learned at a very tender age that being able to make other kids laugh, whether at me or with me, definitely insulated me from insults or threats of bodily harm. One episode that I remember in particular actually earned me some degree of peer acceptance, involving as it did, a confrontation of sorts with one of our teachers.

Hanging on a chain from the ceiling of my homeroom was a large replica of planet Earth. It was lowered to eye level when we studied geography, and returned to the ceiling when not in use. One day, while waiting for Mr. Harrison, our geography teacher, to arrive, I lowered the globe, placed a pair of girl's navy blue shorts on it and hoisted it back up. The shorts, by the way, had lain around the gym unclaimed for some time. Suffice it to say, when Mr. Harrison, without first looking up, released the chain and lowered Mother Earth wearing girl's knickers to the laughter of the entire class, he was not amused. When he asked for the perpetrator of the transgression to stand up and be recognized, my classmates all stared in my direction, which made my confession easy and swifter than I'd planned.

I was immediately dispatched to the principal's office to select a cane. At eight years of age, this was my first encounter with the cane selection process, and I don't remember what kind I chose. However, I do recall that for my "clowning" I received two hefty strokes on each hand, a painful experience that I managed to endure without sound or tears. This probably endeared me to my watching classmates, if not to Mr. Harrison.

For the record, I should confess that the above incident did little to curb my natural tendency to find humor in just about everything. In fact, one year my report card carried the following notation from Miss Jewell, my homeroom teacher, "John is a good student but he takes life too much as a joke." I suspect that if Miss J had known how vital my sense of humor was to my successful interaction with and acceptance by my peers, she might not have offered that criticism.

English schools were not then equipped, nor were they required to provide students with lunch. We were all given one-third of a pint of milk each day, but were expected to bring our own lunch. While bread was the luncheon staple, butter was very expensive. Margarine was much cheaper, but before it was made from vegetable oils, it had a very unpleasant odor that was a great appetite killer when one spread it on bread.

As an alternative, my Mom, like most of her contemporaries, when shopping for meat would plead with the butcher for whatever scraps of fat or suet he'd trimmed from his various cuts, waste items that he'd usually throw away. She'd take home the scraps, heat them on the stove until they melted, and then pour the liquid animal fat into a cup to harden. When spread on bread it became "bread and drip" and passed as a meal in many households. Actually, when liberally sprinkled with salt and pepper it was quite tasty and much preferred over margarine.

Another bread-spread substitute to margarine was "fish-paste," a strange, smelly substance sold in jars. I believe it came in two flavors, salmon or sardine. It had little nutritional value, and only an expert could tell one flavor from the other. Cut-meats, which are so plentiful today, were luxuries that few of us ever experienced, and certainly not in our school lunches.

Instead, reflecting the universal poverty then common to working-class families, "fish-paste" sandwiches or "bread and drip" were the lunches most of us carried to school on a daily basis. This might explain why, for most of my adult years, I've been plagued with elevated blood cholesterol and triglyceride counts!

Few of us ever savored the luxury of an orange or banana, except perhaps at Christmas. Even the lowly apple was a rare and prized treat. I remember that any boy who showed up with one at the school playground would immediately be surrounded, at which point the chanting would begin, "Gimme the core!"

When the owner of the apple decided he'd eaten enough, he'd throw what remained into the air, and in a flash the core, stem, seeds or whatever, would disappear into the mouth of the boy who caught it. I witnessed this playground ritual many times, and more than once I was even lucky enough to make the catch!

In recalling my school days in England, I've concluded that underlying the mission of its educational hierarchy, was the preservation of Britain's entrenched "class" distinctions. For instance, a boy from a so-called "upper class" family was expected to attend a private school during his primary years. At age twelve he would be sent to a boarding school, such as Eton or Harrow, to continue his studies until age eighteen. He'd then be expected to attend one of England's prestigious universities, such as Oxford or Cambridge, or one of its equally renowned military academies.

Children from the so called "middle class" also attended private schools if their parents could afford the tuition. Some, through academic scholarships, could gain admission to the universities that graduated many public and private school teachers. They were also eligible for admission to any one of England's polytechnical institutions, whose graduates provided the country with its engineers, technicians and candidates for middle-management positions in commerce and industry.

Few if any "working class" parents could afford private school tuition, which meant their children had only one educational option, the neighborhood school. This environment guaranteed that they would never acquire the distinctive "posh" accent associated with private school, boarding school or university education.

Given the country's rigid and accepted social pecking order, a person's accent was a dead giveaway as to their "class," and more often than not, that dictated their future career path and job opportunities for advancement. That presumption formed the basis of the neighborhood school's limited mission, to educate and prepare children, not for college, but for "working class" jobs.

To that end, children at age eleven were required to take an exam to divide those who were most academically gifted from those whose records at that stage were less impressive. Children in the first category were placed in an advanced, four year course of study, graduating at age sixteen. Based on their exam results, those not so academically gifted were given a less intensive course of study, following which they could leave school at age fourteen or fifteen and enter the work force.

When we moved to Hornsey, my sister Peg spent only a few months at Stroud Green School before sitting for the required exam, which earned her a four year academic scholarship to St. Aidans School, a private, Anglican-related institution for girls, located a few blocks from where we lived.

While finishing one's formal education at age fifteen or sixteen seems premature by current American standards, in balance, the English school year was longer, with far less time off for holidays and vacation. My recollection is that we were out of school only five or six days during the year for various national holidays, and for summer vacation, just one month in August.

Furthermore, school sponsored extra-curricular activities tended to be rare, with sports participation generally limited to intra-mural competition. Soccer and cricket was available for boys, and net-ball and rounders for girls, the latter games being similar to American basketball and softball, respectively.

CHAPTER 4

Cowboys, Indians and Other Boyhood Pursuits

When out of school and away from its rules and rigid discipline English kids, not unlike their American cousins of that period, were essentially free to pursue their own activities, uncluttered by parental or other adult direction or supervision. When I went out to play with the other neighborhood children, the chance of any parental presence or involvement was zero, assuming that our activities stayed within the law.

For instance, a soccer game could begin with two boys and a ball, escalate in size with the arrival of more boys, and end when enough of the participants quit and walked away. Without formal teams, winning wasn't as important as the opportunity to play.

The good soccer players enjoyed the cheers, while the misfits like me, who had to struggle to keep up and stay in the game, endured and accepted shouted insults as the appropriate reward for our limited athletic abilities. Bodies were occasionally cut and bruised in the process, but absent parental or other adult supervision or criticism, our psyches remained stress and guilt free. Best of all, we all had fun!

In retrospect, I see that kind of environment as a precious childhood freedom, which unfortunately has all but disappeared in this country, thanks to the wholesale intrusion of parents and other well-meaning adults into the out-of-school leisure activities of children at every age level.

While English schools mentioned very little about American customs and history following its erstwhile colony's successful War of Independence, most of the movies we kids lined up to see at the Saturday matinees were made in America, and "Westerns" were among the most popular. As a result, the game "Cowboys and Indians" was played by English boys, probably as often and with as much enthusiasm as it was by their Yankee counterparts.

The required garb for a genuine cowboy consisted of a cowboy hat, scarf, chaps, belt with holsters and two six-guns. A boy who showed up to play without most of the above accoutrements would automatically be put into the ranks of the Indians.

I treasured my cowboy outfit. Thanks to Hollywood's pervasive influence, it guaranteed that in any playtime ambush or pitched battle, I'd always be on the "winning" side. (Obviously we knew nothing of Gen. Custer's "Last Stand" at Little Bighorn).

Actually, when I think back, "Cowboys and Indians," as played in my neighborhood was probably more hazardous for the cowboys than for the Indians. One of my friends had an old, beat-up English peramulator, which thanks to our fertile imaginations, we managed to magically convert into a stagecoach. One or two boys, depending on their size, would clamber into the pram, which would then be pushed to the top of any quiet, sloping street.

When the ambush was in place, a hearty shove would send the "stagecoach" and its occupants careening down the slope in a hail of cap-pistol fire until it hit a curb and turned over throwing the hapless occupants onto the street! While cuts and bruises were the norm, none of us wore helmets or any other real head protection. I don't recall anyone being seriously injured in what clearly was potentially a dangerous childhood escapade. In fact, being chosen to ride in the "stagecoach" was a coveted and often fought over privilege, one which for obvious reasons, we were most careful to keep from our parents!

Another popular English activity was "train-spotting" in which thousands of small boys participated. This strange spectator sport saw groups of us assembled each Saturday morning at various spots along the mainline railway tracks. We each were armed with a notebook and pencil, the purpose being to record the engine numbers of locomotives as they headed in one direction, then watching and recording them upon their return runs.

This was the golden era of the steam train as the premier mode of ground transportation. The "locals" serviced London's sprawling neighborhoods. The "express" trains traveled north to Scotland from King's Cross and Euston Stations and from Paddington, west to

Wales and Lands End in Cornwall. They all ran more frequently than buses do today.

I was fortunate to live close to the mainline of the London North Eastern Railway (LNER), over which tracks ran the "Flying Scotsman" on its daily run from London to Edinburgh. Built in 1923, this beautiful Pacific Class 4-6-2 locomotive, resplendent in its apple-green livery, became world-famous in 1934, as the first steam locomotive to ever achieve 100 mph on a regular run. While we boys dutifully recorded the comings and goings of the many trains which passed by our watchful eyes, most of us were probably drawn to that peculiar pastime by the guaranteed adrenaline rush that came from watching Number 4472 and its elegant coaches and restaurant cars streak by under a full head of steam, on its way to Scotland or on its return to London.

While the origin or purpose of the British ritual of "train-spotting" continues to elude me, it certainly served to keep large numbers of small boys out of mischief. I confess that, for many years, I was a dedicated Saturday morning participant.

Of historical note, a fitting postscript to its forty years of daily service occurred in 1963, when the "Flying Scotsman" was retired by British Rail. A group of private investors purchased the locomotive for the purpose or preserving it in running condition, as an illustrious artifact of the bygone age of steam. In 1969, the group arranged for it to visit the United States, where it was displayed at various locations, including Philadelphia, and viewed and admired by thousands.

Not unexpectedly, given my fascination with steam-trains, one of my early career fantasies was to become a locomotive engineer or fireman. I remember that prospect horrified my fastidious older sister Peg because, at that time, none of Britain's four major railroads provided shower facilities, so engineers and firemen had no choice but to go home from their shift assignments, black from head-to-foot from their exposure to coal dust.

Rare indeed was the child from a working-class family who owned a bicycle. For adults, the bicycle was the main form of personal transportation, but if we kids wanted to speed-up our lives, then roller-skates or scooters were our only options. My big day transportation-wise came in 1936, when, on my 9th birthday, I became the proud owner of a bright green scooter, with spoked wheels and extra thick tires. And so began my "explorer" days!

The London Transport Company at that time, published and made easily available a very detailed map of London's bus routes. Once in possession of a copy, I began to plan Saturday excursions on my scooter that took me miles away from my neighborhood. Carefully following the map, I'd stay on the sidewalk, crossing busy streets only at traffic-lights.

Whenever I came to one of the many multiple intersections, for which London is famous, rather than risking my neck in traffic, I'd find the nearest Tube station, carry my scooter down the entrance steps, head underground to the appropriate exit, climb the steps to the street and continue on my journey.

Neither of my parents knew where I went on my scooter. They probably assumed that while out of sight, I was still in the neighborhood. That worked until the day that I made the tactical error of deciding to follow the bus route that went by my grandmother's house in Walthamstow.

When Grandma's only grandson, a nine year old, suddenly showed up on her doorstep, ten miles from home riding his scooter, she was not amused and insisted that I return home immediately, chaperoned by my Uncle Reg, who rode by my side on his bicycle.

Fortunately, Dad wasn't home when we arrived. My mother was predictably upset, especially after I confessed to her all the other trips I'd made, some much further away than Walthamstow. On my promise to cease my exploration of London's more distant suburbs, Mom agreed to keep my past escapades from Dad, whose reaction might not have been so benign.

As it was, about a month later, while keeping my promise to go no farther than the neighborhood park, I was stopped by two bigger boys who made it clear that they were going to take my scooter for a spin, with or without my permission. Discretion being the better part of valor, I reluctantly complied, and watched the bigger boy pedal off with my prized possession.

After he returned, the other boy took off, but apparently he needed his ride to be more spectacular! He returned going as fast as he could, and went flying by aiming for where the path made a 90 degree turn and banked earth began. He jumped off the scooter a split second before it went over the bank and tumbled onto the roadway below, where it broke into two pieces on impact.

At that point, my two new acquaintances took off, and I was left to carry home both parts of my mortally wounded scooter. As I remember, my Dad (except for getting angry when I told of the circumstances) was otherwise most understanding. He had the scooter fixed by a welder friend, but it never looked quite the same. Sporting a black welding scar and a somewhat lop-sided stance, it lost much of its attraction where I was concerned. So ended the short, happy saga of "Kippers" the scooter explorer!

Whenever we'd visit my paternal grandparents, I'd invariably sneak into their scullery for another glimpse of my Dad's "tin-hat," the only remaining souvenir of his Great War military service. After his discharge from the British Army in 1919, my grandparents, who'd lost their eldest son Albert in that conflict, kept Dad's helmet, despite the fact that after many years the inside leather was rotting and green with mildew. I was never allowed to touch it, but having already read so much about the Great War, I found even this modest artifact of my father's connection to military history quite fascinating.

Equally intriguing, on my way to the library one day was my chance meeting with a boy fourteen or fifteen years of age, who came marching towards me in full British Army regalia, the khaki uniform and cap, puttees, hob-nailed boots, a helmet attached to his knapsack and an Enfield .303 rifle slung over his right shoulder.

From Dad, I learned that this boy attended a nearby private school whose curriculum included a Reserve Officer Cadet Corps program. This required those participating to attend classes once or twice a week in full uniform. Given my insatiable interest in the military, I was quite drawn to this individual, only five or six years my senior, and once I'd figured out his "uniform day" schedule, I'd often position myself along his appointed route, just for another encounter.

As a result, we saw each other quite often, and while always making eye contact, neither of us (with typical British reserve!) ever spoke or otherwise acknowledged the other's presence. This was a truly ridiculous situation that I can't imagine occurring here in

America, and it's something that I later had cause to regret, because a few years after our paths had crossed for the last time, England was once again at war with Germany.

By then, given his ROTC training, my "John Doe" military friend was probably on active duty, and his having lived through that brutal, six year conflict, or surviving without being wounded, would have been highly unlikely.

My interest in the military also influenced my choice of toys. During my early childhood years, through purchase or barter, I managed to collect a veritable army of lead-soldiers, along with a toy 75mm field-gun and a 155mm howitzer, both of which fired caps and small wooden shells, and a rubber-tracked, wind-up tank and a replica water-cooled machine gun and tripod.

While content to spend many hours playing alone with my soldiers, I'm afraid I indulged in a rather bizarre practice which caused more casualties in my make-believe army that my "troops" might have suffered had they been in a real war! When my parents or sisters weren't around, I'd often place one or two of my soldiers close to the kitchen fireplace grate, and watch as they slowly melted and collapsed into shapeless balls of lead.

Remembering that practice now, I'm somewhat nonplussed, and can offer no logical explanation for my conduct. Knowing what the present value of that colorful army of lead-figures would now command, I've wished a hundred times over that I'd been smart enough to have saved them all.

I also had a toy train set consisting of a clockwork, wind-up 040 locomotive and tender, two passenger and three freight cars. The track was limited to two rectangular lay-outs, one inside the other, connected by two hand operated switches. It came with a station, a tunnel and several track signals.

This was not an exciting layout, so at Christmas I'd visit Gamages, a local department store, which always featured an elaborate setup inside its display windows. It had lighted streets, houses, cars, trees, bridges, tiny lead-figures and several electric passenger and freight trains pulled by models of real steam-locomotives. Needless to say, I spent a lot of time with my nose pressed against Gamages' windows, wishing and dreaming!

Academically, I was a good student, always one of the top five in my class, so I enjoyed the learning process. My best subjects were history, geography, literature and English composition. Because I was inherently clumsy and an inept athlete, I hated everything connected with the daily gym regimen, except for the rope climbing exercise. Oddly enough, given my fear of heights, I eventually mastered and actually enjoyed that activity.

However, more than anything, I loved to read and with a public library within walking distance of my home, I was pretty much a certified "book-worm," a condition which tended to aggravate my Dad. He was a soccer enthusiast, and he would have been more pleased had I shared his interest. Unfortunately, I can't ever remember being attracted to any sport as a participant or a spectator.

Not surprisingly then, I had no interest in reading about sports or sport celebrities. I did enjoy detective yarns (Sherlock Holmes and Bulldog Drummond were my favorite sleuths) but my childhood literary genre of choice was "adventure." Whether on land, or sea, or in the air, I was always drawn to tales of derring-do, particularly those featuring men in uniform performing heroic, wartime missions.

The Great War ended less than a decade before my birth, and the library shelves were well stocked with war-related fiction and non-fiction. My interest in that period of history was quite insatiable. Two of my favorite fiction authors were brothers Percy and John Westerman. One wrote sea-going adventures about the British Navy, while the other authored stories featuring the intrepid young men of Britain's wartime Royal Flying Corps.

Perhaps unconsciously I was a "Walter Mitty" years before James Thurber created that character who, in the words of my current dictionary, was a "commonplace, unadventurous person who sought escape from reality through daydreaming." In any event, most of my boyhood heroes, fictional or otherwise, tended to be of the "Duty, Honor and Country" variety. I never tired of reading of their exploits or imagining myself somehow transformed in body and spirit marching bravely in their shoes.

I also loved to write. My dad knew this, and when he could afford it he'd buy me a notepad and I'd happily scribble for hours. I can't recall ever sharing my authorship with family or friends, nor did I retain any copies for posterity. This personal shyness probably saved me from charges of plagiarism, because I suspect that my childhood literary efforts were not exactly original, but more an amalgam of the various plots and characters absorbed by my mind, from the many books I'd read so avidly.

While I have no way of knowing how many other nine year old kids were interested in world affairs, I recall how I'd wait somewhat impatiently for my Dad to finish reading his newspaper so I could get my hands on it and catch up on the news. Once in a while he'd bring home a "Picture Post," a British photo-news weekly, fashioned along the lines of America's "Life" magazine.

Given my voracious appetite for the printed word and my fascination with all things military, there was much going on in the world of 1936 to grab and hold my daily attention.

Japan's invasion of Manchuria and its war with China was four years old. Italian troops had invaded Ethiopia a year earlier, and in July a civil war erupted in Spain. By October, Russian tanks and planes manned by Red Army crews had entered the fray in support of the so-called "Republicans," and in November, Nazi Germany's "Condor Legion," consisting of 6,500 troops supported by tanks and artillery and ninety-six aircraft, came to the aid of General Franco's so-called "Nationalist" rebel forces.

While the rest of the world watched, the armed forces of Japan, Germany and Russia honed their fighting skills, practiced new battle techniques and tested their latest fighters and bombers under real battle conditions. All of these events were covered by war-correspondents, many of whom risked their lives to photograph and report the carnage as it occurred. As a child I might have been forgiven for not appreciating the gravity of the news I absorbed, but I must say in retrospect that any adult who heard or read of these events and didn't see the ominous handwriting on the wall where future world peace was concerned, was definitely in a deep denial!

CHAPTER 5

More on My Parents and Other Relatives

It seems appropriate at this juncture to do an update on my parents, who by 1937 had been away from the United States for nine years. I'm sure, given their hand-to-mouth existence, that they had long since resigned themselves to spending the rest of their lives in England.

Dad was forty years old, Mom was thirty-eight. At 5'8" he was two inches taller than she, and both were rail-thin, as were most of their depression era contemporaries.

Mom had a quiet and pleasant disposition. When she had coins to spare, she liked to go to the movies or buy the penny "romance" magazines popular at that time. Beyond those simple pleasures, her life was committed to being a good wife and mother during one of the hardest and bleakest periods of England's history.

She was also the family disciplinarian, delivering on the spot punishments (slaps to the face or to the behind, whichever she deemed appropriate) for any misbehavior while Dad was at work. I can't remember any physical punishment at the hands of my Dad. Just one of his disapproving looks aimed in my direction was the equivalent of a cop with a gun yelling "freeze." Whatever I was saying or doing at the time came to a screeching halt!

One of Mom's habits that I remember, was that she liked to sing to herself, popular songs of the day, while she cooked, ironed or washed dishes in that incredibly tiny kitchen of ours. Two of her favorites were, "When I Grow too Old to Dream" and "Goodnight Sweetheart." Today, more than sixty years later, if I hear those old familiar melodies, I always think of her with affection.

Dad was somewhat more complicated. First and foremost, he was a kind, gentle father who, when he wasn't clowning around making us laugh, would regularly read us tales from Hans Christian Anderson and the Brothers Grimm. On Sunday mornings he insisted that we attend the local Christian Science Church as a family.

He was meticulous about his personal appearance (a virtue which I happily confess to have inherited), and even during his periods of unemployment, he never left the house without looking his best. While his clothes were sometimes threadbare, he kept them as neat and clean as possible, and he always kept a shine on his shoes, regardless of their age or condition.

Blessed with classically handsome features, a full head of dark hair and sporting a neatly trimmed moustache, he bore an uncanny resemblance to Anthony Eden, who was then an up-and-coming member of the Conservative Party. (Eden went on to become a prominent statesman whose illustrious career culminated in his serving as Britain's Prime Minister from 1955-1957).

Dad's job with an insurance company required him to walk the streets of some of London's poorest and toughest neighborhoods. Despite this, perhaps acting out his "Eden" look, he'd dress for work more like a city banker than a debit insurance agent. He'd wear a white shirt, usually with a bow tie, a black jacket, pinstriped pants and a bowler or homburg hat.

I'm convinced that almost anyone crazy enough to venture into a poor neighborhood dressed like a "toff" would at the very least have lost his hat to a well aimed "horse-bun," but that never happened to Dad. Everyone knew that despite his fancy get-up, he was one of them, born and raised in working-class Walthamstow.

It helped that his personality tended to be more American than British! He was outgoing, friendly and unreserved, traits that he probably acquired during his years in the States. He was a great admirer of all things American and insisted on telling his policyholders, and anyone else who would listen, about his time in America, and how well he'd been treated as a working-stiff with little education, in America's relatively classless society.

Additionally, almost everyone knew of Dad's musical talent, and wherever there was a piano on his debit route he'd be expected to stop, sit down and belt out a couple of sentimental favorites before being allowed to proceed. I remember one day walking home from school on Stroud Green's main shopping street, noticing a crowd outside a local music store, from whence came the sound of a piano being played "ragtime," and seeing my Dad sitting in the store window doing what he liked to do best, entertaining an appreciative audience.

Dad's politics, upon his return to England as an unemployed member of that country's working-class, were predictable. He registered as a member of the Labor Party and became an ardent supporter of Labor's socialistic agenda and of the trade-union movement and its commitment to collective bargaining.

He kept himself informed on political and economic developments, nationally and internationally, by always reading the daily newspaper and listening to the nightly BBC news. His favorite paper was "The Star," which editorially tended to have a Labor Party bias, which was fine with Dad. He would argue politics with anyone and was a regular writer of "Letters to the Editor," some of which our local newspaper published.

Some Sundays after church he'd take me with him to Finsbury Park, where our local "soap-box orators" practiced their avocation. Standing up and sounding off on any subject was an ancient and honored English working-class custom. These amateur public speakers could always count on an audience, and as long as they could hold their own against the hecklers and never criticized the Royal Family (something considered to be very bad form), the soap-box ritual represented grassroots democracy in action. It was a civilized way for citizens without power or position to voice their opinions and vent their frustrations.

Dad loved soccer, and during the season, when he could afford it, he attended the Saturday afternoon home games of the "Arsenal," the local professional team. He never took me with him, having given up the hope I guess, that I'd ever become a sports fan.

Best of all, Dad never forgot that he was a reformed alcoholic, and as such he never spent a penny on booze. This set him apart from many working-class men, who would regularly spend payday evenings at their local pubs. Most were fathers, and when accompanied by their wives, they'd bring their kids along even though children were not allowed on public-house premises.

Consequently, the pavements outside the pubs throughout London were awash with kids of all ages sitting on the curbs in every kind of weather, waiting patiently for the 10:00 pm closing time, when their parents would emerge and take them home. Whenever we'd be out walking and pass a pub, I'd see the children waiting outside and feel very glad that our father never drank and that my sisters and I never had to endure that sad, working-class ritual.

Our leisure activities as a family were limited to Sunday visits to the local municipal park and occasional trips by train to Walthamstow to see my paternal grandparents and Dad's unmarried brothers, Uncles Reg and Bert, who were still living at home. Once in a while we'd get to see Dad's sister Hett and her husband Will when they were visiting at the same time.

Rarely did we get to see Dad's brother Sam and his wife Sarah, who lived in West London. As for his other brother Len, I recall meeting him only once. Len was a career soldier, and during most of my childhood he was stationed overseas at various military posts throughout the British Empire.

We almost always visited my grandparents on Christmas Day, and sometimes we'd stay over for "Boxing Day (December 26), which was a national holiday in England. Sleeping over night in that small, overcrowded house was never much fun. My sister Mary and I were inevitably required to share the same bed, an arrangement we both hated but endured, because Christmas dinner at Grandma's made it worthwhile. Roast chicken, the usual entrée, was a treat we rarely had at home, and even more special, we kids would each get an orange, a luxury item we usually only got to enjoy once a year.

After dinner, everyone would congregate in Grandma's tiny parlor. There, my Dad at the piano and my Uncle Reg with his accordion would entertain us with the popular songs of the day. They'd also get around to tunes that harked back to the Great War, such as "It's a Long Way to Tipperary" and "Rose of Picardy," songs which rekindled poignant memories of Dad's brother Albert, who died in that conflict, thus guaranteeing a spate of family tears.

By now, my maternal grandparents were both deceased, but whenever we were in Walthamstow we'd still visit their house, where our Aunt Ann and cousin Ivy lived. Ann, who never married, was Mom's sole surviving sister. She had been our cousin's guardian since Ivy's mother died soon after her birth in 1918.

While Aunt Ann was a kind and generous soul, she harbored a peculiar notion that pre-teen children were somehow better off not eating what she viewed as "adult" food. She'd invariably make the same simple meal, canned salmon sandwiches (which we kids would have considered a great treat), but when she called us to eat, I can still hear her saying, "Salmon is for the grownups...fruit salad is for the children." As best as I can recollect, "seeing and smelling" was as close as we children ever got to Aunt Ann's salmon sandwiches until each of us, in time, reached the magic age of thirteen!

Our favorite relatives were Dad's only sister, Aunt Hett and her husband, Uncle Will, who either by choice or circumstance never had children of their own. Perhaps that made us special to them, because every summer they'd invite each of us separately to stay at their house for a four or five day vacation. Getting away from one's siblings, even for such a short time, was a heavenly treat that each one of us cherished.

Our Uncle and Aunt were much better off financially then we were. Uncle Will held a management position at the Handley-Page Aircraft Works located in Hendon, a middle-class neighborhood in north-west London. They owned a new, semi-detached home in the suburb of Mill Hill, a few miles from Hendon. Their home was a palace compared to the rented three-room flat located in an old row-home section of London, where our family of five lived.

For example, their house boasted a modern, indoor toilet, hot running water and a bathtub, electric rather than gas lighting and two bedrooms, which meant that at least for a few days of the year, we kids experienced the joy of actually sleeping alone.

Aunt Hett loved going to the cinema, which guaranteed that we'd get to see one or two current movies during our stay. We'd also get to read the many movie magazines she liked and which she'd save for our visits. My sister Mary remembers that she always cried when it was time for her to leave Mill Hill, and while Peg and I never shed tears, we've confessed in retrospect that we sometimes felt as Mary did, about leaving our Aunt Hett.

CHAPTER 6

As War Clouds Loom, A Family Tragedy

In August, 1937 we took our first vacation as a family, five days in a rented cottage on Canvey Island, a narrow spit of land located in the Thames Estuary, several miles from Southend-on-Sea, the most popular holiday destination for London's working-class. While the cottage was old and musty, it was certainly bigger than the flat we called home. From its windows one could see the distant beach and sea, an exciting vista, very different from that to which we were accustomed.

As fate would have it, our first family vacation was destined to be our last! A month later, at age thirty-nine, my mother died from a severe hemorrhage followed by septicemia, the unfortunate medical consequences of a self-induced abortion.

I still remember clearly the day Mom left for the hospital. She turned on the stairs, smiled and waved goodbye. She said that she'd be back in a few days, but I never saw her again. Hospital rules in those days prohibited visitation by children under the age of fourteen, even if and when a close family member was dying.

The day that Mom died, Dad collapsed at the hospital, and was kept overnight suffering from shock and exhaustion, the latter condition no doubt stemming from his giving Mom several units of blood. Consequently, I learned of my mother's death from our landlady, Miss Garner, on arriving home from school that day. I recall taking that unexpected and shocking news in the best "stiff upper lip" tradition of my ethnic heritage, but I also remember that for many nights thereafter, in the privacy of my bed, I shed many tears because I missed my Mom very much.

Needless to say, as an adult, I've always been a staunch advocate of legalized abortion and a woman's right to choose and secure that procedure in a proper medical facility at the hands of a licensed physician. My mother was a gentle, church-going woman with three

49

children, trying to survive in the Great Depression. She was married to a man, who for no fault of his own was forced to work in poverty level jobs, barely able to support his family.

Facing another unplanned pregnancy, I'm sure Mom agonized over what was best for the family. Even though it was illegal and dangerous, she probably saw an abortion as her only choice, and inducing the process herself, the only option she could afford.

Had she been "middle" or "upper" class, with the necessary financial wherewithal, I'm sure that for the right price, a medically safe abortion performed by a physician or someone with some medical expertise would have been obtainable. Morally right or wrong, that's the way it has always been in every country where abortion isn't sanctioned under law. Women with money get them!

That tragic and unexpected event would forever change each of our lives. My older sister Peg, who turned fourteen that month, became the surrogate mother to a brother and sister, aged ten and eight respectively. Mary and I recall that Peg was pretty strict, and that she ran a very "tight ship" when our father was absent. She also assigned to us specific household chores that we were expected to complete in a timely fashion, or else!

Certain of my chores I remember clearly. Each day after school, I cleaned out the living room fireplace grate, and started a new fire before Dad got home from work. Saturdays, Peg did the family laundry, except for Dad's socks, which for some reason were my responsibility. Because we lived in a cold-water flat without any laundry facilities, all clothes needed to be washed and rinsed by hand in the kitchen sink.

I was also charged with shining my Dad's shoes, which wasn't easy given their usual age and condition. On Sunday evenings, he'd draft me to help him cut cardboard shoe inserts from discarded cereal boxes. These he'd fit into our shoes covering any holes that had appeared in the soles, thus extending their life, until he could afford to buy us new ones.

Peg never came home from her school for lunch, whereas Mary and I did on those days when Mom hadn't packed us sandwiches. After Mom died, Mary tried several times to prepare lunch, but Dad ended that experiment the day that she cut herself severely while trying to open a can. After that, he arranged for us to be fed occasionally by Miss Garner, our landlady, or by the lady who lived next door or at a small neighborhood café, whose owner, one of Dad's longtime friends, fed us many decent lunches.

Aunt Ann, our mother's sister, was also a great help during those sad, hard times. She'd visit us regularly, bringing food and items of clothing whenever she determined their need. During the first Christmas following Mom's death, as a devoted member of an Anglican Church in Walthamstow, she took Mary and I to the church's annual Christmas party, where gifts and food baskets were given to needy neighborhood children. Even though we didn't reside in our Aunt's parish, we returned home with our arms full!

From time to time, Aunt Hett also helped out Dad financially. This included paying for our school uniforms when they needed to be replaced. Even our Dad's mother came by after Mom died to see how we were doing. This was quite an extraordinary event, considering that as far as my sisters and I can recall, it was the only time in our lives that she ever visited us!

News emanating from Europe continued to be frightening! In March of 1938, Austria was annexed by Nazi Germany, whose invading troops met with no armed resistance. They were welcomed by most Austrians, who apparently viewed Hitler's stated "unification of the Germanic" people with pride, rather than with concern.

Encouraged by his successful annexation of Austria, the German dictator began making territorial demands on neighboring Czechoslovakia, prompting Britain's Prime Minister Neville Chamberlain to suggest that a meeting of Czechoslovakia, Britain, France, Italy and Germany take place immediately, to avert the possibility of another war in Europe.

Hitler agreed, and scheduled a conference in Munich, for September 29 and 30. Despite the fact that there was no Czech representative present, the leaders of Britain, France and Italy conceded to Hitler's planned annexation of Czechoslovakia's German-speaking province, based on his signed declaration that Germany had no more territorial designs on that country.

Chamberlain returned to England confident that he had secured "peace in our time," but his action at Munich was widely viewed as appeasement, and would haunt him for the rest of his life. Nevertheless, it did serve as a wake-up call for Britain, which began to increase its supplies of munitions, tanks and aircraft. Additionally, it beefed-up its military through compulsory conscription, and implemented construction and procedures aimed at minimizing civilian casualties in the event of another war.

Within six months, the Nazi dictator had broken his Munich promise. On March 15, 1939 he ordered his troops to cross the Czech border and occupy the entire country. Two weeks later, the civil war in Spain ended, and another fascist dictator, General Franco, came into power. In this conflict, approximately 750,000 people died, and 19,000 German military "volunteers" dispatched to Spain by Hitler to assist Franco, participated in the carnage.

At that point, Britain quickened its efforts to bring its armed forces to a state of wartime preparation. Almost overnight, anti-aircraft guns, searchlights and primitive early-warning listening devices were put in place throughout London, and the distribution of gas-masks to the civilian population began.

In June of 1938 I passed my school's scholarship exam, a compulsory exercise aimed at identifying the "academically gifted" children. For the next four years, these children would receive an advanced course of study in the core subjects of math, algebra, geometry, English grammar and composition, history, geography, basic science, chemistry and carpentry, a foreign language (French) and Pittman shorthand and typing.

I'll always remember one early classroom assignment after I successfully passed my exam. We were each told to look ahead ten years and write a composition indicating where we thought we'd be and what we'd be doing at that juncture. That was an easy challenge for me! I confidently wrote that by age twenty-two I'd be in the USA, the land of my birth, and would be rich. As it turned out I arrived back in the States at age nineteen, and while certainly not "rich," one out of two "crystal-ball" predictions wasn't bad for an eleven year old!

In November, 1938, my sisters and I, still mourning the loss of our mother just fourteen months earlier, endured yet another emotional upheaval. Out of the blue, our father announced that he planned to get married again, and one evening he took us to meet Maude Seymour, the woman who was to become our step-mother!

Dad's new wife to be was a 47 year old widow, 5 years older than he, with an eighteen year old, unmarried daughter, Madeline. They lived three blocks from our flat, and over the years, she had been a casual acquaintance of our parents. Apparently, Dad bumped into her soon after Mom's death, and event she wasn't even aware of at the time, and subsequently the two began a relationship. In February, 1939 the relationship culminated in their marriage.

Our step-mother owned a three storey row-home in which she and Madeline lived. As a source of income she had lodgers who rented three rooms on the second and third floors. After her marriage to our father, two of the lodgers were given notice and moved out in order to provide sleeping accommodations for we three children.

For the first time in our lives we were living in a house with electric lights and bedrooms equipped with gas fireplaces. This made for a cozier environment than we were used to, even though we were only allowed to light the gas-fires a few minutes each evening as we undressed for bed. The kitchen was still heated by a tiny, coal-burning fireplace and the second floor bathroom and separate WC (toilet) weren't heated at all. This guaranteed that in the winter, no one lolly-gagged when using either facility!

Hot water for the bath tub was obtained by way of a gas-coil (called a "geyser" by the British), mounted over the tub. A shilling inserted into the gas-meter located in the cellar would usually supply enough hot water for a decent bath.

In the scullery was a large open boiler (called a "copper") with its own firebox and chimney. Every Monday my step-mother would fill the copper with water, and after soap was added, in would go the family laundry. She'd then light the copper fire, and when the water began to boil, she would have to stir the clothes with a stick until she deemed them to be clean. At that time she'd take them out and rinse them in the kitchen sink.

Standing next to the copper was a "mangle," a contraption with two wooden rollers that she'd manually turn by a big handle. After rinsing the wash she would feed it into the rollers which squeezed out most, but not all, of the moisture. In good weather, she'd hang her wash outside on a clothes-line to dry, but, given London's typically damp climate, most days it had to be hung on racks and placed in front of the kitchen fireplace. Here it took hours to dry, and in the process, filled the kitchen with steam.

Not unexpectedly, our father remarrying so soon after our mother's death was a difficult emotional transition, not only for my sisters and I, but also for our new step-mother. Having been a widow for many years and accustomed to being independent, she no doubt enjoyed sharing her household with just her daughter Madeline, who was out of school and working full-time.

To suddenly inherit two school-age daughters and a son, as a consequence of taking a new husband, must have seemed quite overwhelming, once we'd all moved into her home, and it wasn't long before tensions developed and tempers flared. Madeline, as an only child, probably resented sharing her mother's time and affection with a step-father, especially one who came with a brood of his own. I believe that for my two sisters, adjusting to the new family dynamic was more difficult than it was for me.

I always got along with my step-mother, and can't remember that she and I ever exchanged a cross word. Perhaps, it was easier for her to accept and deal with a son than to get used to having two additional daughters. I've gathered from my sisters that their relationship with our step-mother was not as harmonious as mine, and once in a while was adversarial.

I suspect that my sisters also had the same somewhat edgy relationship with our step-sister Madeline, whereas I, as a twelve year old boy, was completely enamoured with suddenly having a petite, attractive blonde now a part of my life! Madeline was smart enough to recognize "puppy-love" when she saw it, and she used my infatuation for all that it was worth. For her, I'd cheerfully handle any chore and run errands any time, a generous side of me that Peg and Mary, prior to that time, probably could not recall experiencing very often, if ever.

In any event, by the summer of 1939, we three kids had settled into our new and certainly more comfortable existence. Madeline, who until then had been going steady with a young man from the neighborhood, met and began dating a career Royal Air Force

Sergeant-Mechanic named Kenneth Stewart Jupp. Ken had just returned to England from an extended tour of duty in India, and it wasn't long before Madeline's civilian boyfriend was history, and she and Ken were making plans to marry.

There was a milestone event in my life too! As an avid reader I spent a lot of time at the local library. On one of those visits my step-mother asked me to pick up some vegetables from her green-grocer, whose store adjoined the library. While the proprietor was checking out my order he asked whether I'd be interested in working on Saturday mornings as a delivery-boy.

Dad thought that my getting a job was a good idea and the following week I became gainfully employed on a part-time basis, working Saturdays from 8:00 am to 1:00 pm. My job required that I load a "barrow" (push-cart) with bushel-baskets of fruit and vegetables, from orders phoned in earlier, and deliver them as directed, and in the process, collect whatever amounts were owed by the customers.

It was hard physical labor for an undersized twelve year old boy, especially pushing the loaded barrow up the one hill on my route, but I guess I always managed it, because I don't recall ever getting any flack from the store owner. For my five hours of work I was paid two shillings, which was then the equivalent of forty cents in American currency.

On my first day on the job, I offered my step-mother half of my earnings and she readily accepted. It was routinely expected during those hard times, that those fortunate enough to have a job and who still lived at home, would contribute some part of their earnings to the collective family income.

Most customers tipped me a penny (one cent) for each delivery. When this was added to the shilling I was able to keep for myself, it made me feel quite rich because neither my sisters nor I had ever received a regular "allowance" from our father.

By then, events were unfolding in Europe that would have a profound effect on our lives, leaving every detail indelibly imprinted forever on our individual and collective memories. On August 23, 1939, governments around the world were shocked and astonished to learn that Nazi Germany and Communist Russia had entered into a non-aggression pact. This agreement included the provision that if either country became involved in a war with a "third power," the other would remain neutral. However, there was more to this unholy, totalitarian alliance than met the eye.

Secretly, both countries had planned and agreed to acts of unprovoked military violence aimed at extending their respective spheres of influence in eastern and central Europe. Russia was to get Finland, Latvia, Estonia and the eastern half of Poland, while Germany grabbed the rest of Poland and Lithuania. As for their "non-aggression" promise, in less than two years, Germany would attack Russia without warning, proving again the truth of that ancient maxim, that "among thieves" there is no honor!

CHAPTER 7

The Second World War Begins

On September 1, 1939, Nazi Germany invaded Poland. Two days later, following Adolf Hitler's rejection of their ultimatum that he withdraw his forces, Britain and France officially declared war on Germany, thus honoring their defense pact with Poland. So began World War II, destined to be history's bloodiest conflict.

For the British people, September 3, 1939 was a never to be forgotten date in their country's long and illustrious history. Twenty four hours earlier, the British Broadcasting Company (BBC) had announced that Britain's Prime Minister, Neville Chamberlain, would address the nation at 11:15 am the following day.

Given the grim war bulletins already filtering out of Poland, I suspect that on that Sunday, families in every British household were sitting by their radios waiting to hear the dreaded news everyone feared but most had anticipated, that after twenty years of an uneasy peace, their country would again be at war.

My family was no exception. With an address by the Prime Minister scheduled, even Dad, who rarely missed attending church for any reason, stayed home that Sunday to hear what Mr. Chamberlain had to say. By 11:00 am we were all in the kitchen gathered around the radio, waiting for the broadcast to begin.

Not unexpectedly, after the passage of more than sixty years, I can't recall everything that the Prime Minister said, but his final words, "We are at war with Germany," remains forever in my mind. I also remember that minutes after his speech ended, our ears were assailed by the loud wailing of a nearby air-raid siren, a totally new sound until then, but one with which we became increasingly familiar.

As shocked as we were by that sudden warning, I recall that nobody panicked. We sat looking at Dad expectantly, no doubt assuming that he'd know exactly what to do. Unfortunately, he was no better prepared for an air-raid than any other Londoner.

It was generally accepted that if war came, London would again be bombed as it was during the First World War. In that conflict, fourteen hundred civilians were killed in over one hundred raids, conducted at random by German airships (Zepplins) and aircraft.

However, on that fateful day in history, there were no designated public shelters in our neighborhood. Furthermore, our row house, like most others, had no basement, just a four foot high crawl-space where our gas and electric meters were located, along with the bunker that held our supply of fireplace coal.

Fortunately, just moments later the siren wailed again, but this time with the "all clear" signal. This was quite different from the one that warned of an approaching air-raid, and for almost six years its clear, non-wavering signal became the most welcome sound in the world, because those of us that heard it knew that once again we were survivors, not victims!

Painful evidence that Great Britain was indeed at war was soon forthcoming! A mere eleven hours after the Prime Minister's declaration, the British passenger liner, "Athenia" (13,500 tons) en route to Canada, was torpedoed without warning in the Atlantic Ocean west of Scotland by the German submarine U-30. Of its fourteen hundred passengers, one hundred and eighteen were lost in that incident, including twenty-eight Americans.

The following day, the Royal Air Force (RAF) began its air offensive, sending twenty-nine twin-engine bombers to attack German North Sea Naval bases. This first raid was essentially a disaster! For one reason or another, only fifteen bombers actually reached their targets, and of these, seven were lost to anti-aircraft fire. Additionally, during the next two days, three more British ships were sunk by U-boats off the coast of Spain.

On the night of September 3, a government imposed "black-out" went into effect. London's street lights were to remain off for the next sixty months. Traffic signals were masked so that only a sliver of red, green or amber light could be seen close-up, and barely seen at all at a distance. Headlights on all vehicles and bicycles were required to be similarly masked.

Persons who ventured outside after dark without a flash-light (which also had to be masked) risked a fall or becoming lost, even in their own neighborhoods. Vehicle accidents and pedestrian injuries increase dramatically, as a somewhat confused populace struggled to adjust to a new and unfamiliar environment.

Additionally, the government mandated that the windows in every home and building be covered with curtains thick enough to prevent the escape of any light to the outside. It also recommended that windowpanes be taped on the inside, to minimize flying glass injuries during an air-raid. I spent hours during those first days of the war helping my step-mother cut strips of gummed tape and stick these "criss-cross" onto all our windows.

I also remember that within a few days, gas-masks and carrying boxes had been issued to every adult and school-age child. Mothers with infants were issued strange looking containers in which the infant was to be placed during a gas attack. It had an air-tight seal and a bellows that the mother needed to pump continuously to force air into the container, where it passed through a gas filter before reaching the infant.

Each day at school, we had a gas attack drill, during which we were required to put on our masks and sit quietly at our desks. It wasn't long before someone discovered that by breathing very hard into the mask, it made a rather crude sound, a "raspberry" to the British or what we Americans might term a "Bronx cheer."

Soon, "raspberries" were being made by everyone in the class, and there was little the teacher could do because there was no way he or she could accurately pinpoint an offender. Too young and naive to fully comprehend the serious implications of our daily drill, we kids enjoyed harassing our teachers because in this rare instance, we were able to get away with it.

There was some positive news on September 3. The government announced that its planned evacuation to rural areas of 1.5 million civilians from London, Birmingham and other cities viewed as probable targets, had been completed in three days without incident. Most evacuees were children and their mothers, women who were pregnant, the physically handicapped and the infirm.

As a result of Britain's experience during The Great War, the threat to its citizens posed by air-raids and their impact on the country's morale, had been studied, reviewed and discussed in detail by the government and various committees appointed specifically for that purpose, begining as far back as 1922.

A clear majority involved in those lengthy deliberations agreed that in any future European war, the evacuation of civilians from England's major cities to its rural areas would be necessary, and if properly planned, was actually feasible. However, there remained an unresolved "wild-card" element in this potentially logistical nightmare, how to properly house and feed a huge displaced population, over an extended length of time.

Evacuations from London and other major cities continued through September, driven by a nagging fear that air-raids were probably imminent, recognizing that Warsaw had been bombed within an hour of the German invasion of Poland. That fear only heightened on September 17, when thousands of Russian Red Army troops suddenly crossed Poland's eastern frontier and advanced westward.

On September 23, three weeks after his forces invaded Poland, Hitler announced that all Polish military resistance had ended. Six days later, Germany and Russia formally signed a "boundary and friendship treaty," following which they divided that stricken and once sovereign country into two occupied regions. The treaty also gave Russia the go-ahead to enter into "mutual assistance pacts" with Lithuania, Estonia and Latvia, an ominous prelude to the Soviet's eventual annexation of the Baltic States.

Along with making its own evacuation plans, the government encouraged citizens who could afford to privately evacuate and relocate to do so. For most urban working families, this was not an option unless they happened to have a relative or friend living in a rural area who was willing and able to take them into their home for an indefinite period.

As circumstances would have it, our step-mother had such a friend in Mrs. Holmes, a widow who lived with an elderly uncle in South Normanton, a small coal-mining village located in Derbyshire, about eighty miles north of London. Two weeks after the outbreak of war, Dad broke the news that he and our step-mother had arranged with Mrs. Holmes for my sisters and I to go and live with her. When we would return home was left unsaid!

Without meaning to cast aspersions on our father, who I'm sure in agreeing to our evacuation, did so primarily out of a concern for our safety, my sisters and I remain convinced to this day that our step-mother was the driving force behind this decision. Despite being married only seven months, she and Dad were already quarreling quite often, and we suspect that the main source of their discord arose from her disenchantment with having inherited three children along with her new husband.

Perhaps, she saw "evacuation" as a good excuse to get us out of her house and have Dad to herself. Also, her daughter was planning to get married that month, and knowing Madeline, I'm sure that she too would have preferred not to have us around as part of that occasion. To this end, our step-mother was clearly willing to cover the travel expenses of a private evacuation, and the continued costs of having us boarded away from home.

Peg, who was about to turn sixteen, had graduated from school in July and expect to soon be employed. Compulsory conscription of all males aged eighteen to twenty into Britain's military had begun a year earlier, following the Munich Crisis, so jobs were plentiful and available to anyone interested and qualified. However, Dad expected Peg, as his oldest child, to accompany Mary and I on this sudden and unexpected exodus, and within the week the three of us were on a northbound train to Derbyshire.

Our journey to South Normanton took most of the day. Britain's four major railways were swamped by evacuation traffic, so all trains were overcrowded and delays were frequent. At Derby, we left the express train that we'd boarded at London's Euston Station, and transferred to a "local" which took us to a small town called Alfreton. There we waited for more than an hour for the bus that would take us to our final destination.

Having grown up on London's crowded streets, the bus ride was a fascinating experience. The route took us over an almost deserted two-lane highway, which wound its way over windswept hills and dales, with the only visible evidence of habitation being an occasional glimpse of a farmhouse and grazing cattle and horses.

I confess here and now that my recollections of the village in which we lived for the next three months are unusually sparse, considering how well my memory has served me with respect to other times, places and events.

I do remember that the widow, Mrs. Holmes, was a kind soul in her late forties who turned out to be a decent surrogate parent. Her uncle who lived with her was a retired coal-miner who accepted our sudden intrusion into his life without rancor. She was a good cook, (Mary remembers in particular her delicious apple-dumplings), and with food rationing not yet in effect, we probably got more to eat there than we'd been used to at home.

However, one bizarre incident involving her kitchen hygiene I'll never forget. Her house was typically English, no ice-box or refrigerator. Perishable foods were kept in a cupboard called a "larder" with a small window open to the outside. In the winter months, the outside air kept the food cool and reasonably fresh.

Unfortunately, during the rest of the year flies entered the unscreened window and did what flies do naturally! One day, I saw Mrs. Holmes take a ham from her larder and scrape live maggots off its surface with a knife before placing it in the oven. Seeing my horrified expression, she assured me that the roasting process would take care of any contamination!

Next to us, lived a blacksmith, an affable neighbor who I enjoyed watching work at his forge, pumping the bellows until the iron he was heating glowed red. Then he hammered and shaped the metal into horse-shoes, and finally nailed these, still hot and smoking, onto the hooves of the horses waiting patiently outside.

The village itself was just a blip on the map, a few houses and stores clustered along both sides of the main Alfreton highway. It boasted a coal-mine, a school (attended by all grades), a tiny cinema and a church, which I recall pealed its bells every Sunday morning to summon the faithful to worship.

In May, 1940, following the fall of France, those bells, along with all other church bells, were silenced for the duration of the war, after the government decreed that henceforth, they were to be rung only to warn the locals that enemy paratroopers were descending from the sky and about to land in their neighborhood.

Upon our arrival, Mary and I were immediately enrolled at the village school, which was within easy walking distance. Peg, having already graduated in London, remained at home and helped Mrs. Holmes with her household chores.

At that point in time, we were the village's first evacuees. While we were treated decently by the teachers, the reception afforded us by the students, was mixed. Some were friendly, most were aloof and a few were downright hostile. It didn't help that the school's curriculum and academic standards, lagged behind those of our school in London.

This probably reflected the reality faced by South Normanton's educators, that many of its students weren't very interested in the learning process, aware as they were, that most boys were destined to toil as farm laborers or coal-miners, while the girls would work in local stores, or help their mothers at home, until such time as they married and became house-wives themselves.

I guess my English teacher was thrilled to have someone in the class who cared about her subject matter, and she'd regularly hold me up as an example for my classmates to follow. This did nothing to endear me to those who already despised me as a "foreigner" from London, and this all came to a head, the day the teacher presented me with a copy of Jules Verne's "Journey to the Center of the Earth" as a prize for one of my compositions.

That afternoon when I left school, four or five classmates were waiting for me, and it wasn't to offer me their congratulations! To get through them, I used my gas-mask box as a weapon, whirling it around and around by its strap, and ran for home under a hail of roadside gravel, thrown in my direction as a parting farewell.

After being forced to run that gauntlet several more times, I began to wonder whether it might not have been safer back home in London, where I would have had only the Luftwaffe to worry about!

Fortunately, a village boy my own age, Norman Cooling, did become a good and close friend, in and out of school. His father and two older brothers were coal-miners, and I remember being at Norm's home one day, when they arrived together, from their shift.

It was a scene straight out of the "How Green Was My Valley" movie! The three came walking slowly up the hill in single file, led by the father, each carrying a lamp and a lunch-pail. All were covered from head to foot with coal dust, as pit-heads in those days were rarely, if ever, equipped with shower facilities.

Anticipating their scheduled homecoming, Norm's mother had been heating kettles of water on the kitchen stove most of the day. Upon their arrival, she filled a large metal tub which stood in the kitchen, into which his Dad stepped first, followed in age sequence by his brothers. I'm not sure how the youngest sibling ever managed to get clean, because by the time he got his turn in the tub, its contents more resembled coal "slurry" than bath-water!

One other event that I recall from my South Normanton days, was a visit to "Robin's Oak", a huge ancient oak-tree in the heart of Sherwood Forest, outside of the nearby City of Nottingham. Here the legendary thirteenth century outlaw Robin Hood supposedly hid from his nemesis, the Sheriff of Nottingham, when he and his band of Merry Men weren't robbing the rich to give to the poor.

Each evening at 9:00pm, we'd all gather around the radio to hear the BBC news, which, following the defeat of Poland, continued to be somewhat daunting. In early October, the German High Command began moving the bulk of its land and air forces westward out of Poland, in preparation for Germany's confrontation with the Allied armies of France and Britain.

At the same time, Russia's dictator Josef Stalin, emboldened by his easy conquest and occupation of Eastern Poland, began making territorial demands on the Baltic States of Lithuania, Latvia and Estonia. Under considerable diplomatic pressure, backed by the ever present threat of military intervention, each country in turn, reluctantly conceded to Russia's demands.

His appetite for territorial expansion now further whetted by his bloodless annexation of the Baltic States, Stalin set his sights on neighboring Finland. The Finns however, in a veritable "David and Goliath" confrontation, stubbornly resisted the Soviet's iron-fisted diplomacy, and on November 30, Red Army troops swarmed across its borders, on three fronts, thus precipitating the conflict which became known as the "Winter War."

As 1939 drew to a close, except for sporadic raids on England's Channel ports and its south-eastern coastal towns, the expected air-raids on London and other major cities, had not materialized. Lulled into a false sense of security, thousands of women and children who were evacuated during the early weeks of the war, began returning to their homes, and in December, with the consent of our parents, my sisters and I also returned to London.

CHAPTER 8

The Quiet Before The Storm

While calamitous events were occurring in Eastern Europe, the French Army, Europe's largest in terms of manpower, remained hunkered down behind its Maginot Line. This was a series of steel and concrete fortifications, built by France along most of its border with Germany, following the First World War. Britain's Expeditionary Force in France, some 160,000 troops, manned defensive positions on France's border with neutral Belgium.

Absent any aggressive effort by the French or British armies to engage the enemy during the first four months of hostilities, this sustained period of military inactivity, was soon dubbed "The Phony War." This was a derisive term which only served to add to the complacency felt by many in Britain, including the famed underwriters at Lloyds, who were then purportedly laying odds that the war would be over before the year's end. Nevertheless, in December, the government extended military conscription to apply to men between the ages of 19 and 41.

I don't recall much about the Christmas of 1939, except that Dad broke with tradition by not visiting his parents on Christmas Day. I suspect that his family and Mom's, were upset when he remarried so soon after her death. My step-mother, probably hurt by their resentment, made no effort to curry their favor. As a result, we children saw our grandparents and our aunts and uncles, who always got together at Christmas, much less often.

Our step-sister Madeline had moved out after her marriage three months earlier, and was now living on an RAF base north of London while Ken her husband, attended Officers Training School. He was subsequently commissioned a Pilot Officer, the British equivalent of an American 2nd Lieutenant.

In those days, very few individuals in Britain's armed services, became officers without first having received an "upper-class" education at a prestigious public school or university. While Ken had attended a prep-school, I don't believe he graduated before entering the RAF as an enlisted man. Imagine our surprise, when he and Madeline visited following his commission, to find that both had suddenly acquired "upper class" accents, no doubt carefully cultivated to match Ken's newly minted military status!

However, despite his having successfully breached the enlisted man/officer barrier, Ken remained a Pilot Officer without flying status, for his five years as an RAF officer. Apparently, while the powers that be let Ken become an officer, they made sure that absent the "proper" education, he would never be promoted.

During my three months away from London, the city had moved to a state of wartime readiness, and this was readily apparent in our own neighborhood of Stroud Green. The familiar blue police call-boxes, were now almost hidden by protective sandbags, as were the many Air Raid Precaution (ARP) posts, which had been established throughout the area, and were now manned twenty-four hours a day, by civilian volunteers.

"Anderson" shelters were visible in many back-yards, and more were being installed each day. The shelter (named after Sir John Anderson, the man responsible for Britain's domestic security) was made available by the government to all homeowners.

The "Anderson" consisted of pieces of curved corrugated steel bolted to steel rails which, when assembled, formed an arch-shaped structure. It was then buried to a depth of three feet, in the back-yard of the homeowner, and its roof covered with eighteen inches of soil or sandbags. It was made to accommodate four to six persons, and while never intended to survive a direct hit, it did provide reasonable protection from bomb blast, flying debris and shrapnel.

Visiting our local Finsbury park, I was thrilled to find that it was now home to a 3.7" anti-aircraft gun and a searchlight unit, both manned by men of the Territorial Army, Britain's equivalent of our National Guard. At a different park location, I discovered a barrage-balloon unit, manned by "WAAFs,", the name given to the volunteer members of the Women's Auxiliary Air Force.

With little happening on the Western Front, the war raging in Finland was front-page news in England. All newspapers featured maps of Finland, with daily up-dates on the battles between the opposing armies, as they swirled back and forth. Even though I knew very little about Finland or the Soviet Union, I remember that I studied the newspaper reports and maps, with interest.

Apparently, Moscow had assumed that launching four armies totaling 600,000 men, against a Finnish army of 150,000 would result in a quick and easy victory. However, it soon became clear that despite its numerical advantage, serious deficiencies existed in the Red Army's leadership, equipment and troop morale. In the face of determined Finnish resistance and aggressive counter-attacks, the Soviets gained very little ground and suffered heavy casualties, during the initial months of the war.

In January, 1940, my sister Peg secured a full-time clerical position in the office of the local gas company, located in Stoke Newington, a municipality close to where we lived, and Mary and I returned to our classes at Stroud Green School. While we were no longer required to carry our gas-masks at all times, we were surprised to find that our respective playgrounds, where we once played during recess, had been excavated and transformed into a series of ugly sandbag-covered trenches, in which we were to take cover, should an air-raid occur during school hours.

Along with the loss of our playgrounds, was the noticeable change in the school faculty, and its curriculum. During our evacuation to South Normanton, some teachers had entered military service, and others had been evacuated with various groups of children, and were now teaching outside of London.

As was mentioned earlier herein, I had passed a scholarship exam in 1938, which guaranteed me a four year "advanced" course of study in thirteen major subjects. When the war began, I'd completed only the first year's curriculum, which hadn't included any algebra, geometry, chemistry, shorthand or typing. Then three weeks into my second year, I left London and spent the next three months in a village school whose curriculum essentially left me in limbo, from a scholastic standpoint.

While air-raids on London had not yet begun, officials in its government and school systems, all assumed that it was just a matter of time, before the capital became a "front-line" city, subject to the same kind of frequent and concentrated attacks from the air, as was the fate of Warsaw, the capital of Poland. Faced with that grim reality, the everyday collective safety of the children became the paramount goal of the authorities, rather than strict adherence to every facet of its pre-war curriculum.

As necessary as this wartime decision was, the children most negatively affected, were those like me who'd received only one year of their four year promised study course. As the war progressed, the "advanced" curriculum was limited or adjusted, and in most London schools, ceased to be offered at all.

In January 1940, the government made two major announcements. Food rationing would begin, with butter, sugar, bacon and ham each limited to 4 ounces per week, and women between the ages of 20 and 30, would be required to choose between working in a defense plant, serving in the Womens Land Army as farm laborers, or volunteering for duty in one of Britain's army, navy or air force womens' auxiliary services.

The government's earlier extension of military conscription of all men between the ages of 19 and 41, had provided limited occupation deferments for farmers, coal-miners and specialized defense plant workers. However, as the war progressed, and the demands of the military increased, the government canceled deferment of miners, and they too, became subject to the draft.

Unfortunately, with the demand for coal at a record high, and mines operating 24 hours a day, this bureaucratic anomaly eventually required that the conscription process be amended again, this time to provide that a certain number of those called to military service, be assigned instead to work as coal-miners.

When this became common knowledge, many young men chose to volunteer for military duty, rather than await conscription and risk the possibility of being chosen to serve their country, not on the battlefield, but deep in the bowels of the earth!

By February, war news emanating out of Finland, indicated that the Soviet's numerical advantage in troops and weapons, was turning the tide in their favor. 35 Red Army divisions were advancing against 15 depleted Finnish divisions, now on the defensive, and losing ground rapidly to the invaders. Sensing a military victory, Russian diplomats began peace overtures, and the beleagured Finns agreed to discuss an armistice.

On March 12, the "Winter War" ended, and a gallant nation lost its sovereignty, yet another victim of Communist imperialism. It was a costly military venture for the Soviets, who lost more than 68,000 men killed, along with 1,600 tanks and 700 aircraft. The Finnish army suffered a loss of almost 25,000 men killed.

Earlier that month, unbeknown to the rest of the world, Hitler ordered his military commanders to prepare for an invasion of neutral Norway and Denmark. He also conferred secretly with Italy's fascist dictator Benito Mussolini who, having agreed to enter the war on the side of Germany, was given the "choice" of attacking either France or Yugoslavia.

Mussolini chose the former, based on his estimate that Italy's share of the plunder would be greater, thus validating Winston Churchill's characterization of the dictator as a "jackal" when three months later, Italian troops invaded France just days before the French gave up the fight, and surrendered to Germany.

By Spring of 1940, the massive Nazi ground and air forces, which had "blitzkrieged" their way to victory in Poland, had been reinforced and were now positioned along Germany's borders with France, and the neutral countries of Belgium and Holland.

On April 8, British and French naval vessels laid mines in the coastal waters of neutral Norway, arguing that such action was necessary to deter German military expansion into Scandinavia. The Norwegian government protested, not knowing at the time, that a German invasion fleet was already in Norwegian waters, a secret well kept, even from British and French intelligence. Twenty four hours later, without warning, Germany invaded Norway and Denmark.

Armed resistance in Denmark was minimal. The Danish army lost 13 dead and 23 wounded, and within four hours, the Danish government capitulated, explaining that it did so, to spare its tiny country the fate that had befallen Poland. The Norwegian army fought the German invaders fiercely, helped by the British, French and Polish troops, who landed in Norway supported by the British naval forces.

Unfortunately, the skies over Norway were dominated by the numerically superior Luftwaffe. Without adequate air support, and after a series of bloody encounters with German forces in the interior, Allied troops began to retreat to the coast. By May 3, almost all had been evacuated, and were back in Britain.

For those of us on the so-called "Home Front," keeping track of these momentous events through our newspapers and nightly BBC bulletins, "good" news was a rare commodity indeed! The German Army's victories as reported, were certainly disquieting, but they weren't viewed as seriously as they should have been. They were even dismissed as irrelevant by those who were convinced that when the Hun faced a "real" army, (the French and British forces), the military outcome would be markedly different.

What the public didn't know (because for security reasons, it wasn't always reported), was the mounting toll being taken on Britain's merchant fleet and naval escort vessels, in its coastal waters and beyond, by German bombers, mines and U-boats. These losses of men, ships and cargoes, truly threatened Britain's tenuous ocean life-line, and by the war's eighth month, the British people were in dire straits, more than most imagined.

Things weren't going well in the Smither household either! My Dad and step-mother, were once again at odds. As a child witness, I don't know what caused the constant bickering, or the days of silence between them, which followed. I do know that for my sisters and I, it was pretty nerve-wracking, trying to get along with both parents, without becoming embroiled in the fray.

I remember my thirteenth birthday on April 14, 1940, for two reasons. As a gift, I received a pair of ankle-length gray flannel pants, the first recognition of my teen-age status. Unfortunately, while I was still savoring the moment, Dad announced he was leaving our step-mother and taking us with him, to live in a small furnished apartment, several blocks away.

I don't recall much about that period of my life, except that on my way home from school, I'd sometimes detour to my step-mother's house. She'd make me a cup of tea and find a biscuit to go with it. We'd chat for a while, then I'd be on my way. I never told Dad of my visits, and probably kept them from my sisters too, fearing no doubt, that they'd spill the beans, and my tea and cookie days would be numbered!

On May 10, (again without warning) Germany annexed Luxembourg and invaded Belgium and Holland. Occupation of the latter countries, insured that when the Nazi legions were finally launched against the Allied armies in France, their flanks would be protected. Upon learning of this latest act of aggression against three neutral countries, Prime Minister Chamberlain resigned following his declaration that "some new and drastic action must be taken if confidence is to be restored...and the war carried on with the vigor and energy which are essential to victory."

He was replaced by the First Lord of the Admiralty, Winston S. Churchill, who promptly formed a coalition government of Conservative, Labor and Liberal members. In his first major speech as Prime Minister, "Winnie" promised the British people he would prosecute the war "at all costs, for without victory there is no survival" offering them "nothing but blood, toil, tears and sweat." The "Phony War" was definitely over!

Chamberlain's resignation as Prime Minister, was welcomed by a majority of British citizens, who by then had concluded that his pre-war peace efforts through a policy of appeasement, however well intentioned, had failed, and that furthermore, his wartime leadership had been weak and indecisive.

Winston Churchill's elevation to that post, was a timely boost to the country's flagging morale. Despite his blunt assessment of Britain's dire straits at that juncture of the war, and his stark promise that things would likely get much worse, I recall that even my staunch socialist father, reflecting the sentiment of the working-class, took comfort in the widespread belief that "Old Winnie" would soon give the bloody Jerries "wot for!"

That faith and confidence in the new Prime Minister, was to be sorely tested during the next thirty days, as German ground troops, closely supported by the Luftwaffe, continued their rapid and seemingly unstoppable advance, through the Low Countries.

Holland's fortifications were easily outflanked, and on May 14, all Dutch resistance ended. A supposedly impregnable Belgian fort protecting the key city of Liege, was overwhelmed in a surprise attack by glider-borne infantry. On the heels of that quick victory, German paratroopers were dropped into north-east France, and panzer divisions supported by infantry, attacked and routed two French divisions, which reportedly retreated in panic.

In London, my sisters and I were still living in a small cramped apartment with our father, who'd not yet reconciled with our step-mother. Peg worked full-time while Mary and I attended school by day, and struggled with our homework at night. At her tender age, I doubt that Mary fully comprehended the daily war news and its grave significance, but for myself, I was totally immersed in the dramatic military events unfolding across the English Channel, less than 200 miles away.

When my father arrived home from work with his daily newspaper, my homework became secondary! I'd devour each page looking for the latest war news, which every day, became more disheartening. However, there was one development that I'm glad never made the news. Mr. Churchill, during his first two weeks in office, came under considerable pressure from influential members of his own Conservative Party, primarily Foreign Secretary Lord Halifax, to seriously consider the unthinkable, namely, if France fell and British forces were routed, what his response as Prime Minister would be, if a "peace with honor" offer was made by Hitler.

Post-war accounts of the so-called "Black Fortnight," the period from May 14 to May 28, 1940, suggest that it was Churchill's unwavering contempt and distrust of the German dictator, plus his indomitable spirit and stubborn conviction that any negotiated peace would inevitably result in an enslaved Britain, that eventually prevailed. His courage and unswerving determination at that point in time, certainly saved Britain and ultimately, thanks to the United States, led to the unconditional surrender of Nazi Germany, and the liberation of occupied Europe.

By May 24, the French town of Boulogne had surrendered and German units were heading hell-bent towards Paris. British and French troops, cut off north of Boulogne, fell back under the Nazi onslaught and were driven into isolated pockets of resistance, where they faced annihilation or capture. Some 380,000 Allied troops were surrounded and trapped by German forces, in a 60 square mile area around the coastal town of Dunkirk.

Two days later, following a BBC report on the attempts already underway to evacuate the beleaguered army, a rag-tag fleet of more than 800 ships and boats of all sizes, headed into the Channel bound for the French coast, to assist in history's largest successful military sea evacuation, a daring and noble endeavor which later became known as, the "Miracle of Dunkirk."

On May 27, the French port of Calais, situated at the Channel's narrowest point, fell to Nazi forces, putting Dover on England's southern coast, within shelling distance of enemy long-range artillery. If this news wasn't bad enough, on the following day, the 500,000 man Belgian army gave up the fight and surrendered.

By June 4, the Dunkirk evacuation, unquestionably an ignominous defeat for the British Expeditionary Force, was over. In that darkest moment of the nine month old war, the "miracle" was seen in the grateful eyes of the 224,585 British and 112,546 French and Belgian soldiers who were rescued, and would fight again. One of those not saved and reported MIA, was my Uncle Len, who'd been a career soldier in the British Army, since his teens.

On the afternoon of that fateful day, Prime Minister Churchill stood before the House of Commons, and spoke to a stunned nation, a memorable speech heard by radio listeners around the world, the final words of which, were to live forever in British history;

"We shall defend our island, whatever the cost may be. We shall fight on the beaches, we shall fight on the landing grounds, we shall fight in the fields and in the streets, we shall fight in the hills; we shall never surrender."

I'll never forget that day, or those words. I remember standing with my father by the radio, and my shock at seeing him trying to hide the tears streaming down his face. I'd never seen him cry before, and at the sight, I found myself crying too!

I treasure an audio tape of Churchill's wartime speeches, given to me years ago by a close friend, now deceased. More than sixty years have passed, but whenever I play that tape and hear that unmistakable voice, and those courageous, defiant and inspiring words, I still find myself reduced to tears, each and every time!

On the heels of the Prime Minister's speech, the government concerned again with minimizing civilian casualties in the event of a hostile reaction from Hitler to that defiant proclamation, ordered London schools to plan for the imminent evacuation of all children under the age of fifteen. Mary and I were given printed instructions in this regard, which we dutifully delivered to Dad.

I don't know whether this event had anything to do with Dad's reconciliation with our step-mother, but several days later, he gave up the apartment and moved us all back to her house. Maybe it was knowing that Mary and I were soon to be evacuated, and that my older sister, holding down a full-time job, would be gone most of the day, while contributing half her pay-check to the family's income, that helped heal the marital rift, but whatever the reason, I for one was glad to be home. Unfortunately, my stay was short-lived. A few days later, Stroud Green school announced that its mandated evacuation would take place the following week.

Meanwhile, the war news continued to be bad. With the BEF driven from French soil at Dunkirk, Nazi forces began to systematically attack, surround, capture or annihilate France's remaining 37 divisions. On June 10, assuming the conflict would soon end with his friend Hitler victorious, the Italian "jackal" Mussolini ordered his army to invade France, and his airforce to bomb French military bases in Corsica and Tunisia.

On June 14, German units entered Paris and captured another "impregnable" fortress, the Maginot Line, by simply outflanking its defenses and attacking it from behind. Upon learning this, Winston Churchill, in another memorable radio broadcast, urged his countrymen to brace themselves for their duties, so that if the British

Empire and its Commonwealth lasted for a thousand years, historians would always say, "This was their finest hour."

Seven days later, on June 21, France gave up the fight! Formal signing of the surrender agreement was witnessed by Hitler, who ordered that the ceremony take place in the same railway car preserved by France as an artifact, in which Germany had accepted its defeat in World War I, twenty two years earlier.

CHAPTER 9

Evacuation, The Second Time Around

The complete subjugation of France and the Low Countries by Hitler's war-machine, a campaign tagged "The Lightning War" by historians, took only six weeks. That Britain would be next on Germany's unblemished record of military conquests, was viewed as inevitable in all of the world's capitals, including our own.

With the fall of France, citizen and congressional debate over America's continued neutrality, increased in intensity. Opinion was unfortunately influenced in part by America's Ambassador to England, Joseph P. Kennedy, father of our 35th President. Kennedy made no secret of his belief that Germany was invincible, and that the British should sue for peace before their country was invaded and reduced to rubble, with enormous civilian casualties.

Having seen in print some of his public utterances during his tenure in London, I must confess that I'm hard pressed to understand why President Roosevelt chose a rather obvious anglophobe to serve in such an important diplomatic post, at one of the most critical periods in British and American history.

Be that as it may, as one who was in London at the time, I don't recall any visible manifestations of panic or defeatism, perhaps due to something everyone remembered from their childhood history lessons, that there had not been a successful military invasion of Britain since the Norman Conquest, in the year 1066!

Spirits were also given a lift by a persistent rumor circulated as a fact, that "the old man" (Churchill), carried a six-shot revolver and had vowed that if England was invaded, he'd shoot five "Jerries" before taking his own life, to avoid capture.

It was during this uncertain but relatively calm environment, that Mary and I were evacuated from London, for the second time in ten months. On a sunny day in the last week of June 1940, we trotted off to school at the usual time, gas-mask boxes looped over our shoulders, each carrying a shiny black shopping-bag purchased by our step-mother for the occasion, into which she'd packed our tooth-brushes and several changes of clothing.

Parents were advised that their children would not be coming home that day, but were not told where they were going. To make the parting "easier," they were also asked not to accompany their children to school, from where the evacuation would begin.

As a result, Mary and I said our "goodbyes" at home, not knowing where we were going, or when we'd see the rest of our family again. These wrenching family breakups were repeated throughout London, yet scores of photos taken at the time, show few public displays of emotion. The legendary British reserve and "stiff upper lips" were certainly much in evidence that week.

My Dad's last words to me were, "look after your little sister," but upon reaching school, we were immediately separated and sent to our respective home-rooms. There, we were issued large tags on which we were told to print our names, before tying these to our jackets. Then we quietly filed onto the waiting buses.

While our ultimate destination remained unknown, our arrival at Paddington Station, gave the older ones of us a clue of sorts. Paddington was the London terminal of the Great Western Railway, the only rail-link to England's western counties and Wales. Now at least we knew that we'd be heading due west. We boarded the evacuation train in the order of arrival, and even though I hadn't seen my sister since early that morning, the constant checking and double-checking by our teacher chaperones, convinced me she had to be on the train, albeit in another coach.

Once the train had left London and it western suburbs behind, its speed increased, and soon we were rattling through open vistas of cultivated fields and emerald green pastures, where cattle and sheep placidly grazed, oblivious to the noisy, smoking monster rushing by. For kids who'd spent their lives on London's grimy streets, these were living and moving picture-book scenes. With noses pressed against the coach windows, most of us watched excitedly and wondered aloud, as rural England flashed by.

Few evacuees had ever been on an "express" train. We were fascinated by the length of its coaches, the way they were divided into separate compartments connected by a corridor, and that each was equipped with the ultimate luxury, a lavatory!

Provided we stayed in our assigned coaches, we could roam the corridors, visit every compartment and mingle freely with other classmates. The re-unions were often boisterous by English standards, and when we were unexpectedly served box-lunches, any heartache from leaving our parents, was temporarily healed.

Speculation as to our journey's end, continued to be hotly debated. Given the perceived Nazi invasion threat, evacuation of women and children from England's southern coastal towns, had already begun, so any destination in that area, was unlikely. Before our train left Paddington, the teachers were talking Reading, in Berkshire, about eighty miles from London, but we went non-stop through that town, and were soon in Wiltshire.

Later, we entered Somerset, and speculation focused on Taunton, where we did stop, but only to be shunted off the main line, to let a regularly scheduled express pass by. At that point, the Devonshire town of Exeter, became the number one choice.

But we passed Exeter without stopping, and it wasn't until the train slowed to a crawl, to cross from Devon into Cornwall, over the famous, but aging Brunel Bridge, that our teachers finally told us that the cathedral town of Truro, was our destination.

At that point, we were given postcards which had been pre-stamped and addressed to our homes in London. On these, we were each expected to print the name and address of our Cornish guardians, and mail these without delay, so that our anxious families in London, would finally know our whereabouts.

It was late afternoon when we reached Truro, tired and grubby, and apprehensive about what would happen to us next. Waiting for our arrival were the men and women, who as surrogate parents, had agreed to shelter and feed us, until further notice.

Most who volunteered to take on this task, did so for patriotic or altruistic reasons. However, some saw evacuees as a ready source of household or farm labor help, and a way to supplement their family income with the weekly billeting stipend. This amounted to 10s 6d for one child, 8s 6d for two or more, paid by the British government, which in 1940, was quite a tidy sum.

Then there were those forced by government edict, to take in one or more children, based on available space at their homes, as determined by a government inspector. They accepted their assigned children reluctantly, and under protest, which made for a less than desirable environment, into which quite a few unfortunate children landed, with little or no support or recourse.

Finally, there was an understandable apprehension felt by those waiting at the station, stemming from news reports that had surfaced during the September, 1939 evacuations. These concerned the filthy condition, lack of personal hygiene and toilet habits of those children who came from the slums of London's East End.

Many had been raised in abject poverty, under horrendous living conditions, and arrived at their new homes, dirty and lice-ridden, often with scabies and rickets. Some came from homes without toilets, and were used to defecating on newspapers, and fully one third, routinely wet their beds. This created a serious housing problem, which the government addressed by adding a laundry allowance of 10s 6d, to the weekly billeting stipend.

Those waiting for our arrival, were lucky, because none of us were "slum" kids! While our parents were all working-class, and poor by any financial yardstick, Stroud Green was considered a middle-class neighborhood, where most housewives, including my step-mother, would, as a matter of personal pride, sweep and pumice-stone scrub their front steps, sometimes daily. And to the best of my memory, none of us had arrived with scabies or lice!

Upon leaving the train, we were put into a line-up, to be "inspected" and then "selected" by the waiting adults, none of whom knew the identity of the children they'd agreed to take, only their genders. In a way, this sad and demeaning ritual, endured by every child evacuee, was akin to the process followed in our own country, at its pre-Civil War slave auctions.

Healthy-looking, attractive children were much sought after, and were quickly chosen and whisked away. Those deemed less desirable by the "shoppers," often faced multiple rejections, until someone from the municipal Evacuee Committee, took them and went door to door, until homeowners were found who would agree to board the children temporarily, until permanent abodes could be found.

Adding to the fear and anguish of the children, who earlier that day had been summarily removed from their parents, was the fact that during the selection process, siblings were often separated, which is what happened to me and Mary, by eleven year old sister.

She and a classmate, Molly Malcolm, were chosen by a couple with a small child of their own, who had specifically requested two girls, while I was destined to be sent to live with a farmer and his wife, who wanted boys. Our new homes were about eight miles apart on opposite sides of Truro, and both were without phones.

Two months would pass before I'd see or speak to Mary again, making the promise I made to my Dad, to take care of my little sister, truly a "Mission Impossible!" Thankfully, neither Mary or I knew at the time, that a full year would pass before we'd see or speak to our parents and our sister Peg.

During the station line-up, a boy named Horace West and I were informed by a lady from the Evacuee Committee, that we'd been assigned to a local farm, and she promised to drive us there as soon as the selection process was over. I had hoped to be paired with a classmate, but Horace hadn't qualified for the advance study course that I'd been taking, so while we were the same age, our paths had not crossed until we boarded the evacuation train.

The sun was low on the horizon by the time we were dropped off at "Seveock Manor," the fifty-five acre farm where we were destined to live, for the next eighteen months. Waiting patiently for our arrival, were James and Florence Grenfell, a couple in their early thirties, who'd been married sixteen months earlier, shortly after the husband became the Manor's latest resident tenant-farmer, on land owned by the Viscount Falmouth.

Our new parents were typical "early to bed and early to rise" farmers, so as soon as Horace and I had been fed, Mrs. Grenfell, carrying an oil-lamp, led us up a huge wide staircase to a room on the second floor, sparsely furnished with an antique chest-of-drawers and two single beds. As tired as we were, I expect we quickly fell asleep, despite the unfamiliar "country" sounds, including the hoots of owls in pursuit of prey, which punctuated the night and invaded our room, through the open window.

I guarantee from personal experience, that anyone who lives on a farm, never sleeps after the dawn's early light, or needs an alarm clock as the means of waking up to a new day. A medley of barn-yard sounds greeted my ears, that first morning on the farm. Roosters crowed, chickens clucked, geese honked, guinea-fowls and pea-cocks screeched, pigs grunted and cattle lowed, on every key!

Sometime between 5:30 and 6:00 am, Horace and I gave up trying to sleep, and wandered downstairs to the kitchen, where a kettle steaming on an ancient cast-iron stove, was the only sign of life. About 7:00 am, Mrs. Grenfell came in from helping her husband and Edgar, their part-time hired hand, milk the farm's seventeen cows. When the men showed up, the five of us sat down to eat breakfast, each surreptitiously eyeing those faces around the table, that were new and unfamiliar.

To me, Mr. Grenfell was the quintessential farmer. Bright-eyed, ruddy-faced, raw-boned and wiry, he tended to be taciturn, no doubt due to the long hours spent working alone, trying to stay current with his infinite farm responsibilities. At that time in England, farming was still very labor intensive, with almost every task performed by hand, as it had been throughout the ages.

Mrs. Grenfell, also tanned from many hours in the sun, was a five foot three bundle of energy! In addition to preparing three meals a day, she baked bread, made delicious pies, churned milk into butter or Cornish cream, made her own jam and fruit preserves, and whenever needed, she was at her husband's side, assisting him in a variety of outside chores, the perfect farmer's wife in every respect.

Edgar, turned out to be younger than I'd thought, only fifteen years old, but taller, heavier and much more muscular than we city boys, a physique acquired during two years of working as a farm laborer, since quitting school early.

While we ate breakfast, Mrs. Grenfell told us that we wouldn't be starting school right away, as the nearest facility had neither the space nor the desks, to suddenly accommodate 30 evacuees from the Stroud Green contingent, who were now billeted in the area.

Needless to say, we boys weren't too upset by this news, which promised us a few days of free time, in which to thoroughly explore our new surroundings. First though, we had to complete the postcards addressed to our parents, and get these mailed, so that they'd know where we were, and who was looking after us.

The nearest post-office was in Chacewater, a village located a mile and a half from Seveock Manor. Mail was delivered and picked up by a postman, whose service to the various farms on his route required him to walk a considerable distance, each day. When he came by that first morning, Mrs. Grenfell introduced us, and while his name now escapes me, I recall that he was about my father's age, and was always very friendly and cheerful, despite having lost one of his arms in combat, during the First World War.

That first day on the farm, we boys trailed Mrs. G as she went about her daily chores. In the process, we became acquainted with the location of the storage barn, the equipment shed, the stable, the cow-shed where the milking took place, the other livestock sheds, the pig-sty and several chicken-houses. And, keeping a respectful distance, we watched the farm's animal population go in and out of the barn-yard, on their appointed summer schedules. Finally, Mr. Grenfell took time to walk us around the farm's perimeter, making very clear his purpose, that if we knew its boundaries, we'd have no excuse to stray or trespass beyond.

In one short day, I'd been introduced to an entirely new and different world, and when I went to bed that night, I was too excited to be home-sick. One thing I missed however, was the daily newspaper. The Grenfells relied on the radio for their link to the outside world, so the BBC's daily broadcasts became my only source of news. Unfortunately, during my eighteen months in Cornwall, war-news for the British was consistently bad and at times their gallant fight to remain free, appeared hopeless.

On June 28, we learned that Britain's Channel Islands of Jersey and Guernsey, located just fifty miles off the coast of occupied France, had been declared indefensible by the government, and those inhabitants who chose not to stay, had been evacuated. By July 1, both islands were occupied by Germany, which gave them the dubious distinction of being the only part of the United Kingdom invaded and ceded to the enemy, during World War II.

On July 2, Hitler issued orders, under the code name "Operation SEALION" for the invasion of mainland Britain. Initial plans called for the landing of airborne and ground forces on or around August 15, along a 200 mile stretch of England's southern coast, from Ramsgate in Kent, to Lyme Bay in Somerset. To this end, the full might of the Luftwaffe was directed at attacking British ships entering the English Channel, and bombing the vital ports and harbor facilities, which were their destinations.

On July 10, as part of this massive air campaign, Falmouth, a busy port on Cornwall's southern coast only 10 miles from where I now lived, was bombed, the first of many raids which were to follow. At that point in time, no bombs had yet fallen in London, so there was a certain irony to my being able to personally witness the not so distant sights and sounds of an air-raid in progress, after being evacuated 300 miles, for my own safety!

History records that the German dictator was so confident that the British, when invaded, would either sure for peace or would be easily defeated on the battlefield, that he further directed his military planners charged with implementing "SEALION," to simultaneously prepare for an invasion of the Soviet Union.

As Britain girded for the inevitable, 1,500,000 men, many World War I veterans too old for the draft, volunteered to serve in the newly formed civilian Home Guard. Their numbers constituted a much needed addition to the 400,000 veterans, who'd earlier been rescued from capture or annihilation from the beaches at Dunkirk.

Unfortunately, the cost in weapons and supplies left behind, was staggering! British troops abandoned 11,000 machine guns, 1,200 artillery pieces, 1,250 anti-aircraft/anti-tank guns, 6,400 tank rifles, 75,000 vehicles and over 500,000 tons of supplies.

Consequently, the Home Guard's civilian army at that juncture, outnumbered the country's available supply of weapons, including serviceable rifles, of which there were only 175,000. This forced many HG units to drill and train for combat, armed with pitch-forks and broom-handles, spectacles which when witnessed by the population at large, did little to raise sagging morale!

Two days after Horace and I arrived at the farm, Mr. Barlow, the only teacher to accompany the Stroud Green contingent, came by to visit the Grenfells. He was accompanied by a member of the Truro Evacuee Committee, assigned to drive him around to all of the homes where his children were now billeted, to make sure that they had settled in, and were getting along with their guardians. He also brought us "good" news, school would begin the next day.

We discovered upon our arrival, that our new school was actually an old barn, which had been hurriedly converted to a one-room schoolhouse, for the sole use of the newly arrived evacuees. It was located in Baldhu, about two miles from our farm, across the road from the village school, which was too small to suddenly absorb our group. It had only one door and three windows, and was referred to as "Ruddy Beams" by the locals, due to the dark red stain applied over many years, to the massive interior cross-members, which supported its ancient roof.

It was on our first day at Ruddy Beams, that I learned that my sister Mary would not be a part of the class. She and her friend Molly, were billeted in Perrenwell, a village too far from Baldhu for them to walk the distance each day, so they were forced to attend a different school, closer to where they lived.

The barn was now equipped with sufficient old desks to seat all of us, plus a table and chair for Mr. Barlow. It boasted several make-shift bookshelves, a cabinet and a well-worn blackboard. It had no sink, fireplace or stove. Each day, water for drinking or washing was carried in a bucket from the village school to the barn, by one of the boy's who'd been assigned that task. On chilly days, we kept warm by wearing our jackets in class.

Outside, at the rear of the barn, two wooden "privies" had been erected, one for boys and the other for girls. Mr. Barlow, in deference to his position, was given access to the teachers' lavatory, located across the road inside the village school.

It was in this incredibly primitive environment, that Mr. B was expected to teach all basic subjects to thirty children, ranging in age from ten to thirteen who in London, had been taught at three different grade levels. In a nut-shell, with all of us now confined to one class, the only way he could hope to hold the interest and attention of the group as a whole, was to teach "down" to me and the older kids, and teach "up" to the youngest ones, a less than ideal arrangement for all concerned.

Needless to say, an assignment like that would easily test the patience, imagination and commitment of any teacher, and for the venerable Mr. Barlow, with a quarter of a century of traditional teaching under his belt, the challenge must have seemed overwhelming.

However, as I look back on my eighteen months at Ruddy Beams, I have to admit that while the education I received there, came no where near providing the "advanced" studies I'd been promised a year earlier, given the circumstances, Mr. B's innovative approach to teaching, was both caring and effective, not unlike that demonstrated by Sidney Poitier in "To Sir With Love."

Those of you who remember that hit movie of the Sixties, will recall that Poitier played a teacher at a run-down school in one of London's poorest East End neighborhoods. His efforts to teach the "3Rs" in a traditional fashion, to a class of fourteen and fifteen year olds, was met with hostility and sullen disinterest.

Frustrated and discouraged, he was ready to quit, but as he got to know his students, he learned about their families and their grim home lives, and the depressing future which most of them assumed would be their lot, as poor working-class adults.

Poitier's epiphany occurred when he concluded that while the "3Rs" were important, his kids had no choice but to leave school in a matter of months, so he needed a different approach. He decided that if he focused on teaching them good manners, personal hygiene, discipline and respect for others, and expose them occasionally to selected museum and art galleries, he might possibly lift their collective self esteem and better prepare them as individuals, for more meaningful and satisfying adult lives, despite their bleak social and economic circumstances.

So it was with Mr. Barlow. Faced with the impossible, he adapted! He would start off each day by reading aloud a passage from the Holy Bible, which he'd then artfully weave into a real life situation, that we could all understand and relate to. Then we'd be assigned lessons to read from our math, history and geography books, after which he'd ply us with questions from the floor. Fortunately, enough text-books were available to take care of the different ages represented in our class, so that we were all able to study and participate, at our own grade levels.

When it came to our "mother tongue," he concentrated mainly on spelling and correct pronounciation, spending little or no time trying to explain the rules of English grammar to such an age-mixed audience. Instead, he'd read to us each day, using works from two of his favorite authors, Arthur Conan-Doyle and Jack London. It should come as no surprise, that of the various characters introduced to us in those reading sessions, Sherlock Holmes and Dr. Watson were the hands down, class favorites!

By the time we'd all gotten to know Mr. Barlow, and were getting used to his "school-in-a-barn" curriculum, July came to an end, and our summer vacation began. We had the whole month of August off, with no school until the first Monday in September.

CHAPTER 10

Seveock Manor and Life on the Farm

Despite my brotherly concern at not being able to see or talk to my sister Mary since our separation a week earlier, I settled down rather quickly, and began to enjoy life on the farm.

First off, I was getting much more to eat than I'd ever gotten at home, simply because farmers, unlike Londoners and other city folk, could grow, raise or produce as much food as they needed. Despite wartime restrictions on the butchering of livestock or poultry for their own consumption, most farm families continued to eat better than their city cousins, for whom meat, bacon, poultry, eggs and dairy products, remained rationed or in short supply during six years of war, and for at least two more years after Germany and Japan had surrendered.

Also, having grown up in a big city, I found that I rather liked living on a quiet lane, lined with trees and wild-blackberry bushes, surrounded by fields of pasture, wheat, oats, barley and various vegetables, with a shallow stream gurgling away within earshot, some 500 feet from the farmhouse.

Seveock Manor itself, was a unique and historic structure. Erected in the mid-1700s, its builder had incorporated part of an earlier dwelling (circa 1600), into the main structure, and much of its interior had survived the passage of time. Many of its 12-pane windows contained their original "crown" glass, and parts of the original kitchen fireplace, were intact. It boasted an immense front-door hallway, and a curved double-wide central staircase with an oak handrail. How many rooms it had escapes me, as many were not in use by the Grenfells, and were kept locked.

According to a local legend, the Manor had once served as a refuge for King Charles II, following the Battle of Tresillian. Given my fertile imagination, I was convinced that had I been permitted to explore its every inch, I most surely would have discovered at least one "secret" room, complete with an ancient sword or musket, and perhaps even a skeleton! Unfortunately, except for the kitchen, scullery, pantry and creamery, where Mrs. G churned milk into butter or Cornish cream, and the bedroom I shared with Horace, most of the rooms in this fascinating relic of a bygone age, remained off-limits during my entire stay.

The dwelling certainly hadn't changed much over the centuries. It had no bath, sinks or toilet facilities. Water for any purpose, had to be pumped by hand from a deep well located outside, and carried inside in buckets, as needed. Oil-lamps were used for lighting purposes, and cooking was done on a wood-burning stove.

The Manor's out-house (a haven for the largest spiders I'd ever seen), was nothing more than a rough-hewed toilet seat placed over a large tub. When the tub was full, its contents had to be manually emptied into a horse-drawn open tank, and carted away to be dumped, I know not where. The men who made their living performing this unpleasant task for the many homes without toilets or septic systems, were called "honey dippers," a strange and somewhat inappropriate euphemism, to say the least!

Within a week of our arrival, Horace and I had explored Seveock Manor's entire 55 acres, and had chosen a spot, away from the house but close to the stream, as our secret "hideaway." We built a primitive hut from saplings which we cut ourselves, over which we stretched old grain sacks, salvaged from those discarded by Mr. Grenfell. Camped out in that home-made hut, miles away from the din of London's streets, it was as if I'd been magically transported into one of my favorite adventure-book worlds.

As I mentioned previously, farming in England in the Forties, was very labor intensive, so not surprisingly, it wasn't long before we boys were expected to toil beside the Grenfells and their hired hand, whenever we weren't in school. We learned how to milk a cow, and were soon helping to perform this task twice a day. We carried feed to the chickens and collected their eggs, fed the pigs and horses, carried heavy buckets of water from the household pump to the stable and cow-sheds, and each day, with a shovel and pitch-fork, cleaned out the animal stalls.

Soon I was working longer and harder than I'd ever done before, but I don't think that bothered me, because what I was doing was new and different from anything I'd been used to in London. Even the four mile round-trip walk each day to school, didn't faze me, except perhaps when it rained, because in those days, any "real" boy, would rather have been caught dead, than carrying an umbrella. If I got wet going to school, I could only hope that during the return trip home, the sun would shine and dry me off.

But central to the manner in which I was able to quickly adapt to my new life, were the Grenfells. They could not have been kinder or more caring, had I been their own flesh and blood. As long as I was polite and well behaved, and did my assigned chores without complaint, which was nothing more or less than was expected of me at home, we got along famously. Given the uncaring and sometimes abusive treatment, which many less fortunate evacuees endured at the hands of their surrogate parents, I was very lucky indeed.

Mr. Grenfell, raised an Episcopalian, rarely attended church, no doubt due to the fact that Sundays on the farm, were much like any other day, as respects his work-load. His wife however, was a regular church-goer, and she insisted that Horace and I accompany her to a tiny Methodist Church, a short walk from the farm.

Horace obviously wasn't used to spending his Sunday mornings in church, and he often grumbled about this, which resulted in his getting to stay home to help Mr. G with his chores. Choosing whether or not to attend church, had never been an option for me at home, so I went willingly. Actually, I even looked forward to church, as that was the only time that I got to wear my long pants. The rest of the week, they remained hidden under the mattress on my bed, an effective albeit primitive way, of making sure they were always neatly creased.

The farm's herd of milking cows fluctuated in number between fourteen and seventeen. The majority of them were tan-coated Guernseys, with several red, white-faced Shorthorns, and one black and white Holstein. They'd all been given names as calves, and after a while, I could tell one from the other, and who was who.

The farm was also home to about twenty yearlings, offspring of the cows who were not yet a year old. The females or "heifers," were being raised for breeding purposes, and at the appropriate time, they'd be mated with the Grenfell's bull. After delivering their first calf, they'd live out their years producing milk twice daily and additional calves as needed. The "steers," males that had been castrated as calves, were being raised as beef-cattle, to be sold at maturity, on the open market.

Seveock Manor's bull was a Guernsey, whose sole purpose in life was to service the farm's cows when appropriate, the heifers as they came of age, and the cows and heifers of neighboring farmers, who didn't own bulls of their own. He had his own stall in the cow-shed, but except for the winter months, he spent his time in a field adjacent to the barnyard, tethered to a long length of chain, which was fastened at one end to a heavy wheel, and the other end, to a large brass ring in his nose.

A Guernsey bull weighs about 1,700 pounds, and the only way to keep that much muscle and surly disposition under control, is by way of his nose, which once it has been pierced and ringed, is probably his most sensitive body part. When in the field, he needed at least two large buckets of water, twice daily, and that chore was generally assigned to me.

As a half-pint city boy, tipping the scales at 97 pounds, I admit to being terrified of this beast, who'd stand pawing the ground and snorting at the farthest point of his chain, awaiting my arrival with the water. I soon learned however, that provided I placed the buckets just inside his perimeter and kept myself out of his reach, he could do me no harm.

Nevertheless, my ability to control my fear of this creature, was sorely tested the day a neighbor farmer showed up with a cow to be serviced, and Mr. G, who was busy at the time, sent me to get the bull. This required that I take him a bucket of water and while he drank, slip two fingers through his nose-ring, unfasten the chain and while gripping the ring firmly, lead him back to the barn-yard. There, Mr. G fastened another chain onto his ring, and walked him snorting with anticipation into the yard to the waiting cow, where he proceeded with his usual enthusiasm, to do that which came naturally.

Fortunately, when the deed had been done, and properly recorded as required by the authorities, and the service fee had been collected,

Mr. G personally escorted the bull back to the field, thus sparing me a second encounter of the scariest kind!

The Grenfells owned two horses, "Tinker" a big brawny Belgian somewhat advanced in age with a friendly docile disposition, and "Titch" a younger, smaller and much livelier animal, probably of Morgan stock. Despite their different bloodlines, they worked well together, when hitched side-by-side to heavy equipment, where maximum horsepower was essential.

Titch was also put into service twice each day, pulling the two-wheel cart in which churns containing raw milk were carried from the farm to the nearest highway, for pick-up by the local dairy. On the trip back, Mr. G would give Titch his head, and he'd break into a gallop, something I never saw old Tinker do. He usually drew the one-horse heavy work, like ploughing, harrowing and raking, where power and stamina counted for more than speed.

Before we arrived on the farm, neither Horace nor I had ever had anything to do with horses, but from his first contact, Horace was clearly more at ease with them than I. He could go into their stalls with bridles and harness, and have them ready to go in no time. One day while Tinker was out grazing, Horace maneuvered him up to an earthen hedge from where he was able to climb aboard and ride the old horse bare-back, around the field.

I could put a bridle on Tinker who'd stand placidly no matter how long it took, but Titch was another story. No doubt smelling my fear the first time that I was sent into his stall to bridle him, he rolled his eyes, tossed his head and moved against me, pinning me between his flanks and the stall.

Mr. G thought this was hilarious, pointing out as he rescued me, that all I needed to have done, was to slap Titch on the rump, and he would have moved. Unfortunately, to a scared kid, slapping the monster's backside didn't at the time, seem like the smart thing to do! Thankfully, from that day on, I was spared any further stall-time with Titch.

The Grenfells owned two dogs, a "Lassie" look-alike named Jack, and Flo, a black and white English Border Collie. Flo, typical of her breed, was a working animal who, twice a day, acting on the whistle commands of Mr. G, would bring the cows in from their pasture, to be milked.

I always enjoyed watching Flo at work. Mr. G would open the gate to the field where the cows had spent the night or the day, and send her on her way. Sometimes the herd would be out of sight, but in no time at all, we'd hear their mournful "moos" and see them lumbering towards the gate, with Flo running back and forth in the rear, occasionally barking at the slow-pokes.

When the milking was over, we'd release the cows from their stalls into the barnyard, and with Flo at their heels, the herd would return to the pasture, to graze for the next 12 hours until Flo showed up again, and the process was repeated.

Jack the older of the two dogs, unlike Flo, had no appointed tasks that I was aware of. He'd sit watching we humans and the animals come and go, and when coaxed, would get up and follow Horace and I everywhere we went. But other than being good company and barking at the mail-man making his daily delivery, Jack's contribution to the well-being of the farm, was minimal.

It was during my first summer on the farm, that I became acquainted with the blood-sucking member of the arachnid family, the tick, something I'd never seen or even heard of in London. As a result of their constant wanderings through the fields and underbrush, the dogs picked up scores of ticks, which Horace and I spent many evenings arduously removing, as best we could.

Given our own outdoor activities, it wasn't long before these little pests were showing up on various parts of our own bodies, making it necessary to also groom ourselves, on a daily basis. Fortunately, other than localized itching at the site where the tick plugged in, we suffered no ill effects from the exposures.

The one true unpleasant thing about Jack and Flo, was their bizarre and disgusting appetites. They'd eat anything and everything! These traits were probably common to most farm dogs, who were expected to live outdoors all year round, and subsist on the family's leftover or discarded food, or forage for whatever other sustenance was available and presented itself.

Two examples! More than once, following the birth of a calf, I saw both dogs feasting on the recently expelled placenta and other afterbirth remains. They would also hang around calves not yet weaned from their mother's milk, waiting for their bowel-movements, which they'd swallow in a flash! These were truly nauseating spectacles, that unfortunately, I've never forgotten.

The farm was also home to many cats, but these were essentially feral, and quite unlike the friendly creatures I'd been used to at home. They roamed at will, existing on the mice attracted to the grain and animal feed stored in the barn and livestock sheds.

Only at milking time did they fraternize with us, drawn to the dishes of warm milk we'd put out for them. After finishing the milk, they'd sit by patiently knowing that at some time, one of us boys would take aim with a teat, and spray whichever cat was in range, and watch the others rush to lick him dry.

Another chore which fell to Horace and I, was the care and feeding of two ferrets. These were housed in separate cages, and kept not as household pets as they are today in America, but as rabbit-hunters, and for that purpose, they were very effective.

The earth and rock hedgerows which dot the English countryside, separating one field from the next, are home to thousands of rabbit families whose burrows form an intricate system of tunnels, with holes to the outside strategically placed, enabling the occupants to hide or flee in any direction, as is necessary.

Whenever Mrs. Grenfell decided to put rabbit-stew on her menu, we'd head out in the evening to one of the fields, carrying the ferrets, plus five or six small nets and a length of primer-cord used in blasting. The noise of our approach, would drive any foraging rabbits back into the nearest burrow, which was exactly where we wanted them. We'd quickly drape nets over all of the entrance/exit holes, and slip in one of the ferrets.

This cousin of the weasel, is a bloodthirsty little predator and the rabbit its natural prey, so its presence in the burrow was guaranteed to panic the occupants and send them helter-skelter for the nearest exit, and into our nets. If Mrs. G wanted only one rabbit, we'd select the biggest and set the others free.

If we were lucky, the ferrets would also exit the burrow into a net, and we could go home. However, sometimes one would catch and kill a rabbit, and then after he'd eaten his fill, he'd decide to take a nap leaving us stuck in the field for hours, waiting for him to wake up and show himself.

That's when the primer-cord came in handy. After making sure that all the exit holes were securely netted, we'd light the cord and shove it into the burrow. Dense acrid smoke would drift out of the holes, and minutes later, a runny-eyed, fat bellied ferret would emerge, somewhat aggravated, but none the worse for wear.

When he was back in his cage, we still had one more thing to do, kill and gut the rabbit we'd caught before delivering it to Mrs. G. I see no point in detailing how we did this, except to say that for me, the act was never easy or guilt free. Nevertheless, during my stay on the farm, it was another task that I learned to perform, and accept as inherent to the business of hunting, when this was required to put extra food on the table.

Hunting also gave Horace and I our first exposure to firearms. Mr. James, who worked one of the adjacent farms, had a sixteen year old son who liked to hunt small game and occasionally, he'd take us along. He owned a .22 rifle and two shot-guns, a single-barrel .410 and a double-barrel 12 gauge. My favorite was the .410, that being the lightest weapon in his arsenal.

As a result of our acquaintance, he gave me an air-rifle which he no longer used, and a supply of pellets. After I'd practiced for a while shooting at cans and other inanimate objects, I took aim at what I thought was a starling sitting in the tree above me, and brought it down with my first shot.

Flushed with pride, I showed the dead bird to Mrs. G who said it wasn't a starling but a blackbird. She then told me that at an earlier time in England's history, blackbirds were considered a culinary delicacy, and promised that the next day, while I was at school, she'd pluck it and put it in the oven, just for me!

I thought she was kidding, because who in his right mind would want to eat a blackbird, but when I returned from school, there on the kitchen table, was a plate containing the roasted bird. Mrs. G sat me down, handed me a knife and fork and waited for me to make the first cut. The bird was so small, I didn't know where to start, and my stomach was already warning me of the probable consequences, should I proceed.

Fortunately, Mrs. G (bless her soul) never intended to force the issue. This was her way of teaching me a lesson, that killing out of hunger or necessity, was one thing, but the random taking of a life to prove one's marksmanship, was something else. And at that, my surprise "roast" became a meal for one of the dogs.

Another lesson I learned as a fledgling hunter, concerned the lowly crow, which I decided was one smart bird! The farm was home to scores of crows, who given their appetite for grain, were viewed as pests and thus fair game for anyone with a gun, who could get close enough to make a kill.

That was easier said than done. Many times, I headed out to where I knew the flock was on the ground scavenging, with my trusty air-rifle cocked and ready, only to see them take off before I got within range, "cawing" away, as if laughing at my efforts. But on those occasions that I'd be out in the field without my gun, I could walk up to the flock and practically be on top of them, before they'd get airborne. Somehow, they had an uncanny instinct as to when my presence was, or wasn't a threat.

Like many English tenant-farmers of his generation, Mr. Grenfell rarely sought the help of a veterinarian in dealing with a sick animal, except where professional involvement was mandated by law, or when the illness and treatment was beyond his own knowledge or frame of reference. As a result, I was present a number of times where his homegrown expertise was put to the test, and two incidents in particular, I'll always remember.

The first was his handling of a young steer who had gone without eating or having a bowel movement for more than 24 hours, a sure sign that all was not well. Based on his years as a farmer, he concluded that the animal had a bowel obstruction, and proceeded accordingly, as he'd probably done many times before.

Mrs. G brought a bucket of warm water and bar of soap to the stall where the steer was chained. Mr. G washed and thoroughly lathered his hand and arm as far as the elbow, then as I watched with disbelief, he gently inserted first a finger, then his hand and then his arm, into the steer's anus, while the hapless animal stomped its hooves and bellowed its head off.

This was a sight and sound for which I was totally unprepared, but about the time that I knew I should get out before I went under, Mr. G's face lit up like he'd found the Holy Grail! His arm slowly emerged, then his hand, which clutched a large ball of excreta, which was immediately followed by more of the same, in liquid form. His diagnosis had been correct, the "operation" a success, and the steer and I had survived the ordeal!

The other example of Mr. G's homegrown veterinarian talents which remains imprinted on my memory, involved the castration of four boar piglets, part of a litter recently born to our resident sow. As usual, Horace and I were drafted to assist in the operation, though neither of us knew why or how, castration was performed.

Mr. G told me to sit down and hold a squealing piglet "belly-up" between my knees. I had no inkling of what was to come, until he produced a straight-razor and with one deft stroke, opened up the animal's scrotum, and with his thumbs, popped out the testes which, as they hit the barn floor, were pounced on and swallowed by Jack and Flow, our omnipresent and always hungry, farm dogs.

Witnessing all of that was too much for me, and I fainted! When I came to, Mrs. G was holding my head in her lap, passing a bottle of smelling-salts under my nose. Fortunately, she'd been on hand, and managed to grab my piglet and hold on to it while her husband, using an ordinary needle and thread from her sewing basket, stitched the incision closed. Horace hadn't fainted at any time during the four castrations, so needless to say, I took plenty of ribbing from Mr. G, Horace and Edgar the farm-hand.

In retrospect, I often wonder what the farm animal mortality rate was back then, when for economic reasons, many farmers doubled as vets, despite lacking any formal training or access to the proper instruments and medications in use by the professionals.

While on the subject of animal husbandry as practiced at Seveock Manor, I'll share another recollection, this concerning a task which

Mr. G actually delegated to Horace and I. During late spring and summer, our cow herd was preyed upon by the "Bot-fly," more commonly known as the "warble-fly" by the locals. This is a large fly which heralds its presence with a loud and distinctive buzz, which when heard by our cows, would send the usually docile animals, into a minor frenzy, with good reason.

The "warble" would usually land on a cow's back out of reach of its swinging tail. Its bite would create a minute incision into which it would deposit an egg, from which a parasitic larvae developed, to feed on the cow's flesh, until such time as its metamorphosis, emerging then as an adult fly.

The larvae presence in the cow was not discernable until its size caused a protuberance much like a boil, to appear on the animal's back. At that point, its growth could be halted before it matured and emerged, and the disgusting cycle repeated itself.

The treatment was simple enough. We boys were expected to check the backs of the herd each day when they came in to be milked. If we spotted the tell-tale "boil," we'd use a small brush to rub into the incision, a derris-powder paste, an insecticide derived from the derris root, a vine-like shrub. This killed the larvae, causing it to eject itself in the process, not a pretty sight. It was another chore we handled, no doubt assigned to us to keep "idle hands from the devil's work," that long hot summer of 1940.

Having a month off from school, didn't turn out to be the "lazy days of summer" vacation that Horace and I had anticipated. August was a very busy time for Cornish farmers, with the annual harvesting of their fields of grain, taking center stage. The timing of this was dependent on each individual's judgment as to when the ears were fully ripened, and when the weather could be counted on to deliver a series of dry, sunny days.

Mr. G owned a "binder," a horse-drawn mower, so called because as the stalks of wheat, barley or oats fell under its oscillating blades, a continuously moving belt carried them to the rear of the machine, where a device tied them into bundles before kicking them out onto the ground. Cutting a clean swath through tight rows of mature stalks, called for considerable power delivered at a fast pace, and this could only be accomplished and maintained for an extended period of time, with a three-horse team.

This required the loan of another horse to work with Titch and Tinker in a triple side-by-side hitch. Mr. James, who operated a farm next to ours, could always be counted on in this regard, and he'd usually stay and help. While Mr. G held the reins of all three horses from his seat on the binder, Mr. James would walk alongside, holding the bridle of the nearest horse, pulling and coaxing the entire team to deliver its maximum effort.

Bringing up the rear, Mrs. Grenfell and I and Horace and Edgar, working as teams, would pick up the bundles of grain dropped by the binder, and stand these on end, six to a stack. This was called "shocking." Many hours of doing this under a hot sun, was not only back-breaking, but also hard on the arms, as constant contact with the sharp-edged spikelets common to the ears of wheat and barley, would leave one's bare arms red and raw.

The harvesting process required that the crop be completely dry, which usually served to postpone the actual cutting until late morning, after the dew had evaporated. This in turn meant that we'd often be in the fields, working non-stop, until dusk.

Meanwhile, the cows still had to be milked on schedule, so at the appointed hour, Mrs. Grenfell would leave the field to take care of that necessary chore. She'd usually take me along to assist her, and later we'd return with a basket of food and jugs of water and milk. After five or more hours of "shocking" in the hot sun, I was always happy to retire with Mrs. G to the cow-shed, sit on a stool and rest my weary head against the warm flanks of a cow, while bringing welcome relief to the beast's swollen udder.

A week after all the wheat, oats and barley crops had been harvested, Mr. G arranged for the local "thresherman" to bring his trademark equipment to the farm, with which the grain would be separated from the ears and stalks. Given my interest in steam-engines, I was thrilled to learn that the threshing-machine's power was provided by a steam-driven traction-engine, so on the day it was to arrive, I waited at the end of our lane.

While I knew what to expect, I'd never actually seen a traction-engine. I recall that when it appeared with the threshing-machine in tow, chuffing along at 3 miles an hour, shrouded in smoke and steam, its gigantic treaded-steel driving-wheels grinding and clanking away, I was suitably impressed.

The thresherman turned out to be a "Barry FitzGerald" look-alike, a tiny wizened old man, smoking a corncob pipe who, when he turned into our lane, stopped the engine and asked who I was. Learning that I was an evacuee, he invited me up into the cab to ride with him, which of course made my day. Unfortunately, what lay ahead, was not nearly as much fun as the ride.

Upon arriving at the farm, the traction-engine was maneuvered into its stationary operating position, to provided power by way of a continuous belt connection from the engine's huge fly-wheel, to the threshing-machine. Threshing was another labor intensive task that everyone faced each year, so by tradition, it was done cooperatively. Farmer neighbors could be counted on to show up and provide the necessary manpower, knowing that when they needed the same kind of help, it would always be forthcoming.

Two-man teams with horse-drawn wagons, would shuttle back and forth between the threshing machine and the fields where the harvested crops were stacked, bringing in the tied bundles. Two other men would toss these bundles to a third, sitting on the top of the machine. He'd cut the twine, and drop the bundles into a chute, where they'd be engaged by the machine's whirring innards.

The machine would discharge the stalks, minus their ears, and another two-man team, wielding rakes, would throw these onto a wagon, to be driven to the barn, and stored as the farm's future straw supply. The grain was discharged through vents into sacks, and as these filled, they too were transported to the barn. Mr. G. would sell some of the grain as animal feed on the open market, but most of what he produced, he kept as feed for his own stock.

The final and most unpleasant task associated with the threshing process, gravitated to Horace and I. Separating the grain from the ears produced "chaff" a dusty waste product that was blown out of the rear of the machine. Armed with rakes, we boys were expected to keep up with the machine's non-stop chaff production, raking it away before it could pile up and block the discharge vent. Standing knee-deep in wheat, barley and oat chaff, we were soon covered from head to foot in this infernally itchy stuff, which got into our eyes, noses, ears and mouths, and glued itself to our sweating faces, arms and legs.

Because the farm had no tub or shower facilities, all we could look forward to before going to bed, was a make-shift bucket-wash. I don't recall doing anything on the farm that I disliked more than being a threshing-machine "rake" boy, and I was grateful that the chore came around just once a year.

CHAPTER 11

Battle of Britain and the "Blitz"

As important and manpower dependent as the harvesting and threshing operations were, all of the daily tasks inherent with a thriving dairy farm, also needed to be taken care of in a timely fashion. As a result, during most of August, the Grenfell household was on a dawn-to-dusk work schedule. Our only time off came before we turned in for the night. We'd gather around the kitchen table to enjoy a last minute snack, and listen to the BBC broadcast the latest war news, which continued to be bad.

The massive air attacks on England's southern coastal ports which began in July, had continued without let-up until August 15 when, as a prelude to Hitler's planned invasion of England, the full brunt of the onslaught on harbor facilities ended, and what was to become known as the "Battle of Britain" began.

Code named "Operation Adlertag" (Eagle Day), by the German High Command, the Luftwaffe's new orders were to severely cripple the Royal Air Force (RAF). On the eve of this historic encounter, its forces in Western Europe numbered 1,514 bombers, 809 fighters and 280 fighter-bombers. Arrayed against this formidable air armada, were 609 RAF fighters, some of which were nearing obsolescence.

The mission of the German bombers, was to destroy RAF bases and airfields, which attacks were expected to entice the RAF's fighters into the air, where Hitler assumed they'd be overwhelmed and defeated by his numerically superior fighter squadrons.

On the first two days of that air offensive, Nazi bombers and fighters, manned by mature pilots, many with previous combat time in the skies over Spain and Poland, flew 3,506 sorties. The RAF's outnumbered pilots, most of whom were in their teens or early twenties with no prior combat experience, rose to engage them, again and again. Surprisingly, losses between the antagonists were remarkable similar. During 3 weeks of continuous daytime battle, the RAF lost 444 aircraft to the Luftwaffe's 443.

As August drew to a close, it must have been clear to Hitler that despite the non-stop bombing of its ground facilities, the RAF was still a viable and potent adversary, so he re-scheduled "Operation SeaLion" for September 21. He'd been assured by his High Command that by then, the RAF would no longer pose a serious threat to his sea-borne invasion forces.

However, on the night of August 23, 10 German bombers, part of a mission to attack oil storage facilities outside of London, strayed off their assigned course, and dropped their bombs within London's city limits. Two nights later, in retaliation for this first raid on London, a force of RAF bombers treated Berlin, Germany's capital, to its baptism of fire.

This and subsequent raids on Germany, so incensed Hitler, that he ordered the Luftwaffe to end its attacks on RAF installations, and direct its efforts into concentrated night raids on Britain's cities. Militarily, that decision was a monumental blunder. Having the Luftwaffe target civilians instead of pursuing its original goal of destroying the RAF in order to guarantee its air superiority over the beaches of England, put at risk any chance of a successful invasion from the sea by German ground forces.

School resumed at Ruddy Beams on the first Monday of September, and after a month of outdoor physical labor, I was more than ready to sit for a few hours at a desk, and exercise my brain for a change, rather than my overworked muscles. Even so, Horace and I were still expected to help with the milking and other farm chores, before leaving on our daily two mile trek to school.

It was good to see my classmates again, but the unexpected and most pleasant surprise was to find among them, my sister Mary who I hadn't seen since we arrived in Cornwall, two months earlier. Mary and her friend Molly, had been very unhappy isolated from the other evacuees, but thanks to Mr. Barlow's efforts, they now lived with a new family in "Lemon Cottage" located in Baldhu, quite close to our Ruddy Beams.

As his first order of business, Mr. B announced that we'd be starting a "Victory Garden" in a plot of ground next to Ruddy Beams, and that we'd all be expected to dig, plant, water and weed, and whatever else was necessary to its success. I still marvel at his stubborn optimism, making plans for a vegetable harvest more than six months off, at a moment in history when an invasion by the world's most successful military machine, was deemed to be inevitable and imminent! However, perhaps that was just his way of helping us kids cope with the latest dramatic turn of events, in a war now entering its second year.

On September 7, a new phase of the "Battle of Britain" began, that was destined to go down in English history as "The Blitz." German bombers, attacking in waves throughout the day and night, dropped massive numbers of incendiary and high-explosive bombs on London. During the next 68 days, with few exceptions, between 150 and 300 bombers returned to the capital and dropped at least 100 tons of explosives, each and every night.

Oddly enough, half-way through that horrendous period, the RAF officially declared that the "Battle of Britain" had ended, but that was of little consolation to those under siege. Air attacks continued unabated during the rest of the year, and into the first five months of 1941, costing the lives of 40,000 civilians and seriously injuring 50,000 more.

Imagine if you can, being a child under fourteen years old, 300 miles away from parents and older siblings, listening every day over a period of nine months, to BBC reports that your home-town had been bombed again, unable to make any contact by phone, and having to rely solely on a weekly letter, to confirm whether or not family members were still alive, or among the casualties.

As evacuees, we were expected to endure this situation without complaint or visible emotional distress, on the basis that we were among the lucky ones, safely away from the actual war-zone, and as I remember it, we proved equal to those expectations, even when news of a family casualty surfaced within our own ranks.

I can't help comparing what we went through with today's society, where any untoward event involving children, mandates that an army of psychologists or therapists be dispatched to the scene, to provide individual and group counseling. Was my generation a tougher breed, or are we underestimating the ability and natural resilience of children to cope with the unexpected, and as a result, could our societal reaction be somewhat overprotective?

Be that as it may, despite the substantial civilian casualties and the enormous distruction of property suffered by many cities, the "blitz" failed to break the spirit of the British people. More importantly from a military standpoint, and to the eventual outcome of the war, it proved to be a major defeat for Germany, as it essentially ensured the survival and growth of the RAF, thus denying Hitler the air superiority without which, he could not launch a successful sea-borne invasion of the British Isles.

Nevertheless, plans to defend against an invasion continued throughout the land, and eventually hit home when Mr. Grenfell, who as a farmer, was exempted from active military service, was required to join the Home Guard. He was issued a uniform and a rifle, and one evening a week, he'd leave the farm for whatever training or guard duty was assigned to his unit.

By October, activities at school were soon following a familiar routine. We began each day with Bible readings, studied our text books individually and participated in discussions as a class, although given our age disparities, these were not always very effective or enlightening. When it wasn't raining, the boys would get in a game of soccer while the girls played rounders, and we willingly put in the allotted hours at our new vegetable patch.

As part of our English studies, Mr. Barlow presented us with a new challenge. He announced that hc planned to acquaint us with the works of Shakespeare by reading aloud from certain of his plays, then having older students memorize and perform selected portions, before the class. Thus was born the Ruddy Beams Drama Club, and as one of the class elders, I was expected to participate.

To introduce us to the Bard of Avon, Mr. Barlow read from Scene II of Act III, of "Julius Caesar," and explained the politics and intriguc associated with the story plot. Then he focused on the section of Scene II that he wanted us to dramatize, a part featuring only three main characters and "extras" aplenty.

In a class with only 10 children over thirteen, securing volunteers for our group's first production, could have been a problem, but Mr. Barlow made it easy. He looked us over, pointed a finger here and there, and in no time at all, casting was complete, and "yours truly" had been chosen to play Mark Anthony!

For me, memorizing the written word had never been a problem, but given my predisposition to becoming tongue-tied when forced to speak in public, the very thought of standing in front of my class, reciting pages of olde English prose, was a nightmare! However, this was not an optional assignment. Mr. B handed out copies of JC to the cast members, and instructed us to begin learning our lines immediately, hinting that he'd be testing us on a daily basis, until we were performance ready.

Those who are familiar with the play, know that Mark Anthony's speaking role in the portion selected to be dramatized, is quite substantial. Many chores awaited me at the farm after school, so finding time to memorize my lines, was limited. My biggest burden however, was the fear and trepidation I endured wondering how I'd ever be able to get all those words I'd memorized, to leave my stubborn mouth on cue.

It was almost Christmas before Mr. B decided that we were ready to act out the lines we'd taken months to learn. Ruddy Beams had no stage, so we had to perform in the front of the class. We were bare-footed, clad in white bed-sheets passing as togas, wearing cardboard cut-outs made by the younger kids, to resemble Roman head-gear. What a rag-tag bunch, but no troup of professional thespians ever heard more enthusiastic cheers and applause, than we received from our classmates.

And that day, standing before the class for the first time in the guise of Mark Anthony, I truly experienced a personal epiphany! My first words, "Friends, Romans, countrymen" tumbled out of my mouth, freely and unfettered by the affliction which had plagued me for as long as I could remember. I learned to my amazement, a reality that changed me and subsequently my future, that when I stepped into the shoes of another person to recite words not mine but imprinted on my memory, that the character I portrayed, didn't have a speech problem.

I think at that moment, I was convinced that the actor's life was for me. Fortunately, at least in retrospect a stage career was not to be. However, my newly discovered talent and flair for the dramatic, and the unexpected impact this had on my ability to talk without stuttering or becoming tongue-tied, prompted me from that point on, to actually volunteer for certain class speaking assignments, which previously I would have assiduously avoided.

This stubborn confrontational approach to an affliction which still occasionally plagues me to this day, has enabled me over the years to accept any public speaking assignment, knowing that as long as I pick and chose my sentence "starting" words with care, the problem will remain a secret and my personal challenge.

December 25, 1940, was the first Christmas Day that I'd ever been away from home, and I quickly learned that in many ways, when one lives on a farm, that day isn't much different from any other. The cows had to be milked twice, all livestock needed to be fed and watered, and in the stable and sheds there was an overnight accumulation of animal waste, waiting to shoveled and removed.

Nevertheless, all field work was postponed, so by farm standards, I guess Christmas qualified as a day off. That's how it was for all of us except Mrs. Grenfell, who spent her day in the kitchen, preparing a sumptuous dinner, roast-goose with all the trimmings and her own recipe English plum-pudding. It was a grand feast but one that I never got a chance to enjoy.

Several days earlier, I'd received from home, a box of assorted chocolates. This was a special treat because by then rationing and routine shortages, had made boxed chocolates highly prized and in short supply. As I recall, between breakfast and dinner, I made the mistake of sampling the box's many different fillings, and my stomach, unaccustomed to this confectionery onslaught, reacted accordingly.

As soon as I sat down at the dinner table and added a slice of roast-goose to my already overloaded digestive system, I probably turned green, because I remember fleeing from the kitchen to the outside, where everything that I'd eaten, again saw the light of day! This unpleasant development didn't sit well with Mrs. G who, having warned me to go easy on the chocolates, was unsympathetic to my plight and immediately packed me off to bed, where I spent the rest of Christmas Day, in mournful and nauseous solitude.

The year ended quietly for those of us living in Cornwall, but for our families in London, on the night of December 29, the blitz escalated to a new level, when the Luftwaffe saturated the capital with incendiary bombs, starting over 1,500 fires. Some months later, when I finally got to talk to my Dad, he told me about that awful night, describing an inferno so intense, that after the bombers had departed and well before daybreak, one could stand outside and read a newspaper, it was that bright!

On that same day, many miles away in Washington, DC, President Roosevelt called upon the American Congress to approve the direct sale of arms to Britain saying, "The Nazi masters of Germany have made it clear that they intend not only to dominate all life and thought in their own country, but to also enslave the whole of Europe, and then to use the resources of Europe to dominate the rest of the world...The people of Europe who are defending themselves do not ask us to do their fighting. They ask us for the implements of war...which will enable them to fight for their liberty and security."

Roosevelt's plea and Congress's approval which was forthcoming, helped Britain survive its darkest days, and subsequently, with America's full scale entry into the war, the stage was set to free all of Europe from Nazi tyranny. On that fateful day, our 32nd President hammered the first nail into Hitler's coffin!

The winter of 1940-1941 was typical for Cornwall, no snow, no extreme drops in temperature, but plenty of rain, which made for a soggy walk to and from school each day. We evacuees were expected to bring our own lunches, but whereas lunch in London tended to be "bread and drip," in Cornwall it was more often a "Cornish Pastie," a food item peculiar to that western county.

The "pastie" was simple enough to prepare. It was made from pie-crust pastry, rolled out flat and cut it into a circular shape, filled with meat and vegetables and folded over. The finished product looked much like a Mexican tacho and could be served hot from the oven, or saved for another time and eaten cold.

It had its origin at the turn of the century, when Cornwall was home to a thriving tin-mining industry, employing thousands of men who toiled many hours a day, far below the region's pastoral landscape. Lunch had to be eaten underground, and the baked meat and vegetable combination, just as delicious when eaten cold, became the lunch-pail favorite, and over time, a Cornish legend.

For the farmer, there are no "slack" seasons, and this became clear to me during the balance of the winter. Before Spring plowing and planting could begin, there was fertilizing and other soil preparation work to be done in the fields, and when Horace and I were not in school, we were expected to pitch in.

The fertilizer we used was in ample supply! Using pitchforks and shovels, we loaded the mountain of manure and straw which had piled up in the barn-yard during the months when all the animals were kept inside, into a horse-drawn "spreader," by which it was transported to the fields, and applied to the soil.

Depending on the special needs of certain crops, some fields also required an application of quick-lime, and what an unpleasant chore that was. We loaded bags of lime onto a wagon, and while Mr. G held the reins and kept the horse moving, we boys knelt at the rear, scooping the lime out of the bags with old saucepans, and throwing it directly onto the ground.

This was a crude and hazardous operation, to say the least. As I recall, we wrapped ourselves in old grain sacks and wore scarves over our mouths, but wind-blown lime still landed on parts of our bodies, with predictably irritating and painful results.

The ploughing and planting of the wheat, oat and barley crops, required special horse-drawn equipment, so this work was always performed by Mr. Grenfell or Edgar, his farm-hand. Certain other tasks fell to Mrs. G and her evacuees, and I remember two in particular, that were real back-breakers!

The farm produced a large potato crop, grown primarily as pig-food. After the area selected had been ploughed, it was our job to place the seed-potatoes into the furrows, by hand. We also had a large area set aside for carrots, turnips, parsnips and kale.

As these various vegetables grew, the furrows in which they were planted, required regular weeding, which was accomplished by the three of us wielding hoes, for hours on end. Finally, when they were ready to be harvested, another labor intensive chore awaited us, picking them by hand to be carried in buckets to a horse-drawn cart. It was probably during one of those sessions, that I vowed not to consider farming, as a viable career option!

The war news continued to be bad! In March, Germany invaded and occupied Bulgaria, following which its troops took up positions on that country's borders with Greece and Yugoslavia. Greece and Yugoslavia had already been invaded by Italian forces five months earlier, and with a German invasion now likely, Britain rushed Commonwealth units from Australia and New Zealand and a Polish Brigade, to Greece from Egypt where they'd been stationed.

In North Africa, British troops, who had been successful in their battles with Mussolini's armies, were forced to retreat under heavy German attacks, following Hitler's decision to send air and ground support to aid his Italian ally, whose army, while losing in Africa, was still trying unsuccessfully to conquer Albania.

On April 2, Germany invaded Hungary and four days later, its armies entered Greece and Yugoslavia. When Greece surrendered to Germany and Italy on April 23, British troops retreated to the beaches, from where 40,000 of its original force of 62,500, were evacuated to Crete and Egypt. Within 30 days, Crete also fell to a Nazi airborne onslaught, from which battle only 15,000 Allied soldiers escaped, leaving three times that many behind.

On May 10, 500 German bombers hit London with its heaviest and deadliest attack of the war. The raid lasted more than six hours, and when the "all-clear" sounded, over 1,400 civilians had been killed, almost 1,800 were seriously injured, and incendiary bombs had started 2,200 fires. After eight months of bombing, it was an attack that apparently came close to finally breaking the spirit of London's indomitable citizens. Fortunately, unbeknown to them or to their government, an unexpected reprieve was at hand.

Following that raid, Hitler moved the bulk of his Luftwaffe to Germany's eastern frontier. There, on Sunday, June 22, 1941, his ground forces invaded the Soviet Union, on a front stretching 1,800 miles, from the Artic to the Black Sea. More than 3 million troops, 600,000 vehicles, 750,000 horses and 3,580 tanks, were thrown into the fray. This gigantic operation, relied heavily on the Luftwaffe to provide air cover and close support over the entire front, an impossible goal had Goering not halted his massive air campaign against London.

The significance of this development, which took Stalin and the rest of the world by surprise, was not lost on Churchill. He saw it as a crucial turning point in the war, postponing indefinitely Hitler's plans to invade and occupy Britain, and providing his beleaguered country the time it needed to rebuild its military for the ultimate clash with Germany, that he knew was inevitable.

The extended 10 week lull in bombing attacks on London which followed, and the fact that Hitler's legions, once poised to invade Britain, were now fighting and dying more than 1,000 miles away, was welcome news for Londoners, whose homes and work-places had been under continuous fire, for more than eight months.

Government restriction on travel, imposed when invasion seemed imminent, were relaxed, so that parents like my own, who hadn't seen or spoken to their children for more than a year since their evacuation, made plans to travel and get reacquainted.

Sometime in June, Horace's mother visited him, and I recall that she did not have a very pleasant disposition. She seemed to look down her nose at the Grenfells, and they in turn, seemed clearly relieved that her stay at their home, was short-lived.

In early July, my Dad, step-mother and sister Peg, came by train to Truro, where they took the Truro to Cambourne bus, which passed close to Seveock Manor, making it easy for them to visit me. However, "Lemon Cottage," where my sister Mary lived, could not be reached by bus, so they walked with me to her place, where the five of us were finally reunited as a family.

During their visit, I managed to get some time alone with Dad, and naturally, took that opportunity to ask him his reaction to Germany's invasion of the Soviet Union. His answer was quick and precise. While thankful for the respite from the bombing of London that Hitler's attack had provided, he warned that someday, perhaps not in his lifetime but certainly during mine, England, America and Germany would be at war with the Soviets.

I still recall that I listened in total disbelief to my father's prediction. At that point in time, I knew little about the Soviet Union and nothing about Communism, but the very thought that England and the United States would ever be allied with the evil power then astride most of Europe, was beyond my comprehension.

In retrospect however, I marvel at the acumen of this working-class man, an avowed socialist and organized labor advocate, whose formal education ended at age fourteen, who in 1941, saw communism as the ultimate threat, even as many upper-class, university-educated men in England and the United States, (Guy Burgess, Anthony Blunt and Alger Hiss come to mind), were duped by communism, even committing treason while under its spell.

I also quizzed Dad on the "blitz" and was shocked to learn of one event in particular which, but for the grace of God, very nearly made Mary and I orphans! Early in the war, my step-mother had balked at the prospect of having her back-yard, with its tiny lawn and flower beds, ruined by the installation of an in-ground Anderson air-raid shelter. When the night raids began, like thousands of other Londoners, she, my father and Peg, would carry pillows and blankets to the nearby Finsbury Park Tube station, and spend their nights sheltered underground.

They did this three or four times, but one night when they arrived, the station platforms were so crowded, that they boarded a train and rode to Bounds Green station located further out in the suburbs, where they anticipated there would be more room. They had settled in for the night, many feet below the surface, when the unexpected occurred. A bomb came down through the station's ventilation shaft, exploding on one of the platforms, fortunately not the one on which my parents and sister slept.

Following the concussion and blast which swept through their tunnel, confused and in shock, my Dad apparently crawled on his hands and knees towards the escalator which inexplicably was still operating, and where he might then have been injured, had my sister Peg not held him back, preventing that from happening. Fortunately, the three of them got out of the station alive and uninjured, but they never again used the Tube during an air raid.

By then, a new "in-house" shelter had been made available by the government, called the "Morrison" named after Herbert Morrison, a Labor MP who served as Britain's Home Secretary. It was nothing more than a reinforced steel table, 7 feet by 5 feet and 30 inches high, with steel mesh, cage-like sides. While it wasn't designed to survive a direct hit, it was a reasonably safe haven if the house collapsed from the blast of a near miss.

My parents had their Morrison installed in the kitchen. They added a mattress, pillows and blankets, and slept in it whenever the siren sounded, for the rest of the war.

Sadly, the visit by my Dad, Mom and sister Peg was all too brief. Within the week, they returned to London, and it would be another five months before Mary and I would see them again. While in Truro, they had their picture taken by a local photographer. While that photo has not survived the passage of time, I remember it well, because the hell on earth that they'd all so recently endured, was graphically etched in their haggard faces and mirrored in their tired, sad eyes.

CHAPTER 12

Final Days In Cornwall, Pearl Harbor Attacked

The second summer that Horace and I spent on the farm, was much like the first, except that a year of "on the job training," had turned us into involuntary farm laborers. When we weren't at school, we were working harder and longer than ever, and the situation became worse, when the Grenfell's hired hand Edgar, left the farm to join the British Army.

A replacement was hard to find given the military draft and the manpower demands of the defense plants, now operating 24 hours a day, seven days a week, so out of necessity, Mr. G looked to us boys to do more. However, he knew that evacuees weren't supposed to be treated like indentured servants, so he decided to begin giving each of us, one half-crown a week.

In 1941, that was 50 cents in American money, not very much considering that our chores before and after school each day, plus what we did on weekends, meant that on average, we were working more than 40 hours a week!

During harvesting time, we worked even longer hours, thanks to "DOUBLE-Daylight Savings Time" which by then had replaced Daylight Savings Time (DST). As I recall, DDST, was adopted by the British wartime government to give city dwellers and defense workers, even more daylight time in the evening, by moving the clock TWO hours ahead of the sun, instead of one.

For farmers, that meant the starting time for cutting hay and grain, which under DST occurred around noon after the dew had evaporated, now had to be postponed until 1:00pm or later, so quite often we were in the fields until 10:00pm. Our cows, who weren't on DDST, needed to be milked by 7:00am the next morning, which made for some rather short nights and many long days!

Our summer evenings were enlivened by sporadic German air-raids on the port of Falmouth, just 10 miles away. We boys would sit outside in the dark, and watch the distant heavy anti-aircraft shells exploding high over the port, and the procession of red tracer rounds climbing skyward, seemingly in slow-motion, from the "pom-pom" guns on the navy vessels, at anchor in the harbor.

One night, after we were in bed, we heard the noise of an approaching aircraft, then as it passed over, the distinctive whistle of an incoming bomb, which luckily missed Seveock Manor, landing just a quarter of a mile away, in a neighbor's field. We boys and Seveock Manor, had finally had our baptism of fire!

The summer of 1941, had another emotional event that I'll never forget. One Saturday morning, when Mr. G went to the stable to feed his two horses, he found Tinker, the big Belgian, lying on his side, unable to get up. A vet was summoned, and while I was not privy to the diagnosis which followed his examination, he advised Mr. G to have the horse put down.

By then, Tinker was quite old, and perhaps the daily rigors of the most recent harvesting activities, were more than he could handle, although given the finality of the vet's advice, I have to believe that his problem was more than his advanced years.

Saying goodbye to this big, gentle creature, was extremely hard on the Grenfells. Mrs. G sat beside Tinker in his stall until the vet was ready, and then she left in tears. Mr. G kept his composure, and remained at Tinker's head, and at my request, he let Horace and I stay with him to witness what went on.

The vet produced a strange device, which Mr. G explained was called a "humane killer." It had a short flared barrel, like a blunder-buss. Placing the flared end against Tinker's forehead, the vet struck the firing pin at the other end with a hammer, causing an explosive charge to drive a large caliber slug into Tinker's brain, killing him instantly. That evening, a man who made his living picking up dead farm-animals, and seeing to their proper and legal disposal, came by and carted Tinker away, leaving us all shook-up and saddened by this unexpected event.

In early September, we began our second year at Ruddy Beams. By then, Mr. Barlow's approach to teaching a class of 30 children, who in London's pre-war schools, would have been separated by age into three grades, had unfortunately reached the age where "learning" for many in the class, had stagnated. In particular, those of us who'd turned fourteen since leaving London, were no longer challenged by a curriculum which was geared out of necessity, to the "middle" age-level children.

I for one, was often bored in class, and as has been well demonstrated over time, bored children, especially those going through puberty, tend to focus on less redeeming, but to them, more interesting activities, and in this regard, "sex" became one of our major pre-occupations. Let me quickly add that sex in that context, had nothing to do with sexual intercourse, something that was still a complete mystery to most of us, beyond its rumored connection to the institution of marriage.

Unlike today's children, who for better or worse are exposed to sex-education as early as grade-school, my generation received no such information at school, nor was it a subject ever discussed at home. For instance, I recall one evening soon after my father remarried, with the family congregated in the kitchen, asking my Dad out of the blue, "Is my belly-button where I was connected to my mother?" That simple question brought giggles from my older sisters Madeline and Peg, and gasps from my parents, but no answer. They probably thought that at my tender age of twelve, this was not information that I had a need to know!

Accordingly, whatever we kids learned in our mutual discussions about female "periods," male "wet-dreams" and masturbation (then delicately referred to as "self-abuse"), we picked up from each other, while unfortunately never knowing for sure whether what we heard was the truth or a lie, or just uninformed speculation.

Classmate Peggy Gravestock, who was already fifteen, was considered to be the leading authority on all of the above "whispered" subjects. Also the tallest and most physically developed female, she liked to prove how strong she was, by joining us boys at recess, in the hay-loft above our classroom. There we'd wrestle with each other, and as I recall, from my bouts with Peggy, encounters with her were definitely softer and more exciting!

She also had an obvious crush on Horace, and one day my jokester mind went to work figuring out what sort of prank I could devise, to take advantage of that situation. At Ruddy Beams, the desks in the back row were reserved for the six oldest boys, Horace, Ray Marshall, the twins Brian and Stanley Little, Peter Laister and me.

Peggy sat in front of us, and when Mr. Barlow wasn't paying attention, she'd turn around and flirt with Horace. It was during one of those times, that I got my inspiration, which I shared with Horace on my way home from school. That evening, we lifted a parsnip from Mrs. G's supply of vegetables, and with a knife, we carefully carved it into a reasonable facsimile of a penis.

Next morning, we got to school early and using red ink from one of the ink-wells, we gave our creation a realistic flesh-like hue. When Peggy arrived, I told her that her boyfriend Horace would have something "special" to show her, when Mr. B stepped outside to smoke his pipe, as he usually did every afternoon.

When that time came and Peggy looked back expectantly at Horace, his hands were out of sight below the desk-top, as if he was fiddling with something. She looked away for a moment, then her curiosity got the best of her and she glanced back again, just in time to see what she assumed to be Horace's exposed penis in plain sight, above his desk. As her shocked eyes focused on that unfamiliar object, I gave it a mighty whack with my ruler and the top half flew into the air, landing on the floor at her feet!

Her reaction I hadn't counted on, but should have expected! She gave a blood curdling scream, scaring the entire class including me. I'll never know how Mr. B, busy with his pipe, could have missed that awful shriek, but obviously he did. When he returned and found us all dutifully studying, he made no comment, and I escaped "six big ones" which I am sure he would have administered with gusto, had he known the details of my latest mischief.

One class activity, Mr. Barlow's earlier commitment to acquaint us with the works of Shakespeare, continued to hold my interest. We were introduced next to "The Merchant of Venice" and as he'd done before with "Julius Caesar," he read aloud excerpts from the play while explaining the gist of the plot.

Finally, he announced that he'd selected Act IV, Scene 1, for dramatization and presentation to the class, specifically the excerpt where Portia, disguised as a male lawyer, confronts Shylock in court, and by using the letter of the law, frustrates his attempt to collect the penalty and forfeit due from Bassanio.

Buoyed with my earlier successful acting debut as Mark Anthony in "Julius Caesar," I actually volunteered for and received the part of Shylock. The role of Portia went to Sylvia "somebody" whose face I still remember, but not her last name. These were both juicy parts, with much to memorize, so Sylvia and I spent as much time as we could at school, going over our lines.

As was the case with our previous production, we had no access to real theatrical props, so when the cast was finally ready to perform, we improvised our costumes as best we could. It was assumed that Shylock, a Jew in Shakespeare's time, would have sported a long beard, which presented me with a problem, which I eventually solved in a rather bizarre fashion.

In Seveock Manor's cow-shed, was a length of rope on which hung an assortment of bovine hair, which had been snipped from the tails of cows owned by the Grenfells, and retained for what reason I'll never fathom. However, I needed whiskers, and this was the only source of hair available. With Mrs. G's help, I tied enough "tails" onto a piece of elastic, which fitted to my face, provided me with a strange multi-colored beard!

I'm sure that to anyone other than my classmates, who were prone to clap and cheer any presentation by the Ruddy Beams Dramatic Society, I would have looked totally ridiculous, but to this day, my sister Mary can still recall my cow-tail beard, so perhaps in my own unique way, I was at least a memorable Shylock!

Most of us older kids kept track of the war news, from listening to the nightly BBC broadcasts. However, theses communications tended to focus on Britain's war with Germany, with very little news concerning Japan's war with China (now in its tenth year), or its increased belligerency towards French Indo China, the Dutch East Indies and the Philippines.

Consequently, it came as a shock, when we learned that the Japanese had attacked Pearl Harbor, an American naval base in the Hawaian Islands, on December 7. Mr. Barlow used the occasion to give us an impromptu geography lesson on that distant part of the world, about which we knew little. That England was also at war with Japan, didn't sink home until a few days later when we got the news that on December 10, Britain's latest battleship, the "Prince of Wales" and its battle-cruiser "Repulse," had been sunk by Japanese aircraft off the coast of Malaya.

The next day, Germany and Italy, in accordance with their treaty with Japan, declared war on the United States. This meant that Britain finally had a powerful ally in its war against the fascist dictators, now into its 27th month. As the only American-born kid in the class, I was an instant celebrity, although much of the attention I received, wasn't always that complimentary.

To some extent, that was my own fault. Listening over the years to my Dad extol the virtues of America, I'd never learned to suffer silently any criticism of the land of my birth. Now that America was Britain's wartime ally, my impassioned defense of all things American, soon had my classmates calling me the "bloody Yank," an intended insult which of course I accepted with pride.

As the year drew to an end, I had learned to accept the fact that as a child of a working-class family, my days at school were definitely numbered. The academic scholarship which I'd earned at age eleven, had assured me of a four year, "advanced" curriculum, but I'd only finished the first year, when the war began.

The expected air-raids on London, had caused most its schools, including my own, to cancel the advanced study courses. With the conflict now in its third year, with no end in sight, kids of my age were encouraged to leave school and join the work-force and contribute their part to the United Kingdom's war effort.

In this vein, Mr. Barlow took me aside one morning in early December, and recommended that I apply for a job that he knew was open, at a farm implement and seed store in Truro. The owner had indicated that he was looking for a bright lad my age with good penmanship, a much sought after virtue at that time, when ledgers and other business records, were all transcribed by hand.

The next day, on the strength of Mr. Barlow's say-so, and without giving it much thought, I borrowed Mr. G's bicycle and rode into Truro to apply for a position. I was interviewed and hired on the spot, at the grand sum of fifteen shillings ($3.00) a week. Returning to the farm, I went by the school to announce my good fortune, and was genuinely surprised and touched by the response of my classmates, who made it clear how much I would be missed.

That evening, when I broke the news to the Grenfells, I guess I was completely taken aback by their reaction. They asked me where I planned to live, pointing out that once I left school and was no longer and evacuee, the weekly government subsidy they'd received for housing and feeding me, would immediately cease.

I was stunned! When I took the job, I had assumed that I'd continue to live on the farm, and ride the bus each day, or use Mr. G's bike until I could purchase my own. I never realized what my decision would do to my status as an evacuee, but certainly Mr. Barlow would have known, and he should have explained this when he was urging me to leave school, and go to work.

I brooded over this development most of the night, and in the morning I told the Grenfells that I'd changed my mind about the job in Truro, and planned instead to seek employment in London. There I knew I could live at home, as long as I paid something for my room and board. Once again borrowing Mr. G's bike, I rode into Truro to explain my predicament to the store owner, who had hired me 24 hours earlier. That done, I pedaled to school where my unexpected return was loudly cheered by my classmates.

The week before Christmas, Horace and I said goodbye to the Grenfells, and accompanied by most members of our class and Mr. Barlow, we boarded a train for London. For me, and those also nearing their fifteenth birthday, our formal education was over, and none of us returned to Ruddy Beams.

When Mary and I arrived home, Dad agreed I should get a job. Given Mary's health problem (unsanitary conditions at "Lemon Cottage" had left her with a bad case of impetigo), he refused to send her back to Cornwall, and when the Christmas holidays were over, she returned to the Stroud Green School, to resume her studies.

On December 23, Wake Island, a tiny American outpost 2,300 miles west of Pearl Harbor, fell to the Japanese. A U.S. force on its way to relieve the island's handful of Marine defenders, was just 425 miles away, when it was unaccountably ordered to return to Hawaii. With the loss of Wake, the U.S. had no base remaining in the Pacific between Hawaii and the Philippine Islands, which were already reeling under Japanese massive air, sea and land attacks.

On Christmas Day, Britain's garrison in Hong Kong surrendered, after suffering more than 11,800 combat losses. Many civilians were also killed and 2,079 wounded. There was not much to celebrate in the United States or the United Kingdom, as the New Year dawned!

CHAPTER 13

Education Ends, Gainful Employment Begins

Once home from Cornwall, I recall being glad that I was out of school, where for 18 months, as an erstwhile honor student, I'd been subjected to many hours of repetitious studies, with few opportunities to be academically challenged. Entering the adult world with all of its responsibilities was an important milestone in my life, one that I welcomed rather than feared.

Mary and I were surprised to discover that while we were away, our step-mom had rented out the two rooms on the third floor of our house, to a married couple in their late forties. The man worked for the BBC, purportedly in a "security" position so sensitive, that his surname could not be revealed, and we were required instead to always refer to him as "Mr. H."

After meeting the man, I found that story a bit hard to swallow! Besides being untidy in appearance and the owner of a generally unpleasant disposition, he and his wife were both heavy drinkers, often getting home after we'd all gone to bed, usually arguing loudly, as they stumbled up the stairs to their flat. "Mr. H" was hardly the kind of citizen to be trusted by the BBC with anything, much less wartime security.

London was still a "front-line" city and subject to frequent night attacks by the Luftwaffe. Seeing the bomb damage already inflicted on my neighborhood, was a grim reminder that my future would be uncertain and often life-threatening. However, given the awesome events that unfolded during the next 41 months, being in wartime London was an incredibly exciting experience. As I look back, I know that I would not have traded my front-row seat to that period in history, for anything in the world.

I didn't have to wait long before becoming gainfully employed. Dad contacted his twenty-six year old brother Bert, who worked in the Sales Department of the Cork Manufacturing and Flexo-Plywood

Companies, in Chingford, the suburb where my parents and Peg and I had lived when we came to England from the States, in 1928.

Before the war, the firms had produced cork gaskets used in the production and maintenance of industrial internal combustion engines, and metal-faced plywood products used by the building and construction industry. Now, both companies sub-contracted for the aircraft and small naval-craft manufacturers, which by then, were fully engaged in meeting war and defense production needs.

Thanks to my Uncle Bert's efforts, I was hired without an interview, as an "office boy" at a take-home pay of twenty-seven shillings ($5.50) a week, beginning the first Monday of January, 1942, four months shy of my fifteenth birthday. My hours were 9:00 am to 5:00 pm, with a two hour round-trip commute. Each morning, I'd walk a mile to Finsbury Park and catch a trolley-bus to Edmonton. There I'd transfer to a Chingford bus which made a stop outside the CM/FP factory's main-gate. The best thing about London's surface transportation system, even during the war, was that most routes had so many buses in service, that if I ever ran for one and missed it, another would appear minutes later.

My new job, including the commute, meant 10 hour work-days, which didn't faze me, given my previous 12 hour days of hard labor in Cornwall. I would read a book on the way to work, and for the trip home, I'd buy an evening newspaper and relax while catching up on the war news, which was usually bad. In fact, Britain's first victory of the war over German troops didn't occur until late 1941, during its Eighth Army's campaign in North Africa.

In that offensive, General Erwin Rommel's Panzer Group Africa, suffered a severe defeat, with 28,000 casualties. However, by January 6, 1942, the British advance had halted, and two weeks later, Rommel launched a counter-offensive, winning back most of the desert real-estate he'd lost earlier, forcing the Eighth Army to retreat into Egypt, home to the vital port of Alexandria and the Suez Canal, an equally important life-line.

There would have been some good news to report closer to home, had the government not kept it a secret for security reasons. On January 26, the first ship-load of American troops to reach Europe, arrived in Northern Ireland, and the U.S. headquarters was established in London for its ground, air and naval forces which were to follow.

When the news of this milestone event, which occurred a mere six weeks after Germany declared war on the U.S.A. was finally made public, it lifted the hearts of us all.

I'll never forget my first day at the office! My Uncle greeted me in the lobby of the plant's two-storey office building, and took me to his office on the second floor, which was crowded with other men, who I innocently assumed were also there to greet me, but no such luck. It was then that I learned there was a "tradition" involved, which required that every male of my age entering the office work-force, endure an initiation.

With my Uncle leading the throng, I was hoisted off my feet and carried into the men's rest-room, where I was unceremoniously held upside-down and held by my ankles over the toilet-bowl. Then, with my head just inches away from the water level, the bowl was flushed to the cheers of everyone present!

The apparent purpose of this ritual, was to impress upon me that my position was the lowest of the low, and to ensure that my future conduct would reflect my acceptance of my place at the bottom of the office's established pecking order.

While that experience seemed traumatic at the time, I later had reason to count my blessings, after talking with Brian Little who'd been a classmate of mine in Cornwall. Brian began work that same week as a "shop-boy" at a furniture factory, and his first day initiation, made mine seem like a walk in the park.

The manpower needs of the military by 1942, had stripped the factory of most of its male help, so many of its machines were now manned by women. When Brian arrived, he was sent onto the floor and told to ask the foreman for a specific tool. This "tool" was really a code-word for the initiation to begin, and he was immediately surrounded by a crowd of laughing women. While some held him, others pulled down his pants and undershorts, at which point, another dipped a brush into a nearby pot, and proceeded to paint poor Brian's genitalia with hot glue!

With my initiation behind me, Uncle Bert took me to an office on the ground floor, and introduced me to the four women with whom I would work. Edie Davies, the office manager, was a matronly woman in her forties. The other three were attractive teenagers, Joyce Wilmot, nineteen, Gwen Harding, eighteen and Joyce Turner, seventeen. With most eligible young men their age now in the armed services, they seemed to like having a male in their midst, even one as young and innocent as I.

Afflicted as I was, by the raging hormones common to every teenage male, finding myself in the company of three attractive older females, was the stuff my dreams were made of, and I thoroughly enjoyed the experience. To add to my contentment, these young women even proceeded to spoil me. Whenever they went to a movie together, they'd always invite me, and those times that I accepted, they invariably pick up the tab for my ticket.

As the office boy, my job was to pick up the outgoing mail from the various departments, fold and stuff it into envelopes, seal and stamp these for mailing, and distribute incoming mail to these same departments, promptly upon its receipt. I also carried mail and other papers to and from the outlying offices located throughout the plant, that were responsible for providing the production teams with their daily work-orders.

All the various office staffs were by now 85% female, so I considered a job which required me to spend much of my time "visiting," a prime assignment. While it certainly kept me busy and on the move, I don't recall that I ever complained.

At the end of my first week on the job, I received an envelope containing 27 shillings in cash. Pay-checks were then rarely used. Upon arriving home, my step-mother and I sat down to negotiate how much I'd pay for my room and board. I agreed to give her 12 shillings a week, which left me with 15 shillings ($3.00), to cover the cost of all my personal needs, including clothes, transportation costs and entertainment.

From that day on, neither of my parents ever gave me any money. Buying on credit was then not an option for the working-class, so when I needed extra cash, to buy a suit for example, my step-mother would give me what I needed, with the understanding this was a loan that I was expected to pay back, which I always did. Thanks to her, I learned an important lesson, that whatever I needed or wanted in life, I should expect to pay for it myself.

With only $3.00 a week to spend, my options were limited! This was the reason I never smoked, even though most teens of my generation, took up the cigarette habit upon leaving school, almost as a rite of passage into adulthood. Tobacco had to be imported, at a time when British ships carrying much more vital cargoes were being sunk by U-boats at an alarming rate. In an effort to reduce demand, taxes on tobacco were greatly increased.

By the end of the war, cigarettes cost 3 shillings a pack, or 20% of my weekly available cash. I had to decide whether I'd rather smoke or date, because I certainly couldn't afford to do both. For me, the "fairer sex" was always the more attractive option, and given what is now known about the hazards of smoking, it's obvious that I made the correct and healthiest choice.

The factory complex where I now toiled, boasted a cafeteria, which served hot lunches every day, to plant and office workers alike. Unfortunately, its entree selections were limited, relying heavily on the chef's ability to invent new ways to serve boiled potatoes and cabbage. After two years of meat rationing, that drab combination became synonymous with British wartime cuisine.

Nevertheless, we all knew better than to pass-up a free meal, and given the opportunities to socialize during the lunch-time break, I became a faithful attendee. However, the cafeteria's standards for the handling of food, left much to be desired, and as its staff didn't take kindly to any criticism of their cooking or serving techniques, I learned not to complain, even when I discovered (on more than one occasion), a boiled caterpillar among the cabbage leaves on my luncheon plate!

Food rationing had begun in Britain two years earlier, with sugar, butter, bacon and ham, the first foods affected, with adults rationed to 4oz a week. By 1942, tea, margarine, butter, cooking fat and suet were included, (2oz of each per week), with jam, marmalade, honey, syrup and lemon-curd spreads, rationed at amounts ranging from 8oz to 2lb per month.

The adult weekly ration of cheese was a measly 1oz. and eggs were rationed to "one half" to 2 a week, when available. (I've often wondered, how does one buy half and egg?) My step-mom thought she was lucky if, after waiting in line for hours at more than one store, she was able to get four eggs a week, for the five of us.

And the sugar ration was so small, that I got used to drinking unsweetened tea, and to this day, I prefer it that way. I also recall eating a lot of "red" oatmeal for breakfast, the odd color being a result of my using jam as a sweetener, rather than sugar.

I'll confess, that many times after I returned from Cornwall, I remembered fondly, how well I'd eaten as an evacuee. Cornish pasties, bread spread with fresh-churned butter and home-made wild blackberry jam, bread with thick Cornish-cream and jam, plenty of milk and eggs, chicken and rabbit often, and once, when Mr. Grenfell had one of his pigs butchered, we ate pork in all of its many variations, just about every day for a month.

Clothing too, had been rationed in Britain since the early months of the war, and in 1942, the per person allowance was reduced from 60 to 48 coupons a year. At that level, a man's basic wardrobe, a suit, shirt, pair of shoes and a top-coat, required more than 48 coupons, so men were forced to stagger their purchases of these necessary items over several years, or settle for second-hand clothing which could be bought without coupons.

I had arrived home from Cornwall with a pitiful wardrobe, two sets of overalls, called "boiler-suits" by the British, my school blazer and gray flannel slacks, both of which I'd outgrown, and a pair of rubber farm boots. In my new job, even as a lowly office-boy, I was expected to wear a suit or jacket and slacks, with a shirt and tie, and somehow, probably with coupons donated by my parents, I put together an acceptable wardrobe.

Over the next three years, I managed to get by with one new single-breasted suit, the jacket complete with fake pockets and pants minus cuffs, the standard government dictated design, aimed at saving material for other more vital war-related needs.

I owned three shirts, all with detachable and reversible collars, which enabled me to wear the same shirt for longer periods, and an assortment of second-hand clothes, including a sports-jacket, several pull-over sweaters, and a pair of brown shoes whose original owner I was told, was killed in an air-raid. I made the mistake for sharing this information with my teen-age cronies, who delighted in asking me how it felt to wear "dead-man's" shoes!

Fortunately I guess, we were all in the same boat, forced to make do as best we could, with whatever clothes we were able to get. Shoes were re-soled and heeled as often as possible, and when constant wear put a hole in the seat of one's pants, or in the sleeve of one's jacket, it was patched with whatever material came close to providing a decent match. Thanks to my step-mom, who as a young woman had been trained as a seamstress, the patches on my jackets and pants, always looked very professional.

And finally, soap was also rationed, 4oz a month, per person, a measly allowance guaranteed to influence the bathing habits of the average household, for the duration of the war. To any ex-GI reading this narrative who served in England at the time, who ever wondered why British civilians tended to look universally shabby, and at times even grubby, now you know.

British and American civilians found little solace in the news emanating from the Far East and Pacific war zones, where Japanese military successes continued. Britain's garrison in Singapore surrendered on February 15, after a series of defeats in Malaya, in which it lost 138,000 British, Australian, Indian and local indigenous troops, most of whom ended up as prisoners of Japan.

On February 19, Japanese bombers attacked Darwin in Northern Australia, and two weeks later, in the Battle of Java Sea, a combined fleet of American, British, Australian and Dutch warships, was decimated in what was then considered to be the worst Allied naval defeat of the war.

American morale finally received a welcome boost, with the news that on April 18, sixteen of its B-25 medium bombers had been launched from an aircraft carrier in the Pacific, 800 miles from Japan, and had bombed Tokyo and three other Japanese cities. But the really great news came six weeks later, when a U.S. navy force of 3 carriers and 8 cruisers, engaged a Japanese fleet of 11 battleships, 8 carriers and 23 cruisers, on its way to invade and occupy Midway Island, a vital American base in the mid-Pacific.

Despite suffering horrendous losses of men and aircraft in their initial attacks on the enemy, bombers from the American carriers eventually sank 4 Japanese carriers and a cruiser. Apparently shaken by the unexpected loss of half his carrier force, Admiral Yamamoto, who had conceived and planned Japan's devastating sneak attack on Pearl Harbor, ordered his remaining vessels to break off the engagement and retreat at full speed to their homeland.

The June 4-6 Battle of Midway, at the cost of one carrier and a destroyer, was an incredible American victory. It marked the end of Japan's expansionist dreams of a Pacific Empire, thwarting its planned invasion of Australia, and dramatically altering the future course of the war, in that strategically important region. Two months later, on August 7, the United States launched its first ground offensive in the Pacific, putting Marines ashore on Guadalcanal and four other beaches in the Solomon Island group.

Much closer to home, on August 29, a force of British Commandos and troops of the Canadian 2nd Division, supported by British Navy and RAF units, attacked the strategic French Channel port of Dieppe. Heavy casualties were suffered by the 5,000 man Canadian contingent, with 900 killed and nearly 2,000 taken prisoner.

Churchill, when criticized for ordering the attack, described it as a costly but not unfruitful "reconaissance-in-force," which had provided the Allies with a wealth of necessary experience and tactical military information, vital to a full-scale invasion of occupied Europe, plans for which were already being formulated.

More bad news followed on the heels of the Dieppe raid. The British people learned that on August 25, the popular Duke of Kent, younger brother of their King, had been killed in an air crash in Scotland, while serving on active duty with the RAF.

I can't remember how soon after returning to London, the sirens sounded, heralding my first air-raid. (I didn't consider the "one bomber/one bomb" Cornwall incident, as an air-raid despite how close to the farm that solitary bomb landed). German bombers usually approached London from the south-east, so the bulk of its anti-aircraft defenses were concentrated in that general region, so as to bring down as many attackers as possible, before they arrived over the densely populated, Greater London area.

My neighborhood was located on the city's north-side, so we'd first hear distant gunfire, which increased in noise and volume as our local AA guns joined in the barrage. True to form, what goes up must eventually come down, and before any enemy bombers were directly overhead, we'd hear shrapnel from the thousands of shells fired into the air, falling like hail onto our roof-tops, and bouncing around in the street, and on the sidewalk.

These pieces of red-hot metal, ranged in size from microscopic slivers to chunks large enough to penetrate a roof. All were lethal and could kill or seriously injure anyone caught outside not wearing a steel helmet, or other heavy protective gear.

While the date of that first air-raid experience escapes me, I'll always remember how mortified I was by the way my body reacted. I wasn't surprised when suddenly awakened by the wail of a siren, to note that my heart rate had increased dramatically, but I wasn't prepared for the involuntary trembling of my extremities, triggered by the noise of London's substantial anti-aircraft defenses in action, and the drone of enemy aircraft overhead.

I guess having been an avid reader of adventure stories, always enthralled by the fearless exploits of heroic characters who were apparently never plagued by bodily tremors, no matter how life threatening their circumstances, I was embarrassed by what I assumed was a sure sign that I lacked courage, when under fire.

In subsequent raids, my hands and legs would often tremble despite my best efforts at control, and I continued to be haunted by my perception of what this reaction said about my character. Many years later however, after talking with combat veterans and reading the personal accounts of others, including the exploits of those who were awarded medals for bravery, I understood and appreciated the words attributed to Mark Twain, that "courage is resistance to fear and mastery of fear, not absence of fear."

In any event, compared to the massive air-raids endured by Londoners from September 1940 to May 1941, the 1942 raids on the city, were sporadic and limited, with little damage or loss of life. However, Bath, Birmingham, Bristol, Exeter, Liverpool, Norwich, Plymouth, Portsmouth, Southampton and York, were all bombed numerous times, apparently on the personal orders of Hitler, in retaliation for the RAF's nightly raids on Germany. As a result, most civilian casualties in 1942, 2,980 killed and 3,766 injured, occurred not in London, but in those 10 cities.

I confess that I enjoyed working as an office-boy at the CM/FP companies. My "work-station" was nothing more than a table and chair located in the front office, in full view of everyone who entered or left the building. On either side of the main doors, were the Executive Offices, and to the far right, was a large room in which the Directors held their periodic Board meetings.

With this much "brass" always coming and going, I learned to watch my behaviour, and to curb my natural born tendency to clown around, or poke fun at those hide-bound British office customs, which in those days were considered sacrosanct by management.

Halfway through each morning and afternoon, the tea-trolley arrived, and we all stopped whatever we were doing, for a "cuppa" and a slice of cake, courtesy of the cafeteria. This ritual was duplicated in all offices and the plant too, where machines were shut down and production temporarily ceased. Even under siege with their backs to the wall, the British always stopped for tea!

Because of the ever present threat posed by the Luftwaffe, the plant had its own fire-fighting detachment and equipment, and a team of "fire-watchers" who, whenever the air-raid siren sounded, were charged with the responsibility of manning positions on the flat roofs of the plant and office buildings, and keeping watch for any incendiary bombs which might land on the premises.

In order to provide the necessary 24 hour coverage, all male employees 18 years and older who were not serving in the Home Guard, were required to stay over a certain number of nights a month, and to accommodate them, several areas were converted into make-shift dormitories by the addition of metal cots, as needed.

Too young to serve as a fire-watcher, I knew little about the on-duty habits and antics of those who did, except that I gathered from office gossip, that on raid-less nights, long-lasting poker sessions were more the rule, than the exception.

In this vein, the Chief of the fire-fighting detachment, who was also required to regularly stay overnight, was known for his legendary ability to sleep through any noise or commotion. In fact, he'd even sleep through the wail of the air-raid siren, if one of his crew didn't shake him awake. This was an amusing personal foible, which not unexpectedly, was finally exploited.

One morning, arriving at the plant, I saw a circle of laughing employees congregated outside the main office entrance. Drawing closer, I saw within the circle, the Chief, clad in pajamas and snoring away on his cot, which earlier had been carried outside by members of his crew, without disturbing his shut-eye. After several photos had been taken, the poor guy was finally awakened, and his expression at finding himself still in bed, but outside the building, was one we laughed and talked about for months.

Mr. Charles Dobson (referred to as "Dobbie" by the rank and file), served as CMC's Corporate Secretary. His office on Executive Row, was immediately to the left of the main entrance, so I saw him often, and vice versa. He was short, portly and pompous, and had never spoken to me, but always glared in my direction in passing, so one day in September, when I was summoned to his office after only eight months on the job, I assumed that I was in trouble.

Actually, that wasn't the case. Mr. D pointed out that my formal education had been drastically short-changed as a result of my evacuation to Cornwall, so perhaps I should consider attending night-school. Taking this as an order rather than a suggestion, I signed up at Crouch End School, located just a few miles from where I lived, for Business English and Accounting, the two courses Dobson had recommended.

Two nights a week, when I got home from a 10 hour work-day, I'd rush out again, catch yet another bus, and spend two hours in class. I did this for nine months and gained some useful knowledge, despite the fact that if the air-raid siren sounded, classes halted and we all headed for home or to a shelter.

Formal night-school graduation ceremonies were unheard of. Students attended as best they could, under very difficult circumstances, getting whatever education was possible from the time and effort they each expended. I'm afraid this describes my one-term, and somewhat dysfunctional, night-school experience.

I don't recall the cost of my classes, but it was mine to pay with no financial help from my employer. The fee and the round-trip bus cost, on top of what I spent on daily transportation to and from work, took the lion's share of my $3.00 a week available cash, and I knew this couldn't continue.

The only solution was to invest in a bicycle, and I was able to do this through a friend Clifford Sparkes, who sold me a used Raleigh at a price I couldn't refuse. However, when I took it home, my step-mother refused to let me park it in our hallway, as I'd planned. With no access to the back-yard or the scullery, except by carrying the bike through the kitchen, which Mom also vetoed, I turned again to Cliff. He owned a small garage a block from my home that he used as a storage facility, and was kind enough to give me a key and permission to park my bike there anytime, which conveniently solved my transportation problems.

The accommodating Mr. Sparkes, who sold me a bike and provided me with free access to his garage, was a truly unforgettable character. We met after I returned from Cornwall and soon became good friends. He was 18 months older than I and lived in nearby Highgate, a more upscale neighborhood than Stroud Green.

Cliff was thin, with black hair and very pale skin, and almost always wore a white shirt, black tie, dark pin-striped pants and a black jacket. This somber "funeral director" appearance was belied by his quick, acerbic wit, an infectious laugh, and a natural inclination to play practical jokes on the unsuspecting, three examples of which I can still recall.

Cliff and I were both movie fans, and at least once a week, we'd arrange to see a double-feature at one of our local cinemas. Given the distance of my commute, I'd usually meet him there without going home first, and knowing this he'd often bring me a sandwich or a piece of cake, to tide me over.

One evening, as the auditorium darkened and the movie began, he handed me a bag which he said contained a fish-paste sandwich. Sitting there in the dark, with my eyes focused on the screen, I took him at his word, biting into the sandwich several times, before I realized to my discomfort, that in between the slices of fish-paste coated bread, Cliff had placed a layer of cellophane! I could have chewed that booby-trapped sandwich for hours, without success, a predicament which Cliff viewed as hilarious.

He had another trick he'd often play as we mingled with the crowed exiting the cinema, onto the blacked-out street. He'd toss a handful of farthings into the air, just for the fun of watching people search frantically with their flashlights, in case the coins they heard hitting the pavement, belonged to them.

While the farthing was worth less than half of an American cent, it was about the same size as an English sixpence, which had a value equivalent to an American dime. In those hard times, most Londoners who thought they'd accidentally dropped one or more sixpences, would certainly always take time for a search.

Finally, I remember the Saturday that Cliff and I, accompanied by Ray Marshall, a friend from my evacuee days in Cornwall, went into the West End on the Underground. By the time that our train was nearing Leicester Square Station where we'd planned to get off, our coach was standing room only, so tightly jammed that at one station, several passengers who wanted off, couldn't get through to the door and were transported farther down the line.

Taking stock of this, Cliff saw an opportunity for another practical joke. He whispered his idea to Ray and I, and as the train slowed down at the Leicester Square Station, Cliff suddenly slumped over in his seat with his eyes closed, as if he'd passed out. On cue, Ray yelled at the top of his voice, "This man is unconscious, we need to get him to a doctor!"

As soon as the train stopped, all the passengers in the doorway spilled out onto the platform, followed by many of those who'd been blocking the center aisle. This gave Ray and I enough room to lift up our "unconscious" friend by his shoulders and feet, and carry him through the coach and off the train, whereupon he opened his eyes and leaped to his feet, taking off at a run with Ray and I following, for the exit escalator!

As I remember it, looking over my shoulder as we ran, the passengers on the platform who'd made room for us to get off, stood for a moment in stunned silence at this "miracle" before elbowing their way back onto the train, no doubt cursing the fact that they'd been suckered by three teen-aged jokesters.

Actually, Cliff's somewhat bizarre sense of humor, masked some very real and impressive talents. At age sixteen, he had already acquired a little shop in Stroud Green. I never asked him how he was able to have his own business at such a tender age, but he was an only child, and his father held a middle-management position at the Kodak plant in London, so very likely he was the source of Cliff's start-up capital.

In any event, thanks to his intrinsically shrewd business sense, his shop did very well with the bulk of its revenue coming from mail-order sales of fishing gear, rods, hooks, flies and such, to customers who lived outside of London.

In addition to the store, Cliff had several profitable side-lines, one of which involved his showing "silent" movies to church groups and at social affairs of other organizations. He owned a substantial number of old movies, featuring Laurel and Hardy, Harold Loyd, the Keystone Cops, and many other stars of Hollywood's silent era. His Dad had obtained these for him several years earlier, when the Kodak plant where he worked, decided to purge its library of these bygone classics.

Amazingly, this facet of Cliff's business was so busy, that he offered to pay me to accompany him on many of these outings, to help carry his equipment on and off the buses which were our only transportation, and set up and dismantle this at our destination.

Another of his lucrative side-lines, was selling ladies' cosmetic and bathroom articles, such as perfume, face-powder, lipstick and fancy soaps. All these items were in short supply and hard to come by, circumstances which after three years of war, had spawned an "underground" market, a source to which I assumed Cliff had a connection, in order to obtain his regular supplies.

One day, at his suggestion, I took samples of his merchandise to work, and showed them around the office. Not surprisingly, I was an instant hit with the predominantly female staff, and returned to Cliff with a large order. I can't recall how much commission I earned on that first big sale and the many repeat orders that followed, but helping him with this venture and his movie shows, provided me with some much needed extra income.

My Parents, London 1916

My Uncle Albert, London 1914
(He was KIA in World War I)

With My Parents and Sisters, London 1934

Stroud Green School Evacuees and Mr. Barlow
(I'm standing at the far right). Cornwall, 1940

With Horace West and Jim and Florrie Grenfell.
Seveock Manor, Cornwall, April 1941

Cliff Sparkes and me.
London, March 1945

CHAPTER 14

At Last, War News Worth Hearing

By 1942, women in Britain were drafted at age nineteen and chosen at random, for service in the military, or to work in defense plants, or as farm laborers. My cousin Ivy was already serving in the RAF's Womens Auxiliary Air Force (WAAF), and in September of that year, when my sister Peg turned nineteen, she too volunteered for military service in the British Army's Womens Auxiliary Territorial Service (WATS).

She was lucky enough to be assigned to the Army Finance Corps, where she served for 43 months at a unit based in the Moorgate section of London. As a result, although always required to be in uniform while on duty, she was able to live at home during her entire service career, commuting to work each day on the Underground, just as she had done as a civilian.

As 1942 drew to an end, after more than three years of war, the long suffering British people finally had something to cheer about, when the Desert War in North Africa turned in their favor. On October 23, Britain's 8th Army, under its new commander, General Bernard Montgomery, broke out of its defensive line at El Alamein in Egypt, and attacked with superior numbers of troops, tanks and aircraft, a massive offensive from which Rommel's vaunted Africa Corps never completely recovered.

By November 5, Montgomery was able to announce that his army had won decisive victory in Egypt. Three days later, the world learned that American and Free-French troops had landed in West Africa, on the beaches of Algeria and Morocco, an invasion which put Rommel's retreating army at risk of assault from two sides.

America's entry into the African campaign, took Hitler and his military by surprise, as did Britain's success at El Alamein. These two heartening events prompted Churchill, speaking to the House of Commons on November 10, to comment in his own inimitable style,

"This is not the end. It is not even the beginning of the end. But it is, perhaps, the end of the beginning!"

At the same time, news from the Eastern Front, appeared to validate the Prime Minister's sentiment. Three German armies which on Hitler's personal orders had invaded the Soviet Union eighteen months earlier despite the misgivings of his military commanders, ground to a halt outside Moscow, Leningrad and Stalingrad. All had suffered enormous casualties in men killed and wounded in fierce, unrelenting battles with the Red Army, and from the killing and disabling effects of their exposure to the legendary harsh elements of two Russian winters.

At the time that Hitler had launched his surprise attack on Russia, few in Britain knew anything about the Soviet Union or communism, even though the British Communist Party had been a recognized and legal political organization, for many years.

However, almost overnight following the invasion, literature extolling the virtues of Britain's new ally, appeared in book-stores and on news-stands, including a weekly newspaper called the "Red Star," devoted to reporting the Red Army's heroic and seemingly always victorious exploits, against the Nazi hordes.

At the risk of being labeled a "fellow-traveler" more than half a century later, I confess that I was a regular reader of that publication not out of any interest in communism, but as a result of my fascination with military matters, especially with an allied army engaging in a life and death struggle with Nazi troops, who might otherwise have been used to invade Britain.

While the "Red Star" was likely more propaganda than fact, it did trigger my curiosity about Russia, a country which less than forty years earlier, had been a monarchy, much like Britain.

Browsing in the public library one day, I discovered Mikhail Sholokov, a Russian author who had penned a fictional trilogy, based on the actual events leading to the Bolshevik Revolution in 1917, and the bloody communist dictatorship which followed. Hooked on Shokolov's first book "And Quiet Flows the Don," I subsequently worked my way through his two companion volumes, "The Don Flows Down To The Sea" and "Virgin Soil Upturned."

I concluded from all that I read, that Sholokov's books had probably been banned in the Soviet Union, because they certainly did nothing to promote or enhance communism, serving instead to bring an element of reality, to the "gift-wrapped" version of that cruel and Godless doctrine, to which I'd been exposed, as a young and innocent reader of the "Red Star" weekly.

On February 14, 1943, progress by the Allied forces in Tunisia suffered a setback, when Rommel's Afrika Corps launched a powerful counter-attack on infantry and armored units of the U.S. Army's II Corps, as they advanced across the desert plains of the Kasserine Pass. This first bloody encounter between our green and untested troops and the combat-wise, battle-hardened German forces, resulted in a costly and embarrassing American defeat.

In light of the disparity in the combat experience of the two armies, the battle's outcome was not unpredictable. Nevertheless, in Britain, the news media's criticism of American military leadership, and its snide comments on the fighting qualities of our troops, was rampant. I well remember those newspaper headlines and critical editorials, which given my obsessive devotion to all things American, I took somewhat personally!

Apparently, Britain's press had conveniently forgotten that in the first three years of the war, German forces drove British troops out of France, Belgium, Norway, Greece and Crete, and until El Alamein, had almost driven the British 8th Army out of North Africa! Under the circumstances, their unbridled criticism of the U.S. Army's performance during its baptism of fire, against one of Germany's most elite and combat-experienced armies, was uncalled for and hypocritical, to say the least.

As it was, less than two weeks later, American forces had regained the ground lost at Kasserine, and by February 28, the German advance was stopped in its tracks. The cost to the Allies however, had been high, 10,000 casualties of which 6,500 were American, compared to 2,000 casualties suffered by Axis troops.

On March 6, 1943, General George S. Patton, Jr. whose legendary aggressive leadership would earn him the reputation of being the Allied field commander the Germans most feared and respected, took command of the U.S. Army II Corps. Two months later on May 2, German General Von Armin, who earlier had replaced Rommel, surrendered all Axis forces in North Africa, which sent a total of 238,243 German and Italian prisoners, into Allied POW camps.

With no end to the war in sight, keeping up civilian morale was crucial to Britain's homefront efforts. Many large companies, especially those engaged in defense or war related production, instituted all kinds of social activities aimed at lifting the spirits of their employees.

For example, management at the plant where I worked had discovered enough musical talent within its employee ranks, to form a company dance-band. While it wasn't Glenn Miller quality-wise, it played the tunes which by then had made Miller as popular in England as he was in the States, imitating faithfully his orchestra's unique sound and distinctive arrangements.

Dances were held in the company cafeteria, which was cleared of tables for each occasion, and decorated so as to more resemble a commercial dance-hall, of which there were many throughout London and its suburbs. As I recall, the company band played two or more Saturday nights a month, always to an enthusiastic crowd of employees and their guests.

After my first company dance, I knew that if I planned on being a regular attendee I needed to learn to dance, so I signed up for waltz, quickstep and fox-trot lessons at a studio near my home, run by two elderly spinsters. More than one evening lesson was interrupted by the air-raid siren, but I finally "graduated," and from that point on, was able to ask any girl to dance, with confidence. To this day, whenever I hear the strains of "Sleepy Lagoon" or "Moonlight Serenade," two songs from my dance-school days, I sentimentally remember those two dear old ladies.

While on the subject of dancing, let me say that I believe the British have always approached this pastime, more seriously than we Americans. In fact, during the friendly wartime "occupation" of their country by our forces, some Brits were convinced that if an American, out of uniform and dressed in civvies, went to a dance-hall, he'd be identified as a Yank immediately.

GIs when dancing, would invariably remain in place, rocking back and forth, barely moving, whereas most British men would steer their partners around the ball-room, meticulously quick-stepping or fox-trotting in unison with the other couples, a sight rarely seen in this country except in professional dance competitions. But when "jitter-bugging," the Yanks could always hold their own.

As a morale builder, the company dances were certainly a great success, particularly from my standpoint, as they provided me with an opportunity to meet and socialize with the teenage girls I'd see during my daily work related trips through the plant.

The only one of those young ladies that I can still remember, is Phyllis Greenleaf, who worked as a typist on the second floor of the Main Office. Phyllis was seven months older than I, a petite and pretty blue-eyed blonde, and from the moment I laid eyes on her, I was smitten!

However, when Edie Davies, my office manager, learned of my "crush," she told me in no uncertain terms, that Phyllis was off-limits as she was already involved with a young man currently serving with the Royal Navy. Forewarned, I set my romantic sights elsewhere, but Phyllis and I became good platonic friends, and at the Company dances, we often teamed up as partners.

(As an aside, in 1947, Phyllis married Eddie Gillam, the young Navy man I'd been warned about. She remains the sole connection to my teen-age days in England, and over the years, whenever I've been in London, I've always taken time to visit her and Eddie, and to this day, we still exchange Christmas cards).

Despite my hectic schedule, I found time to pursue the acting-bug which I acquired playing Mark Anthony and Shylock, during my final months at school in Cornwall, and I spent many Saturday afternoons at Foyles, studying books on acting and the theater.

Foyles of Charing Cross Road, was London's most famous bookstore, where one could browse for hours and pick up all sorts of new and used literary bargains. I recall purchasing a book on stage make-up, another on stage sound-effects, and one titled "How To Form An Amateur Dramatic Society." I concluded from reading the latter, that realistically, the only way I'd ever get a chance to be an actor, was if I wrote the play myself, with a part in it for me, and then produced and directed it too!

To that end, I contacted SGS class-mates, Eileen Frewin, Graham Woods and Peter Laister, who'd been in my class in Cornwall, and Yvonne Ude, a gorgeous girl who I'd always worshipped from afar, and Len, a boy whose last name I can't remember, who was a talented pianist who already had his own small dance-band.

I managed to persuade all five to sign on as cast members, and around this troup of somewhat reluctant thespians, I wrote a play entitled "Let The People Sing," in which I played not one, but two characters, an American called "Stewy Stubbs" and an Englishman with the unlikely name of "Sir Tainly Knott." Perhaps not surprisingly, both men were identical look-alikes!

I can't recall the details of my first play, except that Len my musician friend insisted that the plot include an opportunity for his band to play "Elmer's Tune," one of the popular songs of the day, and to ensure his participation as a cast member, I wrote the script accordingly. This was just as well, because from an audience appreciation standpoint, his band's rendition of that number, was clearly the high spot of the entire production.

Eileen took on the chore of typing copies of the script as I wrote it, and we got together at her house to read and rehearse our parts whenever we could, which wasn't easy as we all had full-time jobs. Finally, I convinced the Pastor of Holly Park Methodist Church in Stroud Green, to let us use his Church's recreational hall, which was equipped with a real stage.

One Saturday evening in May, the first and only production of "Let The People Sing," played to a small audience, primarily of friends and relatives of the cast and a few Holly Park Church members, on hand no doubt to monitor our use of the facility.

Real news must have been in short supply that evening, because the event was actually covered by a reporter from the "Hornsey Journal" our local newspaper. His generally neutral comments on our performance appeared under the heading "Sixteen Year Old Dramatist," and I carried that clipping in my wallet for many years. I wish now that I'd kept it, because it turned out to be the only formal recognition of my very brief theatrical career.

Several months later, not knowing at the time that my first production was also destined to be my last, I began work on another play, which I decided, even before having a plot synopsis, would be a mystery titled "Murder Hath Charms."

Several days a week, I'd stay late at the office writing and rewriting, trying to produce an original murder mystery script. Eve Allen, a secretary to my Uncle Bert, would faithfully type my pages of long-hand, never commenting, one way or another. Her silence in this regard should have been a clue to the possibility that my play was probably not "Tony" material!

In any event, as I struggled to write a plot which if staged, would actually represent a "mystery" to the audience, Eve suddenly announced she had enlisted in the Womens Royal Navy Service (WRNS). After she left, with no one else willing to transcribe my scribble, I never did finish "Murder Hath Charms."

Two year later, home on furlough from the U.S. Army, I read the unfinished "Murder" script and my first play "Let The People Sing," and was so embarrassed by how amateurish my efforts as a sixteen year old playwright were, that I destroyed both scripts.

My sister Mary's days at Stroud Green School ended in June of 1943, four months after her fourteenth birthday. As was then the custom, she was interviewed by the school's Employment Counselor whose task it was to steer those children whose education was about to end, into jobs for which they seemed to be best suited.

Mary was tagged as a "clerical" person, and sent for an interview at a local office of the London Insurance Company, where she was immediately hired at a salary of 25 shillings ($5) a week, starting two days after leaving school. Just as Peg and I did before her, she gave more than half of her paycheck to our step-mother for room and board, and paid for all of her other personal expenses, including transportation, clothes and lipstick.

Mary still remembers how she hated her first job at the insurance company, and after ten months, she left to work as a switch-board operator at an import-export firm in Holborn. This position she enjoyed until another girl was hired to replace her as the telephonist, and she was re-assigned to the typing-pool.

While appreciating the opportunity to become a typist, she soon became bored with preparing invoices all day, and when a clerk-typist position opened up at the Bond Street establishment of a Turf Accountant (bookmaker), where a good friend of hers was already employed, she changed jobs again.

In 1943, while significant ground battles were being fought in Africa, the air offensive from England against Germany, carried out by the RAF at night and the U.S. 8th Air Force by day, had intensified, with 1,000 bomber raids becoming more frequent.

Getting 1,000 four-engined bombers into the air without mishap, was an extraordinary logistical feat. Putting the many units into their respective battle formations, before they headed for the target, was an equally challenging process. Usually the first planes off the ground, were required to "mark-time" circling the area, until the entire fleet was fully assembled and ready to go.

With most of the Allied airfields located in East Anglia, this process was one with which all Londoners became familiar. As darkness fell, we'd hear the drone of thousands of aircraft engines, as the unseen RAF formations assembled overhead. On our way to work in the morning, we'd hear and see the silver B-17s and B-24s of the "Mighty 8th" heading out in formation, their numbers literally filling the sky, from one horizon to the other.

Witnessing these frequent reminders of Allied airpower was a great morale booster, particularly for those who had earlier endured and survived the many air-raids on Britain. Where the citizens of London were concerned, turnabout was fair play!

For me, there was another more personal aspect to the mounting American presence in England. By then, for security reasons tied to the planned Allied invasion of occupied Europe, and to keep secret the number and identity of its divisions in Britain, the U.S. Army issued very few passes to London, to its ground troops.

Everyone however, including the enemy, knew that the U.S. 8th and 9th Air Forces were stationed in England. When the men of those organizations were given leave, London was their favorite destination, so that on most week-ends, the West End was awash with Yankee fliers, intent on having a good time.

Often, on a Saturday or Sunday, I'd take the Tube into Leicester Square, and stand in one of the area's many amusement arcades, watching as American officers and enlisted men bantered freely with one another, (very un-British!), and listen to the many different "Hollywood" accents. I guess in some strange way, I was homesick for the land where I was born, but had never known.

My sister Peg was also a frequent week-end visitor to the West End, joining the thousands of other Allied servicemen and women at the British and American "canteens," located around Piccadily, which were open to all hours for tea, coffee, donuts and dancing.

On one of these visits, she met an 8th Air Force flyer, Staff Sergeant Herbie Sohns, from Scranton, Pennsylvania, who she invited home to meet Dad, knowing that he'd be thrilled at the prospect of once again chatting with an American.

Tall, dark and handsome, Herbie was quiet spoken and polite. He'd been a member of the Pennsylvania State Police before enlisting in the Air Force, and already had 15 combat missions under his belt as a B-17 "Flying Fortress" waist-gunner. He seemed to enjoy his visit as much as we did, and promised to come again.

Peg and he began to correspond, which led to an amusing incident, when she ended one of her letters with a British expression, which to an American, would have a very different connotation. The words Peg used, "keep your pecker up," was a common British salutation during the war years, a universally accepted way of saying to a friend or relative, "don't let the war get you down."

Needless to say, when Herbie got a letter from Peg telling him to "keep his pecker up," he was so surprised that he shared it with the other members of his crew. They of course thought the whole idea was hilarious, and when he took his next leave to London, most of them insisted on accompanying him, so they could meet this English girl, who'd given him such unusual advice!

As I recall, it was during the summer of 1943, that my Dad quit his job as a debit-agent for the Mutual Property Life and General Insurance Company, and took an entry level position in an office of the British equivalent of our Internal Revenue Service, where he continued to work until his retirement in the Sixties.

On July 9, two months after the fighting in North Africa had ended, the Allies launched their campaign to carry the war to Mussolini, Hitler's cohort. Powerful airborne forces parachuted into Sicily, located at the "toe" of Italy, and 24 hours later, 12 divisions of the U.S. 7th Army and the British 8th Army, were put onto its beaches from ships and landing-craft.

This combined air and sea assault caught the 350,000 Axis troops on the island by surprise, German intelligence having falsely concluded that Sardinia would be the likely invasion target.

On July 25, anticipating that a full scale invasion of Italy was imminent, a coalition of Italian generals and politicians, ousted Mussolini and placed him in exile, under house arrest. Three weeks later, Sicily fell to the American and British forces, but 60,000 German troops escaped across the Straits of Messina to Italy, to form the nucleus of an army that would engage Allied forces in fierce and costly battles, for the next 21 months.

On September 8, the formal surrender of Italy was announced, and on the following day, elements of the U.S. 5th Army, comprised of the British X and U.S. VI Corps, were put ashore at Salerno.

CHAPTER 15

New Duties At Work, A Close Call At Home

It was in September 1942, that I incurred the wrath of corporate Secretary Mr. Dobson, over an innocuous incident which nevertheless led to my transfer from the Main Office to the plant Production Office. As I previously indicated, meetings of the CMC Board of Directors, were held in a room opposite my work-station. All the directors were "upper-crust" males, and when they were around, we employees were expected to be on our best behavior.

Following one routine Board session, as the directors filed out of their room, one of them, a retired British Army Major who always sported a large cigar, accidentally slipped or tripped and landed on his backside, right in front of my desk.

It was a classic Keystone Cops pratfall, and unfortunately, I reacted accordingly! While the Major wasn't physically hurt, his dignity took an awful blow, no doubt compounded by seeing the lowly office-boy laughing at his discomfort, rather than running to his rescue, as did everyone else in the vicinity.

Next day, "Dobbie" called me into his office, and let me know in no uncertain terms, that my behavior would have gotten me fired, had I not been the nephew of the Company's Sales Manager. Thanks to that connection, I still had a job but would be immediately transferred to the plant Production Office. There I'd be far enough away to not again be an embarrassment to the Main Office, and where I'd be given one last chance to redeem myself.

While my transfer was clearly intended as a punishment for my unacceptable behavior, it actually turned out to be a blessing in disguise. I'd been an office-boy for 21 months and given my restless personality, I needed something more challenging with some real individual work-related responsibilities.

My new boss, the Production Office Manager Frank Crawford, was a short, stocky gentleman whose thinning black hair was strangely marked with snow-white streaks. I learned that these streaks had manifested overnight, during the hours he was trapped in the bombed-out ruins of his house, during the 1940-41 Blitz.

I suspect that he had been apprised by Mr. Dobson on the reason for my sudden transfer to his jurisdiction, as he made it clear during his short speech of welcome, that any more monkey-business on my part, would lead to immediate dismissal. He then introduced me to the other office men, Assistant Manager Bruce Hewitt, Sales Representative Len Bayliss and Ted Hicks, Senior Production Clerk, my direct supervisor.

Ted was an affable seventeen year old, who'd already given notice that on his eighteenth birthday, he planned to enlist in the RAF. With that event just months away, I knew that I'd need to learn without delay, all that I could about being a Production Clerk.

Bayliss, in addition to his sales and customer liaison duties, was also charged with reviewing all orders for CMC products as they were received, before turning these over to Ted and I. Our job as Production Clerks, was to translate customer orders into factory work-orders and then expedite these through the plant, while monitoring their progress from production to shipping.

In those days, work-orders were prepared in long-hand on small lined pads using carbon-paper to produce the required triplicate copies. On these sheets, we'd indicate the specific material needed, and on repeat orders, the proper machine-tool to be used. On first-time orders, we'd also have to write out the customer's specs and give these to the template/tool makers, so that the necessary machine tools could be designed and produced.

I liked working with Ted and enjoyed my new duties which were certainly more interesting and challenging than those I'd been used to as an office-boy. While the actual preparation of each day's new factory work-orders took up most of my time, the job also required that I meet and confer with the various factory foremen and tool-makers as well as the machine-operators, most of who were girls my own age, or a few years older.

I remember thinking that the sexual chemistry between me and one flirtatious girl called Betty Monks, was particularly intense and for me as a sixteen year old, that's how it probably seemed. However, that imagined attraction was abruptly cooled after I learned that Betty was already dating Ted my supervisor. First Phyllis and now Betty, it seemed as if every young female who stole my heart, was destined to belong to another!

In October, my Uncle Bert was drafted into the British Army, and after finishing his basic training, he was shipped to Italy as an 8th Army artillery unit replacement, where he served out the balance of the war. After he'd left, I learned that his wife, my Aunt Alice, was pregnant with their first child.

It was in October, that I made myself very unpopular with my sister Peg by infecting her with chicken-pox, which I'd picked up from a girl at my office. Peg was 20 years old and serving in the military, and was particularly mortified being stricken with what she viewed as a childhood ailment. Possible trying to assuage my guilt in this regard, I remember that as she lay spotted and itchy in her bed, I sat and read to her for hours on end, from various novels of her choice.

I wasn't required to do anything equally altruistic for Mary, because she had her bout with chicken-pox as an evacuee in Cornwall. However, during the two weeks I was house-bound, I recall that my step-mother and I really got to know one another, establishing an affectionate relationship, which I'm happy to say withstood the test of time.

Every afternoon, she'd make a pot of tea, and we'd sit and talk about many things, including of course my obsessive desire to some day leave England and return to America. During one of these sessions, Mom confided that many years earlier, a friend had shown her how to "read" tea-leaves. In those days, tea was always made in a pot, never from a bag, so every cup when drained, contained a tea-leaf sediment.

My step-mom, bless her, always played into my Yankee yearnings. From the first time she peered into my tea-cup, and each time thereafter that I prevailed upon her to do another "reading," her predictions remained the same, "your leaves say that you will travel to a faraway country where you'll be very successful," which of course was exactly what I wanted to hear!

In November, an event occurred which I still vividly remember. One of the worst "pea-soupers" in Britain's history, blanketed the Greater London area, paralyzing all surface transportation and pedestrian traffic alike, for 48 hours. That first morning, the visibility wasn't that bad for a London fog, but for safety reasons, I took the bus to work, rather than ride my bike.

By late afternoon when I left the plant, the fog was so dense, most buses had stopped running except for those trying to make it back to their depots. These were forced to crawl along at a snail's pace, the drivers following the conductors, who walked ahead of their buses carrying tar-soaked torches, to illuminate the way.

I was lucky to get on a trolley-bus heading for Finsbury Park, where I got off, after a nerve wracking ride which took over two hours, instead of the usual 30 minutes. I walked the last mile home, using my flash-light and carrying a piece of wood that I dragged along the privet-hedges outside of the row homes, to keep me on the sidewalk, which because of the fog and wartime unlighted streets, was totally invisible to the naked eye.

When I entered the house and saw myself in the hallstand mirror, I looked like something from a horror movie! I had bloodshot eyes rimmed with black soot, a soot-filled runny nose, a sore throat and hacking cough! This was a fog, which before it dissipated, was to claim many lives, particularly among the elderly.

Sometime before Christmas Ted Hicks my supervisor and Betty Monks were married, and Ted enlisted in the RAF. His departure from the CMC, elevated me to his position as the Senior Production Clerk. Bernard, a fifteen year old just out of school, was hired as the new Junior Clerk and a girl the same age called Sheila, was assigned to assist us. Both were subject to my direction and supervision, and I recall that even at the age of sixteen, I was quite comfortable with those new responsibilities.

On December 24, U.S. Army General Dwight D. Eisenhower, was appointed Supreme Commander, Allied Expeditionary Force (SCAEF). British General Bernard Montgomery was named his Deputy and Commander of the Allied ground forces then being assembled for the planned 1944 cross-channel invasion of occupied France.

These appointments no doubt help trigger the oft-repeated British comment, that the million plus American troops in their country were "overpaid, oversexed and over here," to which criticism, Americans reacted in kind, by pointing out that the British troops were "underpaid, undersexed and under Eisenhower!"

At year's end, the British tallied their civilian casualties in 1943 from German air-raids, 1,484 killed and 2,168 injured. Despite this toll, there was a feeling of optimism in Britain, now in its fourth year of war, that there was a light at the end of the tunnel, where the conflict with Germany was concerned.

In the USSR, Hitler's armies, suffering massive losses in men and material under a relentless Soviet offensive, were being driven back towards the Polish border, while in Italy, in the face of continuous American and British assaults on their defensive positions, his troops were being forced to retreat to the north.

Thousands of miles away on the other side of the globe, the bloody and costly island battles being fought in the south west Pacific by American and Australian forces against fanatical Japanese defenders, received scant attention in Britain, where speculation concerning the anticipated Allied invasion of Nazi occupied Europe, overshadowed all other war news or concerns.

New Year's Eve has always been celebrated in England as festively as it is in the USA, but during the war years, New Year's Day was not an English national holiday. This was pretty hard on those celebrants who, after singing Auld Lang Syne and partying well into the early morning hours, were expected to show up for work "bright-eyed and bushy-tailed," at the usual time.

Public transportation was not generally available after midnight, so at the crack of dawn, those who'd partied away from home, took the first available bus or train directly to their place of employment. In my case, the fact that the CMC/FPC held a New Year's Eve dance at its plant, made my showing up for work on time on that first day of 1944, real easy.

None of us celebrating at that time however, had any inkling of the death and destruction which we'd soon face during a new wave of Luftwaffe bombing attacks, or from Hitler's secret "V" weapons which were launched against Britain over a nine month period, beginning six months later.

By 1944, Britain had been transformed into the world's largest military installation. It housed more than one million American troops plus hundreds of thousands of British, Canadian and other Allied forces. Acres and acres of English countryside from Essex to Cornwall were packed solid with tanks, trucks, artillery, ammunition, gasoline and other military supplies.

The build-up was so enormous, it was speculated by some that had it not been for the hundreds of barrage-balloons tethered over London and other strategic locations, that the island itself may very well have sunk, under the weight of the men and materials!

That an Allied invasion of occupied Europe was now imminent, was not lost on the German High Command. Its few bomber units which were still operational were passed into service, with the knowledge and expectation that no matter where their bombs would fall, they'd land on a target of military significance.

Given Britain's greatly improved air defenses, the massive bomber formations favored by the Luftwaffe during its 1940-41 blitz were no longer feasible, and it relied instead on its fast bombers (usually JU-88's), flying independent sorties. Regardless of their assigned targets, these lone intruders tended to jettison their bombs as soon as they ran into concentrated anti-aircraft fire, before high-tailing it back to their bases, hoping not to run into any RAF night-fighters along the way.

During January, air-raids on Britain cost the already depleted German bomber force, 57 aircraft, a number it could ill afford to lose. Despite these losses, on February 18 it launched a new wave of bombing attacks on London, a period referred to as the "Little Blitz" by the capital's air-raid hardened citizens.

Riding to work the morning after a night-time raid, I had to stop several times to re-inflate the tires on my bike that kept going flat. On the ride home, I went through the same frustrating exercise, to a point where I gave up trying to ride, and walked my bike instead. When I arrived at the garage where I stored it overnight, I removed both tires and tested the inner-tubes for leaks by immersing them inflated, in a pan of water.

I found three small holes in each tube, which I patched, and then I carefully examined both tires before remounting them. It was well I did, because imbedded in each tread, were scores of tiny, razor-sharp slivers of shrapnel, which had obviously fallen into the streets, from the hundreds of anti-aircraft shells fired into the sky during the previous night's raid.

After that experience, I always left my bike at home and took the bus to work, on mornings following a visit from the Luftwaffe. Records indicate that the British civilian casualties during those first two months of 1944, totaled 1,068 killed and 1,972 injured.

Dad and Mom went back to sleeping each night in the Morrison shelter, which unfortunately was only large enough for two. I continued to sleep on a sofa-bed in the parlor, while my sisters slept next door in my parent's bedroom. When the air-raid siren sounded, all that we three could do, was to pray! My favorite supplication to the Almighty was the 23rd Psalm, which I recited aloud with genuine passion, more times than I can now recall!

I do remember all too clearly, that one of those February, 1944 hit-and-run raids, came much too close for comfort. One night, after we'd all gone to bed, I awoke to the mournful wail of the air-raid siren, and the distinctive "throb-throb" engine noise of an approaching German bomber.

Simultaneously, our local AA batteries opened fire, and the pitch of the bomber's engines changed as it dived to evade the hardware fired in its direction. Then, as I lay transfixed in my bed, I heard the unmistakable whistle of a falling bomb, followed by a loud explosion which sent a shower of dust and ceiling fragments onto my upturned face. As it turned out, a large bomb had landed just one block away from our house.

My sisters and I left our beds in a hurry, and ran to the kitchen, where we bumped into our parents who'd left their shelter, and were on their way to check on us. At that point, our lodgers, Mr. H and his wife, both in a high state of anxiety, came downstairs and we all went to the front door, and peered out. We saw several neighbors heading down our street, presumably towards the bomb-site to view the damage and help in the rescue efforts. When Dad announced he planned to join them, I begged to go along and he consented.

The bomb had apparently landed dead-center in the back-to-back yards of a four-square block of homes, and the acrid smell of the explosive, still hung in the air. The rear of almost every house had been ripped open or had collapsed from the blast, and as most yards were home to Anderson in-ground shelters, there had to have been a number of deaths and serious injuries. I'm convinced that had we lived any closer to the point of impact, we would probably have lost our home too, and perhaps our lives.

By the time we arrived on the scene, the air-raid rescue teams had everything well under control, and our help was not needed. However, we ran into a family Dad knew whose house had been badly damaged, and he invited them home to stay the night with us. No one could sleep, so we all crowded into the kitchen, talking and drinking tea, while the work outside to locate and rescue those not so fortunate went on.

In the morning, I went to a pay-phone and called my office to report what had happened, and to confirm that I wouldn't be in that day. I'm proud to say, that was the only time during the war that I didn't show up for work, as a result of enemy action.

The "Little Blitz" continued through March and April, but the raids became sporadic and less deadly. Civilian casualties for the two month period were 425 killed and 859 injured, and in the month that followed, for the first time in four years, no civilian casualties from enemy action were recorded.

Early in May, S/Sgt. Herbie Sohns, Peg's 8th Air Force friend, visited us for the last time. Having completed his required bombing missions, he was about to be shipped back to the States for re-assignment to an Air Force training facility, as an aerial-gunnery instructor. He told us that since we'd last seen him, his B-17, returning from a raid over Germany, crash-landed in the English Channel, where he and his crew were picked up by RAF Air-Sea Rescue. Herbie was one of the lucky ones. Some 50,000 American airmen died fighting alongside their British allies.

His visit occurred over a week-end, and on Sunday afternoon, he and I took a walk to Finsbury Park. When he saw the lake, he decided to rent a row-boat, and the two of us spent a leisurely hour, he on the oars and I at the tiller, while he regaled me with stories about his combat missions, his home in Scranton and his pre-war life as a Pennsylvania State Trooper.

When it was time for him to leave, he presented us with a few souvenirs, a carton of American cigarettes, a box of Band-Aides, which I found absolutely fascinating because until then, I'd never seen such a product, umpteen American candy-bars and packs of chewing-gum, and especially for me, an 8th Air Force shoulder patch, which needless to say, I treasured.

My sister Peg continued to correspond with Herbie after his return to the States. In late 1945, we learned that he had been discharged from the Air Force, was married to a young woman he'd met in Tennessee, and was again living in Pennsylvania, working as a State Trooper.

CHAPTER 16

Normandy Invasion, London Under Siege, Again

By the end of May 1944, rumors and speculation concerning the long awaited Allied invasion of occupied Europe were rampant, and the tension was almost palpable. Southern England and all of the Channel coastal areas were off –limits to civilians, and as anyone with one eye on the sky could tell, the daily USAAF and RAF sorties against the enemy, had reached a record high.

Not unexpectedly then, most of us were more relieved than surprised, when we tuned into the BBC on Tuesday morning, June 6, and heard the news we'd waited for so long. In history's greatest combined air/sea operation, a force of 156,000 American, British, Canadian and Free French troops, had been dropped or put ashore into Normandy. A great and honorable military crusade to free occupied Europe from Nazi tyranny, was finally underway!

What we didn't know from those initial broadcasts, was how precarious the beach-head was, or how serious the American losses were on Omaha Beach during that famous "Longest Day." Nor did we know how easily our forces could have been driven back into the sea, had German armored units in Normandy not been held back by Hitler himself, who remained convinced during the first 72 hours, that the Normandy attack was a diversion, and the main invasion would be launched further up the coast, on the beaches at Calais.

I recall that on that morning, I decided to take the bus to work rather than ride my bike, and was glad I did. When I boarded the trolley-bus at Finsbury Park, it was packed as always, but something was decidedly different. Everyone was talking excitedly to everyone else, whether they knew them or not, which for the average British commuter was uncharacteristic indeed.

At Edmonton, where I needed to make a transfer for the remaining leg of my trip, another event occurred that still hasn't faded from my D-Day memories. While I waited in the bus line, a convoy of trucks carrying British troops rumbled by, on its way to one of the invasion embarkation ports.

Everyone began to wave and cheer, and then suddenly, up and down the line, laughter rang out as the crowd saw the hand-made signs on several of the passing trucks. They read, "Don't Wave At Us Girls, We're British," a somewhat cynical jab at the well known popularity of American GIs, with British young women.

Sadly eclipsed by the massive newspaper coverage of the events of June 6, was a barely noticed communiqué from Italy, reporting that just two days earlier, U.S. 5th Army troops had marched into Rome, making the "Holy City" the first Axis capital to surrender.

One had to have lived in wartime Britain during those dark days when enemy invasion seemed inevitable, death and destruction from the sky was commonplace, and victories for its armies were rare indeed, to have been able to appreciate the elation that D-Day brought to its citizens, despite their sober acceptance that the campaign to liberate Europe, would be long and costly.

That first week, we all listened to the BBC's nightly invasion updates, and followed intently the progress of the Allied forces in Normandy, by checking the maps which appeared in every daily newspaper. Adding to the general euphoria, was the realization that no civilian air-raid casualties had been reported during the entire month of May, a welcome lull that many embraced as a good omen, and indication that attacks from the sky were probably over.

Unfortunately, those of us living in London and the counties of South Eastern England, were in for a rude awakening! During the early hours of Tuesday, June 13 our neighborhood air-raid sirens wailed, and once again, thousands took refuge in their Morrison or Anderson shelters. With no shelter available, my sisters and I stayed in our beds and hoped for the best.

It was a night to remember! After a while, the "all clear" sounded, but before we could relax enough to sleep, another "alert" sounded, and this sequence of sirens was repeated several more times. We heard no aircraft overhead and our local air-defenses remained silent, but throughout the night, we could hear the faint rumble of distant AA guns and explosions. What none of us knew at the time, was that the third "blitz" on London had begun, a siege that would continue over a period of nine months.

During the next 72 hours, sirens wailed day and night, but for those of us living in North London, the AA gun fire and many explosions that we heard, remained in the distance. Rumors abounded that the explosions came from German aircraft that had been shot down, and had hit the ground still carrying their bomb loads. And if one believed the gossip, apparently all of the planes that had crashed, had "funny-sounding engines" and went down with flames shooting out of their tails.

On June 16, the British government officially confirmed what we civilians had already concluded, that we were under attack from a new and unknown source, rather than from conventional aircraft. The V-1, the first of Hitler's secret weapons which he often boasted would win the war for Germany, had made its debut!

"Vergeltung" or "revenge weapon," was a designation assigned by the Nazis to several of their top-secret unconventional weapons, which on Hitler's orders, were launched against London to punish the British for the bombing inflicted on Germany, by the RAF.

The V-1 was an unmanned robot "flying bomb." Those of us unlucky enough to be on the receiving end, referred to it as a "buzz-bomb" on account of its weird engine noise, although some called it the 'doodle-bug" which I thought inappropriate, because that name made it sound like an insect, or a child's toy.

It was approximately 25 feet in length with short stubby wings, carried 2,000lbs of explosive in its nose, and was propelled by a simple ram-jet engine, enclosed in a large hollow cylinder mounted in the rear above the fuselage. When in flight, this gave the weapon its distinctive pulsating rumble, which most of us thought sounded like the engine of a very large motor-cycle.

Along the coast of occupied France, the Nazis had built scores of specially designed ramps, from which this weapon was launched. Once airborne, it climbed to an altitude of 1,200ft, at which point its course was determined by pre-set magnetic compass and gyroscopic controls. It's top speed in level flight was more than 350 mph, and its fuel capacity gave it a range of approximately 160 miles, just far enough to put it over England's capital.

If the bomb made it all the way to London, its flight was terminated by two simultaneous robotic activations. A tiny guillotine cut the fuel-line, and the elevator and spoiler-flap controls were forced down, a combination of events guaranteed to send it into the ground, where its explosive cargo detonated.

It didn't take long for everyone to figure out that there was a time lapse, between the moment we heard the fuel-starved engine cut, and the resultant explosion. I'm convinced that no matter where we civilians were, when we heard a buzz-bomb speeding in our direction, we'd all begin to silently mouth the same word, "go! go! go!" as if we could somehow "will" this infernal-machine to fly a few extra yards further before its engine quit.

I've always thought how lucky I was to have lived in North London at that terrible time, compared to those living and working south of the Thames, an area which became known as "buzz-bomb alley," where most of the carnage and destruction occurred. However, two incidents I'll never forget, did come very close to home.

One night in bed, I heard that sound I'd learned to hate, getting closer and closer, seemingly at roof-top level. No doubt in concert with all of the neighbors, I began my "go! go!" mantra, and just as the bomb rumbled over my house, the engine quit.

I remember in those split seconds before the huge explosion which followed, hearing my sisters in the next room hit the floor, as they sought cover under their bed, an option I didn't have as an occupant of a sofa-bed. In the morning, we learned that the bomb had landed four blocks away on Granville Road, narrowly missing St. Aidans Church and School, where Peg received her education.

A few days later, about a mile from home returning from work on my bike, I heard an approaching bomb. The street I was on was residential except for several blocks, where it was bounded on one side by Finsbury Park, and on the other by railway tracks. That's where I was when I looked up, and saw this ugly black object with its "tail on fire," heading in my direction.

As the engine went silent, I recall dropping my bike and throwing myself face-down into the gutter, seconds before the bomb ploughed into the park and exploded, showering me with chunks of turf which left me dirty, but without injury. I was lucky! Had the bomb landed on the macadam road instead of the park, the debris which rained down on me, would certainly have been lethal. I walked my bike the rest of the way home, too shaken to ride!

During that terrible summer, the plant where I worked had someone on the main office's flat roof 24 hours a day, to watch for flying-bombs, and if one was spotted heading in our direction, we'd be alerted by the plant's siren. When that happened, all employees were supposed to seek cover under their machines, benches or desks, and stay there until the "all-clear" sounded.

One morning, after the siren had wailed, and I was under my desk waiting with the others in the office, our collective fingers crossed, the tea-trolley lady appeared. Bomb alert or not, she was right on schedule, and at that, we all left our desks, which wouldn't have been much protection anyway, and our tea-time went on as usual. Even under fire, we Londoners knew our priorities!

The V-1 bombardment of England, continued day and night for three months, with such frequency that the public air-raid sirens were no longer used to alert us of their approach, so instead we had to rely on our ears and eyes to warn us of danger.

England's AA defenses at the time, which had been set up to meet the threat from conventional bomber attacks, were re-structured. Half of the 1,000 guns deployed around London were moved to the southern coastal region, where 500 guns were already positioned. These weapons engaged any V-1 that successfully made it through the massive gauntlet of RAF fighters, on patrol over the Channel.

Those flying-bombs not shot down over the coast, were allowed to continue on course, as London and the countryside in between was so densely populated, that deaths and injuries from AA shrapnel, would have added to any casualties caused by the falling bombs.

London's last remaining line of defense, were the hundreds of barrage-balloons flown at various heights around the outskirts of the city. These were credited with bringing down over 200 V-1s that collided with their steel cables, while in flight.

Post-war records have revealed that 58% of the estimated 6,700 flying-bombs launched against England, were destroyed. About 2,300 landed in London, killing more than 5,000 people, injuring over 18,000, and destroying more than 23,000 homes.

The psychological impact of being held under siege 24 hours a day by a "robot" bomb, was hard on many citizens, particularly those who'd survived the earlier Luftwaffe blitz. Many who were able, left London along with thousands of school children who were evacuated to safe areas, out of the weapon's range.

However, leaving town wasn't an option for the great majority, so we each learned to cope in our own way, and life went on much the same. Theaters remained open, and I can attest to the fact that their business was near normal, because my friend Cliff and I continued to see at least one movie a week, as we'd always done.

I believe that most theaters posted an usher outside to listen for flying-bombs. When one was reported to be in the vicinity, management would alert the audience by halting the movie and projecting on the screen, a slide which warned of approaching danger, while assuring those who chose not to leave, that the show would go on. I can say from personal experience, that most people, having paid fourpence or more for their seats, usually opted to stay, not very sensible under the circumstances, but typical of the spirit of most Londoners, during that time.

Sometime in June, my aunt Alice gave birth to a son Peter, her first child. With my Uncle Bert overseas in Italy, she and Peter were living alone, a difficult situation for any new mother, made much worse by the danger posed by the V-1s. Alice lived in Ilford a suburb not far from Chingford, so I visited her often during that awful summer, and stayed overnight, which she appreciated.

One thing that I still vaguely recall from those visits, was helping my aunt practice gas-attack drills with her baby. While poison-gas was never used by Germany, the threat always existed. To protect babies not old enough to wear a mask, new mothers were issued a contraption that looked like an infant-sized tent, into which the baby could be placed in the event of a gas attack.

It was probably made of rubber with a plastic transparent panel, so that the baby could be observed, and when zippered shut, it was gas-proof. I think that once inside, the infant's air supply was provided by the mother using the small hand-operated bellows attachment, that forced in outside air through a gas-filter.

In retrospect, having since been a parent myself, that must have been a depressing ritual to have to practice, but during the war, it was one that all new British mothers had to accept and endure.

By early July, most of the Allied troops and supplies that had been concentrated throughout England's southern counties prior to D-Day, had been moved to Normandy, and government restrictions prohibiting civilian travel in those areas, were finally lifted.

I was among the thousands of Londoners who quickly responded to this unexpected development, by taking some hard earned vacation away from the city. I headed to Paddington Station and rode a crowded train to Truro, Cornwall, to visit Seveock Manor and the Grenfells, whom I hadn't seen for 31 months.

I knew from my own experience on the farm, that no matter the season, if I expected to see anything of Jim and Florrie, I'd probably have to follow them to the fields and help with whatever they were doing, and I was right.

They had several acres of grass that had been recently cut and left to dry. It was ready to be raked and taken by wagon to a site closer to the barn, and built into a hay-stack which would serve as winter-feed for the Grenfell's livestock. I was put on the stack to lay and pack down the hay, a mundane task which on that particular day, was not without an exciting moment.

By late afternoon, the stack was about 20 feet high and almost complete, when we heard the roar of approaching aircraft. Four American B-26 medium bombers returning from a combat mission, came thundering over the tree-tops, flying in a ragged formation so low that those of us on top of the stack, thought we'd had it!

While I'm certain that flying at zero altitude was frowned upon by the USAAF, the exuberance displayed by the young men who'd managed to beat the odds and make it home again, was something that as a seventeen year old, I could easily understand.

I did find time to make a sentimental visit to Baldhu and "Ruddy Beams," where I'd spent eighteen months attending school as an evacuee. Alas, the black-board and desks were gone and the school-room had again assumed its original identity, as a barn.

On my walk to Baldhu, I came upon a convoy of U.S. Army medics and ambulances. The unit had spent the previous night parked along the roadside en route to Falmouth, its port of embarkation to France, and as always, I couldn't pass by a contingent of Yanks, without stopping to chat.

Despite being thousands of miles from home and only 24 hours away from the Normandy battleground, these young men were typical Americans, cheerful and friendly, and after I'd told them that I was born in Ohio, they loaded me down with candy and chewing gum. By the time I returned to the farm, the convoy had departed.

I stayed in Cornwall four days, working with the Grenfells and filling up on some of the food that I fondly remembered from my evacuee days, eggs, bacon and freshly baked bread spread with Cornish cream and homemade jam. And it was like old times to work outdoors instead of behind a desk, and I thoroughly enjoyed it.

For six weeks following D-Day, the progress of our armies in Normandy was thwarted by stubborn German resistance which was greatly enhanced by the impenetrable natural defenses formed by the "bocage," century old hedgerows which turned every pasture into a deadly killing field, for those troops trying to advance.

On July 25, the stalemate was finally broken by a massive Allied ground offensive preceded by a coordinated attack by some 3,000 aircraft. For the first time, heavy-bombers were used as close support weapons, saturating the area in front of the massed infantry and tank units, with 5,000 tons of high explosives.

This unprecedented aerial assault, demoralized and totally decimated the enemy forces in its path. The tactic, conceived by U.S. Army General Omar Bradley, was opposed by top Air Force commanders as too risky, and their concerns proved to be correct.

A number of bombs fell short causing the worst "friendly fire" incident of the war, killing more than 100 American soldiers including Lt. General Lesley J. McNair, and wounding approximately 480. Despite that tragic outcome, "carpet-bombing" in close support of advancing Allied infantry, was used several times in subsequent weeks, causing many additional "friendly" casualties.

On August 2, the newly deployed U.S. Third Army, under the command of Lt. General George S. Patton, attacked on a wide front, led by the legendary commander's armored units, whose wide ranging and aggressive tactics were limited only by the logistical problems inherent in meeting their fuel, supplies and ammunition demands.

About that time in England, where Patton was almost as well known as Eisenhower from press coverage of his exploits in North Africa and Sicily, an article appeared in the "London Illustrated News" which featured a full-page picture of the General, wearing his trademark scowl and his ivory-handled revolvers.

I remember thinking when I saw that unforgettable face, that we finally had a battlefield commander aggressive and audacious enough to strike fear into the enemy while inspiring his own troops, leadership qualities which to me, seemed lacking in many British field commanders, including Field-marshal Montgomery.

I kept that picture of Patton and one of Winston Churchill, for the duration of the war. All teen-age boys have their heroes, and those two were mine. Whenever I looked at their pugnacious "never surrender" faces, I knew that Hitler didn't have a chance!

On August 15, the U.S. Seventh Army commanded by Lt. General Alexander M. Patch, invaded southern France, landing American and French troops by air and sea on its Mediterranean coast near Cannes. Patch's objective was to link up with Allied forces in the north, while neutralizing any effort by the German High Command, to move its troops from the Italian front into France.

Resistance was relatively light, when compared to the Normandy invasion. Many of the German troops previously stationed on the Riviera, had been moved to the north, and as our men fought their way through the region's world-class vineyards, the operation became known as the "Champagne Campaign." This was an unfortunate choice of names, as it caused those unfamiliar with our many bloody encounters with the enemy, to assume that it was an easy campaign with few casualties, which was certainly not the case.

On August 15, Paris was liberated by Allied troops led by the French 2nd Armored Division, and two weeks later, Pennsylvania's own 28th National Guard Division, marched in formation through the capital, to the cheers of thousands of Parisians. By the 5th anniversary of the outbreak of the war, Hitler's armies were retreating with enormous losses in France, from newly liberated Belgium, in Italy and the occupied areas of the Soviet Union.

By now, the ramps in the Channel coastal areas of France, from which the V-1s had been launched, had been over-run by Allied forces, and the flying-bombs were no longer a serious threat to London. However, this weapon was now being launched from inland locations, against military targets in Belgium, notably the strategically vital port-city of Antwerp, through which the bulk of the invasion reinforcements and supplies passed. Casualties from these V-1 attacks totaled more than 14,000 killed and injured, of which close to 3,000 were Allied military personel.

On September 6, the British government ended the blackout, and for the first time in five years, homes could be lighted without shades or curtains, after dark. This event, together with good news from the war-fronts, caused some optimistic souls to speculate that the war with Germany, was just around the corner.

Unfortunately, what was "just around the corner" was the fourth blitz on London! 48 hours after the black-out ended, the first of Germany's second unconventional weapons "Vergeltung 2," rocketed into the sky from a secret location in France, before plunging earthward and exploding in the West London suburb of Chiswick.

The V-2 was a gigantic rocket, 46 feet long. It weighed over 28,000 lbs. and carried a 2,200 lb. explosive warhead. Unlike the V-1, the V-2s were launched from mobile pads, which were almost impossible to pin-point and destroy from the air. The rocket was able to reach a height of 50 miles before exhausting its fuel, and gravity pulled it back to earth, to land on its target.

On impact, it was traveling at 3,800mph, five times the speed of sound, so the only indication of its approach was a sonic boom which came five seconds AFTER it had struck and exploded. In other words, if you heard it coming, you weren't at ground zero!

Unlike its predecessor, the V-1 which on impact made a relatively small crater, the V-2's tremendous weight and speed enabled it to pass through most buildings, and penetrate streets to a great depth before exploding. This caused considerably more havoc to London's trolley-tracks and below-ground gas, electric and water lines, than the damage attributed to the flying bomb.

As was the case when the V-1 first appeared, Londoners endured 72 hours of terrifying explosions and untold casualties, before the British government formally announced that the city was again under attack, but this time from long-range enemy rockets, for which there was no warning system or means of defense.

During the period from September 8, 1944 to March 28, 1945, approximately 1,200 V-2s were successfully launched against England. Of these, more than 500 fell on London, while an equal number landed elsewhere in Britain. Casualties were considerable, over 2,500 killed and close to 6,000 injured.

A wartime research study done by the U.S. Army of troops who'd been under fire in combat, sought answers to the question, what weapon did the men find most frightening. People who know that I lived in London during the war, have asked me the same question.

I can answer that easily. As a civilian, I endured a number of air-raids by conventional aircraft, and all of the V-1 flying-bomb and V-2 rocket attacks on London, and if I ever had to live under enemy fire again and had the luxury of choosing which of those three weapons I'd prefer to face, I'd pick the V-2.

Why? Because when death or injury from the sky is likely and inevitable, I found that not knowing when this was going to happen, was easier to take than listening to an enemy aircraft overhead, waiting for it to drop its bombs, or hearing the scary sound of an approaching flying-bomb, and wondering when and where it's going to fall. It's the sweating out of those moments time and again, that's the roughest part of being under fire.

Absent any warning of an approaching V-2, we were spared the mental and psychological trauma we had experienced during attacks by flying-bombs and air-raids by conventional aircraft. After a while, most Londoners recognized the advantage in not knowing in advance when their number was up, and they went back to attending the theaters and dance-halls, falling in love, getting married and starting families. Life went on as before, despite the daily explosions and the casualties, because there was no other option.

Sunday September 17, dawned sunny and warm, coaxing thousands of Londoners and Allied servicemen and women on leave, into the city's many parks. I was among the crowds in Finsbury Park that morning, when the tranquility was shattered by the roar of many aircraft engines, and soon everyone was gazing skyward as a fleet of 5,000 fighters, bombers and troop-transports towing 2,500 gliders, moved slowly overhead.

It was a sight I'll never forget! The column of aircraft filled the sky, and took more than an hour to pass over the city. We were witnesses to the greatest airborne armada of troop-carrying aircraft in history, and later that day we heard from a BBC broadcast, of a military operation, code-name "MARKET GARDEN."

"MARKET GARDEN" was a bold and daring operation, the brain-child of British Field-Marshal Montgomery, which was surprising in light of Monty's reputation as a conservative, risk-averse field commander, who usually attacked only when success was assured. It called for 20,000 troops from the British 1st Airborne Division, the U.S. Army's 82nd and 101st Airborne Divisions and the Polish 1st. Parachute Brigade, to be dropped behind German lines in occupied Holland, a maneuver fraught with considerable risk.

As envisioned by Monty, the operation was to take no more than four days, and called for five river bridges located across Holland, to be captured intact. Its main objective was to outflank Germany's Siegfried Line defenses, which meant that the farthest bridge at Arnhem, which crossed the Lower Rhine into Germany, was the most important. When all five bridges were in the airborne army's hands, the British 2nd Army poised in Belgium, was to drive swiftly across Holland and spearhead a massive invasion of the Ruhr, Germany's industrial heartland.

It was an audacious, imaginative operation, and had it succeeded, it might very well have ended the war in 1944. Unfortunately, that was not to be. While the objectives of the two American divisions were realized, the British 1st Airborne Division's efforts to capture the Arnhem bridge failed, and after nine days of heroic combat, the division was almost entirely decimated.

Three problems contributed to the Arnhem defeat. First, was Montgomery's failure to give credence to information he received from Dutch underground contacts, that substantial German infantry and armored forces were encamped in the area; secondly, the inability of the British division's commander and his troops to communicate with each other due to faulty radio equipment; and finally, the failure of Britain's 2nd Army to reach and rescue its beleaguered airborne troops, before they were over-run.

It was a very costly operation, the details of which were later immortalized by American author Cornelius Ryan, in his post-war book "A Bridge Too Far." Over 17,000 airborne and ground troops were killed, wounded or reported missing. Of these, more than 13,000 were British and close to 4,000 were American.

Despite the failure of that operation to bring a quick end to the war in Europe, Eisenhower's armies continued to advance on all fronts, but their progress was slow and casualties high, as the embattled German troops who were now defending their own towns and villages, fought stubbornly and with renewed vigor.

At this stage of the war, American and British ground commanders, with their greater undisputed air superiority, always had more available tactical options, than did the enemy. Despite that advantage, military historians have pointed out that certain Allied engagements, given their limited military value and their predictable cost in men and supplies, should never have been attempted, and without question, could have been avoided.

The battle fought in Germany's Huertgen Forest, was a bloody case in point. Its steep, forested hills with deep ravines and no roads to speak of, made it the perfect place to defend and the worst terrain on which to mount an attack. Absent any compelling tactical value to its capture, the Huertgen should have been bypassed, and its dug-in defenders left to wither on the vine, cut-off from reinforcements, ammunition, food and other supplies, until surrender was their only choice.

Instead, on November 2, U.S. troops were ordered into the Forest where, for 15 days, they fought and died in the snow, fog and below freezing temperatures, in a battle reminiscent of the trench-warfare of World War I. Bearing the brunt of the fighting was Pennsylvania's 28th Division, which during that short, bloody and unnecessary campaign, suffered a 75% casualty rate.

All through the V-1 and V-2 blitz, I continued to faithfully attend the Saturday night employee dances at my work-place, although during those perilous times, rather than taking any chances while riding my bike home after midnight, I usually stayed overnight in Chingford, at a friend's house.

To encourage attendance, the company even sponsored dancing lessons by two outside instructors, for those employees interested. Having already taken waltz, foxtrot and quick-step lessons on my own, I didn't sign up until the tango lessons began, and found myself partnered by the instructors, with teenage Sheila, who worked with me in the plant Production office.

Delicately put, Sheila was a "big" girl, a tad taller than I and much heftier, and I worried that given our weight difference, I might not be able to hang on to her, during the "dips" associated with the tango. My concern was unfounded, because on the dance-floor, Sheila was as light as a feather, and we did very well together. This was important, because as I previously indicated, dancing in England is taken seriously, and whenever the orchestra played a tango, the floor would always be crowded with couples, each doing justice to that very beautiful dance.

I recall one company affair in particular, which didn't turn out to be quite the fun I'd anticipated. In early December, to celebrate the approaching Christmas season, the CMC announced it would hold a Fancy Dress Ball, and I decided that I'd go as "Uncle Sam," a choice which probably didn't surprise anyone.

Working from a picture of that American legend, my step-mom using skills she acquired during her seamstress years, fashioned a jacket, vest, pants and hat, replete with red, white and blue stripes and stars, into an authentic Uncle Sam costume.

When it was finished and I tried it on, I was convinced that my costume was a winner. Unfortunately, two days before the Ball, I came down with the flu, which kept me in bed for three days and off work for a week. I felt bad for my Mom, who'd put in so much time on her sewing-machine on my behalf. Since then, I can't recall ever having the flu again. Talk about bad timing!

Germany's defeat, which after D-Day had been viewed by some as a year's end possibility, had not materialized. Nevertheless, most in Britain went about preparing for the holiday season, convinced that their 6th wartime Christmas would be the last, at least where the war in Europe was concerned.

That conviction even helped sustain the morale of those of us in London who, as a consequence of the V-2 rockets which continued to randomly fall without warning in our midst, saw ourselves as involuntary participants in a grim, daily lottery, in which the only "prize" was one's individual survival.

I'll always remember December 16, 1944, as the day that all over Britain, celebratory plans for the holidays were marred by a BBC broadcast that evening. We learned to our surprise and dismay, that sometime before day-break, thousands of Hitler's crack troops and hundreds of tanks, had swept out of the fog-bound, snow-covered, heavily-wooded Ardennes area of Germany, in a massive offensive aimed at re-capturing the port of Antwerp, whose facilities were absolutely vital to the Allied cause.

The "Ardennes Offensive" was conceived by Hitler, and launched on his specific time-table, over the misgivings of his top Generals. If his planned 100 mile long blitzkrieg through Belgium to Antwerp had succeeded, he might have also realized his other equally important objective, to drive a wedge 40 miles wide, between the U.S.1st and 9th Armies, while his troops in Northern Holland drove south with the goal of cutting-off and eventually encircling, the British 2nd and Canadian 1st Armies.

That Germany was able to assemble an army of 300,000 men plus hundreds of tanks and weapons, within a few miles of the American lines without its presence being discovered, was a logistical miracle, and a major factor leading to the unpreparedness which characterized the American response to the sudden onslaught.

The element of surprise was helped by the wooded terrain which provided perfect concealment, and the rain, snow and fog which grounded Allied reconnaissance aircraft for several days before the attack, and during the first critical week of fighting. Contributing to the lack of American military preparedness, were several decisions made by Lt. General Omar Bradley, who was in overall command of the U.S. First, Third and Ninth Armies.

Bradley, having decided sometime earlier that the Ardennes was a "quiet" sector, ordered the U.S. 28th and 4th Infantry Divisions there to recuperate, after the Huertgen Forest bloodbath. Also in the area, spread in a dangerously thin defensive line, was the U.S 106th Division, newly arrived and lacking combat experience.

He further compromised the situation several days before the attack, by ignoring a warning by U.S. Army Major/General Kenneth Strong, Eisenhower's personal intelligence chief, that a German offensive was brewing in that region.

Bradley apparently chose to ignore the warning in favor of the position espoused by his own G-2, that no attack was likely or possible. Based on that faulty intelligence, Bradley made no effort to reinforce his defenses in the Ardennes, nor were his division commanders placed on a heightened state of alert.

During the first seven days of the offensive, all the news we received in Britain was bad. We were told that the U.S. Army's defenses had collapsed, its troops routed, and the Nazi Army was unstoppable. Initially, much of that was true, but post-war records show that on December 19, just four days after launching the attack, Hitler was told by his top Generals, that it was unlikely any of his objectives would be realized.

The reason for that startling admission, was clear from interviews with German survivors of the attack. Hitler's time-table was irreversibly disrupted in those first critical days, by American GIs, fighting in deplorable weather in the coldest winter in recorded history, in squads, platoons or companies, and often as individuals, stubbornly refusing to surrender until casualties or depleted ammunition, left them no other choice.

Twenty-four hours after the offensive began, the U.S 82nd and 101st Airborne Divisions were trucked into Belgium to defend vital road junctions and villages. The most notable of these was Bastogne, where units of the 101st. refused to surrender, despite being surrounded and under constant enemy fire for nine days, until tanks of the U.S. 4th Armored Division, broke the siege.

In two weeks of heavy fighting, SS troops and panzers had created a "bulge" in the U.S 1st Army's defensive perimeter, thus giving America's largest ground battle of the war, its historic name, "The

Battle of the Bulge." However, Hitler's forces were still approximately 50 miles away from Antwerp, their prime objective.

They also faced an acute shortage of gasoline, and their flanks were now under aggressive attack by General Patton's Third Army. Although fighting was to continue into January, 1945, Hitler's grandiose plans in the Ardennes and to the north, where British forces halted German attacks from Holland, had completely failed.

Before the six-week battle ended, 600,000 American, 50,000 British and 550,000 German troops, had been involved, and losses on both sides, including those taken prisoner, were staggering. Allied forces suffered 81,000 casualties most of whom were American, German casualties were 125,000. On January 18, 1945, Prime Minister Winston Churchill in an address to the House of Commons, commenting on the end of the Ardennes offensive said, "This is undoubtedly the greatest American battle of the war and will, I believe, be regarded as an ever-famous American victory."

Given Britain's close proximity to the fighting which raged on the Continent during the last half of 1944, it was not surprising that the British news media focused most of its attention on the European theater-of-war. As a result, the progress being made by U.S. Navy, Marine and Army forces in the Pacific, failed to get the recognition and press coverage in Britain it deserved.

The Marshall Islands were the first of Japan's pre-war territories to fall into American hands, followed by Saipan, Tinian and Guam in the Mariannas, major island prizes from which hundreds of B-29 "Super-Fortress" bombers would be launched in massive day and night raids, against the Japanese homeland.

On October 20, the U.S. Sixth Army led by Lt. General Walter Kreuger, invaded the Japanese occupied Philippine Islands, and several days later, in what has been referred to by some as the greatest battle in naval history, an American Fleet operating off the Philippine coast, dealt the Imperial navy a defeat from which it would never recover. In the Battle of Leyte Gulf, 34 Japanese warships were destroyed at the cost of only 6 American vessels.

During that same 12 months, steady military gains were made in Burma by British, Commonwealth, Indian and Chinese troops. By successfully halting and defeating Japan's forces in Burma, the Allies essentially thwarted it's planned invasion of India. It could be said that 1944 saw the beginning of the end for Japan!

CHAPTER 17

Holocaust Horrors And The Iwo Jima Bloodbath

With German forces retreating before Eisenhower's armies in the West, and the relentless advance of the Red Army in the East, Britain's war-weary citizens greeted 1945 with renewed hope and conviction that the defeat of Nazi Germany was finally at hand. For Londoners, however, the war remained close-up and personal.

While V-1 flying bombs no longer menaced the city, the V-2 bombardment continued through January, February and March and some days were definitely worse than others! On January 26, thirteen rockets fell on London over a 24 hour period, compared to an average of four each day, during February and March.

The toughest part about that time, was the anguish we went through as a family because we didn't have a telephone, and neither did our nearest neighbors. As a result, each day while at our respective work-places, my Dad and two sisters and I, would hear one rocket explosion after another, with no way of knowing their exact location, and until we arrived home each evening, we never knew if our house had been hit, or whether or not we were all still alive and uninjured.

The last recorded V-2 rocket attack of the war, occurred on March 28. Casualties from this weapon during the first 3 months of 1945, were 1,275 killed and 2,578 injured. In April, with the Nazi regime in its death throes, there were no reported civilian casualties from enemy action. By then, Britain's civilian losses during 68 months of war, were 60,585 killed and 86,175 injured.

By the end of January, Stalin's armies had wrested most of Poland from German control, and their most northerly units were less than 150 miles away from Berlin. On January 27, the Red Army entered a small town which, prior to Germany's 1939 invasion of Poland, was known as "Oswiecom" but had been re-named "Auschwitz" by its

Nazi conquerors, a name (to paraphrase Franklin D. Roosevelt), that would forever live in infamy!

It was no secret to any of the Allied governments, that "death-camps" had been constructed in Germany and Nazi occupied Poland, for the specific purpose of exterminating Jews, gypsies, the physically and mentally handicapped, homosexuals and all those persons deemed "undesirable" by the Nazi regime.

However, until the Auschwitz-Berkenau camps were liberated by the Soviets, the world at large was privy to few details, and I can vouch for the fact that what little we in Britain had learned in this regard from the BBC or from our newspapers, was too ghastly and unimaginable for us to comprehend, much less believe.

When the Soviet troops entered the Auschwitz-Berkenau camps, the Nazi guards had already fled, leaving behind approximately 7,600 emaciated survivors, and over 600 abandoned corpses awaiting cremation in Auschwitz's huge ovens. For some reason, Russia waited more than two weeks before officially commenting on the existence of the camps, and over the next five weeks, all requests by Britain's Foreign Office for details, were ignored.

By then, confirmation from the Soviets wasn't needed! Between April 4 and May 6, Allied troops advancing through the German heartland, liberated 12 additional camps and the newsmen and camera-crews who followed, finally provided the world with graphic evidence of the horrors uncovered, at each location.

I for one, will never forget one evening at the movies, watching in complete disbelief a news-reel filmed a day earlier, at the liberation of Buchenwald, a camp less than 100 miles from Frankfurt. The camera slowly panned over the stricken faces of the barely alive inmates, before focusing on a British Army bull-dozer pushing huge piles of skeletal remains of those who hadn't survived the camp's brutality, into a trench for mass burial.

Thank God for all this firsthand, indisputable print and film evidence. Without it, I suspect that no civilized country would have believed that atrocities of this magnitude could have even occurred, much less at the hands of individuals who, when their daily shifts at the gas-chambers or ovens ended, were apparently able to leave the camp and return to their homes, and enjoy a quiet meal and "quality-time" with their wives and children!

With Teutonic efficiency, Hitler's murderers recorded in detail their barbaric activities. Thus by the war's end, from the Nazi's own records and the testimony of thousands of camp survivors and Allied soldiers who liberated them, a shocked world learned of the "Holocaust" in which more than 10 million people, including some 6 million Jews, died horrible and agonizing deaths.

On February 19, thousands of miles from Britain, on the other side of the globe, U.S. Marines of the 4th and 5th Divisions stormed the volcanic-ash beaches of Iwo Jima, while the Marine 3rd Division lay off-shore in reserve. An 8 mile-square patch of land 700 miles from Tokyo, the island stood directly in the path flown by the B-29s of the U.S. 20th Air Force, at the half-way point of their 2,500 mile round-trip missions to bomb Japan, from their bases on Saipan and Tinian.

Though a mere blip in the immense vastness of the Pacific, this tiny military outpost boasted a radar-station and 3 airfields. While the garrison's radar provided Japan's mainland defenses with timely warnings of every air-raid, its fighters rose and engaged the outbound B-29s. Hours later, the mission survivors were attacked again, as they straggled back to their distant bases, often heavily damaged, carrying wounded and low on fuel.

Iwo Jima's bleak terrain reeked of sulphur and was dominated by Mt. Surabachi, an extinct volcano from whose flowing lava eons earlier, the island had its birth. With less than 3 miles of beach suitable for an amphibious assault, its defenders knew exactly where the Marines would land, and had planted their mines and zeroed-in their machine-guns and artillery, accordingly.

Iwo's 750 major defensive installations, had been pin-pointed by U.S. reconnaissance flights and subjected to constant bombing and Navy shelling prior to the landing. However, not known to the Marines as they waded ashore, was the fact that its 22,000 defenders had constructed an elaborate system of underground rooms with multiple entrances and exits, all connected by more than 16 miles of tunnels.

The Japanese commander had deliberately placed his machine-guns and artillery in heavily fortified positions, well back from the beach, to permit as many Marines as possible to crowd onto the narrow landing area, where the rounds from his hidden guns could cause the most casualties and confusion. During the Navy shelling, his troops remained underground and invisible to the Marines, who were pinned down on a volcanic-ash surface so loose and powdery, they couldn't even dig fox-holes for protection.

The beach was destined to become a slaughter-house! By the end of the 2nd day, 3,650 Marines were dead, wounded or missing at the hands of an enemy few had seen, and their progress was measured in yards. It took 34 more days of bloody, hand-to-hand fighting before the entire garrison was rooted out of its hidden caves and tunnels, and annihilated. Nearly 6,000 Marines died, more than 17,000 were wounded and 27 were awarded the Medal of Honor, our country's highest military decoration for bravery in combat.

Without a doubt, it was one of the America's most costly and heroic victories. Thankfully, the sacrifices so many Marines made, were not in vain. Over the next six months, Iwo Jima served as an emergency landing-field for 2,400 B-29 bombers damaged during raids on Japan, thus saving the lives of 27,000 crewmen, who might otherwise have perished in a watery grave.

Early in March, my sister Peg arrived home with some news that would instantly impact on my future, and set the wheels in motion for the realization of my life-long dream, to return to the land of my birth. That day, when learning that Peg had been born in the United States, an Army friend told her that had she formally "declared" American citizenship before becoming subject to Britain's wartime draft, she could have avoided military service, as women were not subject to conscription in the United States.

This was correct. Peg and I, having been born in the United States of British parents, were "dual-nationals" under the laws of both nations, and as such, we had the option of keeping that status, or choosing to be either American or British citizens.

However, when my sister enlisted in the WATS, she was required to swear allegiance to the Crown, which automatically made her a fully-fledged British citizen. This voided her option to choose American citizenship, a situation reinforced by the 1907 U.S. statute in effect at that time, which provided that "any American citizen would be deemed to have expatriated himself when he had taken an oath of allegiance to any foreign state."

Fortunately, a wartime reciprocal Agreement between the U.S. and Britain allowed Americans who had sworn allegiance to Britain in order to serve in its military, to undergo a simple voluntary ceremony following their discharge, to re-affirm their allegiance to the United States, thus restoring their American citizenship.

It was this Agreement, which made it possible for 243 young American men to go to England in 1940 before our country entered the war, and volunteer to fly with the RAF as the "Eagle Squadron," without forfeiting their precious Yankee birthright.

While Peg's opportunity to declare herself an American, would have to wait until her discharge from the British Army, my dual-national status was intact, and I could exercise that right whenever it suited me. With my 18th birthday just six weeks away, and the possibility that I could be drafted into the British Army on that date, time was suddenly of the essence.

Accordingly, on Saturday, March 17, 1945, I rode the Tube into the West End, and clutching my Ohio birth-certificate, I marched into the American Embassy (then located on Russell Square as I recall), and announced to the young American woman who greeted me inside the entrance, that I'd come to enlist in the U.S. Army.

I was amazed at how quickly and easily, my wish was granted. After examining my birth-certificate, the woman took me to an office staffed by U.S. Army personnel, where an officer handed me an enlistment form to complete and sign.

That done, he said that within 30 days, I'd receive a telegram ordering me to report to a specified location in London, where I'd be required to pass a U.S. Army physical, before being sworn in. I was assured that the notice would give me at least 14 days in which to get my affairs in order, and given how limited my "affairs" were, this was more than enough time.

Needless to say, March 17, 1945, is a date I'll never forget. I walked "on a cloud" to the nearest Tube station to take a train home. It was there that I first became acquainted with a custom peculiar to the United States, that of celebrating the birthday of St. Patrick, regardless of one's ethnic origin. Arriving West End trains, were disgorging crowds of American GI's on leave, all in high spirits, many clearly under the influence of bottled spirits, and most sporting a flash of green on their uniforms.

While history tells us that the patron saint of Ireland was a 5th Century English prelate who, on a pilgrimage to the Emerald Isle, converted the "heathen" population to Christianity, St. Patrick's Day is not celebrated in England, and even in Ireland, not with the same degree of enthusiasm it arouses in the States.

I remember when I got home that day, telling my Dad what I'd seen at the station, and how surprised I was that so many Americans were of Irish descent. That's when he remembered his time in Cleveland, and explained how once a year on March 17, everyone in the United States becomes "Irish" for a day.

By the beginning of April, the end of Hitler's Third Reich appeared imminent. On the Western front, American, British, Canadian and Free-French troops had crossed the Rhine, and were sweeping across Germany. To the East, a weary and outnumbered Wehrmacht was in full retreat, overwhelmed by a massive vengeful Soviet Army, while its besieged troops in Italy retreated before a major offensive, launched by the Allied Fifteenth Army Group.

We in Britain couldn't wait to get our newspapers, whose head-lines now gave us cause for hope and elation, rather than the despair we'd endured, when bad news was the order of the day.

When I returned from work on the Monday following my enlistment in the U.S. Army, I decided to keep that fact a secret until I received my orders to report for duty, figuring that I'd still have enough time then, to give my employer two week's notice.

But this wasn't something I wanted to keep from Sparkes and my other friends at the Stroud Green Baptist Church, that I attended at that time. When I broke the news, everyone seemed somewhat shocked, but after years of listening to me talk about returning to America, they probably weren't surprised. Actually, I was the one surprised when Pastor Butler announced a "birthday-going-away" party for me at the Church Hall on Saturday, April 14, my 18th birthday.

On April 12, I received the much awaited telegram from the U.S. Army, ordering me to report for duty on Monday, May 2. During the evening of that same day, several thousand miles away in Warm Springs, Georgia, Franklin Delano Roosevelt, the 32nd President of the United States of America, died at the age of sixty-three.

Given the time difference between our two countries, it was very early the next morning, when my Dad, who always got up at the crack of dawn, woke me with tears in his eyes, and gave me the shocking news, which he'd just picked up on his radio.

That day, as the word spread throughout the land, Dad's heartfelt grief at Roosevelt's death was universal. Most British people accepted the fact that when their country stood alone following the fall of France, it might not have survived and prevailed, without FDR's unwavering support.

They also knew of his demonstrated political activity on their behalf, which in March, 1941, led to U.S. Congressional approval of the President's unprecedented commitment to Britain's survival, the legislation known as the "Lend-Lease Act" under which, payment for arms and other war supplies shipped to Britain, could be deferred until after the war ended.

At the time of his death, no American President had ever been more admired and respected in Britain than FDR, and his passing was genuinely mourned, particularly because his opportunity to savor the hard-fought, imminent Allied victory over Germany, to which he'd contributed so much, was sadly denied him.

Some days later, after the shock had lessened, Dad kidded me that the President must have found out about my call to duty in his Armed Forces, and the knowledge of this had precipitated his untimely death, but I never bought into that scenario!

The day after receiving my Army orders, I reported this to my boss Mr. Crawford, and gave him two weeks notice of my leaving. While he had assumed that he'd lose me to the British draft as soon as I turned eighteen, he was very surprised to find out that my military service would be in the U.S. Army, and that following my discharge, I planned to live in the United States.

In any event, his reaction was very positive. He even suggested that given my unusual circumstances, he'd accept just one week's notice, so that I'd have more time at home before leaving for the

Army. I spent my last work day, wandering around the plant and the Main Office saying farewell, and promising to visit whenever I got my first Army furlough. I remember in particular getting an memorably passionate kiss goodbye from co-worker Betty Hicks, its warmth I suspect, not kindled by me leaving, but from the fact that Betty hadn't seen her RAF husband in months!

The next week, I received another surprise, a communication from my onetime nemesis "Dobbie," Secretary of the CMC. I still have his letter, tattered and yellowed by age, which reads as follows:

"Dear John:

In view of your departure to join the United States Army and your decision to settle down in the States when demobilized, the Directors feel that they would like you to accept the enclosed cheque for 25 pounds as a parting gratuity.

I would like to take this opportunity of wishing you the very best of luck, and we hope that you will look us up whenever you are this way. Yours sincerely, C.B. Dobson, Secretary."

That most welcome gift was the equivalent of $100, more money than I'd ever had as a lump sum, in my life. It really came in handy, because with two more weeks at home before I left, I knew my Mom would still expect me to pay my room and board, as always.

I'm quite sure that I enjoyed being unemployed for a change. Counting my days as an evacuee laboring on a farm in Cornwall, plus my time at the CMC, I'd worked at least 8 hours a day for almost five years, despite having just turned eighteen.

One event from that period of leisure, remains imprinted on my memory. Peg received a letter from a U.S. serviceman who she'd met at a dance, before his unit was shipped to France. She hadn't anticipated seeing or hearing from him again, but apparently he'd been wounded in action, and was now in a U.S. Army hospital in England, and was hoping she would pay him a visit. Peg asked me to go along and keep her company.

I can't recall whether the hospital was in Surrey, Kent or Sussex, but I know that we took a Southern Railway train from Waterloo Station, so it had to be located in the South-Eastern corner of England. We had quite a distance to walk after getting off the train, which was no problem, but we certainly weren't prepared for what lay in store for us, at our destination.

The hospital was the temporary home for U.S. soldiers who had been grievously wounded, a "way-station" where they could recuperate sufficiently to withstand the stress of the long journey back to a Stateside military hospital. Peg's friend was in a ward with about twenty-five other young men, most of whom were in their late teens or early twenties. Many were missing hands, arms, legs or feet, and some had multiple limb losses.

These were men who'd left their homes as boys, celebrating their physical prime, who were now disfigured and perhaps crippled, and no doubt tormented with personal fears about how they would be greeted and accepted by their families and loved ones, while contemplating a future that none had likely ever imagined!

While Peg chatted with her friend, I wandered through the ward, pretty much in a state of shock. I was the same age as most of these men, and in less than a week I'd don their uniform, to serve as an infantry replacement in a war not yet over in Europe, and far from being won in the Pacific.

It was truly a grim and sobering experience, not helped I guess by the comments I received when I announced that I had just voluntarily enlisted in the U.S. Army. Everyone told me that I must have been crazy, and as I left with Peg, a chorus of "you'll be sorry" chants followed me. It was a subdued and silent ride back to London, as my sister and I sat immersed in our own sad recollections of our close-up look at the price so many young men had paid, in the noble crusade to restore freedom to Europe.

On April 28, Italy's deposed dictator Benito Mussolini and his mistress Clara Petacci, were caught by partisans as they tried to flee the country. Both were summarily executed by machine-gun fire, and their bodies hung upside-down, for public display.

Two days later on April 30, Nazi dictator Adolf Hitler and Eva Braun, his bride of 24 hours, committed suicide by swallowing cyanide capsules. News of Hitler's ignominious death was greatly welcomed in Britain, whose citizens saw it as a sign that the surrender of Germany, was finally just days away.

Chapter 18

Duty Calls, As The War In Europe Ends

Early on the morning of May 2, 1945, as a proud enlistee in the U.S. Army, I not only said goodbye to my family, but also to the country where I'd grown up and lived for seventeen years.

As I was giving my step-mother a final hug outside our house, the next door neighbor woman, whose name I've long forgotten, came out and proceeded to chastise me for "becoming an American" while predicting that when I "came to my senses" I'd return to England where I belonged! I don't know what triggered that diatribe, because she hadn't spoken a dozen words to me in years. Perhaps she was jilted by a Yank in the first World War, but in any event, her outburst upset my Mom, already in tears at my leaving.

I walked to Finsbury Park Tube Station and took a train into Russell Square, to a large house adjacent to the American Embassy, then occupied by the Army unit to which I'd been ordered to report. Somewhat to my surprise, I found a dozen other young men from the London area, who like me, were American citizens by birth, and had volunteered for service in the U.S. Army.

Our first order of business was to pass the Army physical. This required that we strip down to our undershorts and parade before a Medical Officer and his NCO medics, who peered, prodded and frowned, before declaring us all fit for duty. I suspect at that point in time, with the invasion of Japan probably already in the planning stage, that few enlistees were ever rejected.

Once again clothed and decent, our induction ceremony began. An officer had us raise our hands and repeat the oath of allegiance to the United States, following which he welcomed us as American citizens into the U.S. Army. As a further indication that none of us were expected to fail our physicals, he presented us with our individual G.I. "dog-tags" already indented with our names, blood types, religion (P, C or J), serial numbers and "T" for tetanus.

We were told us to memorize our serial numbers, because we'd be ordered to repeat them often during our basic training, advice that I obviously took seriously, because "10602168" still tumbles off my tongue as easily now, as it did 58 years ago.

The officer explained that we'd be staying in London overnight, and then taken by train to a U.S. Army Reinforcement Depot in Lichfield, a small town about 20 miles north of Birmingham, where we'd be issued uniforms and receive our required inoculations. He warned that while we still wore civvies, we were servicemen on active duty in a war zone, forbidden to go anywhere without specific Army orders, emphasizing that to be absent without leave (AWOL), was an offense punishable by court-martial.

With that, we were taken next door to another large house, which had been converted into a make-shift dormitory, with each room now home to three or four Army cots. I was assigned to a room with three others, and began the process of becoming acquainted.

That day in London, I ate my first U.S. Army food, or "chow," the GI name for all meals, whether prepared in a mess-hall by a cook, extracted from a can or served in a box. While I've forgotten my first main course, I do remember two things, a huge helping of fruit-cocktail dessert, and the coffee.

Fruit-cocktail was a luxury few in Britain had savored during five years of war, and coffee, which had a low wartime import priority, was often adulterated with ground, roasted chicory root, to stretch the supply. This gave it an unpleasant, bitter taste, so growing up I drank very little coffee, but with tea not an option, I reluctantly filled my canteen-cup with American "java." To my surprise, I liked it, and while I still enjoy tea on occasions, I remain a confirmed black-coffee drinker.

Trying to sleep on an Army cot for the first time, in a room with three guys I hardly knew, was a challenge. Awake most of the night, I finally dozed off only to be awakened at dawn, by a corporal who went room to room, banging on doors and yelling "drop your c—s, put on your socks." I'm pleased to report, that was the only time I heard that particular wake-up call. Sleep in the Army was usually interrupted by a recording of "reveille" played at maximum decibels, over the camp's PA system.

Our quarters were typically British, no showers and limited bath, sink and toilet facilities. 40 guys trying at the same time to get spruced-up for the day, took some maneuvering. Fortunately, some of us weren't yet growing facial-hair at a rate to warrant shaving every day, so that cut down on the busy sink traffic.

After breakfast, we were assembled outside, picked up by a chartered bus, taken to Euston Station and put on a train to Birmingham. There we transferred to a local train to Lichfield, where Army 6x6 trucks were waiting at the station, to take us to our destination, the U.S. Army 10th Reinforcement Depot.

The 10th RD had taken over the Whittington Barracks in Lichfield from the British Army in September 1942, when the first American troops began arriving in England. Since then, more than 300,000 troops had passed through its facilities, the majority as replacements for casualties suffered by the 60 U.S. Army infantry, armored and airborne divisions, deployed in the European Theatre.

A huge sign greeted us at the Depot's main entrance. "IF YOU GO AWOL FROM THIS CAMP SOLDIER, YOU'LL BE SORRY. COLONEL JAMES A. KILIAN, COMMANDANT." That was enough of a warning for me. With just 36 hours of soldiering under my belt, I decided not to leave the camp, even when offered an evening pass. With a rigidly enforced curfew in effect, I figured that with my luck, I'd miss the last truck back, and end up in the guardhouse!

Eight months later, I had reason to applaud my decision, when the significance of that cryptic warning became clear. The U.S. Army's newspaper, the "Stars and Stripes," reported that Colonel Kilian and others on his staff, had been arrested and were being court-martialed for "cruel and inhuman treatment of GI prisoners" who had been housed over the years, in the 10th RD guardhouse!

The Whittington Barracks, where the Depot's permanent cadre of officers and men lived, was a dark and depressing collection of Victorian-style buildings, circa 1880, typical of that period. Transient troops however, were housed elsewhere on its grounds, in a sprawling

191

tent-city. There we spent a week, eight or ten men to a tent, along with an additional 30 new inductees.

While most of us had been living somewhere in the United Kingdom, our group included a young man from Sweden, one from newly liberated Luxemburg, a Japanese-American who'd grown up in California and a Brooklyn native who, before enlisting in the U.S. Army, had been a sailor in the U.S. Merchant Marine. The latter two, were the only ones who actually spoke with an American accent! It was at the 10th Depot that I met Douglas "Scotty" McClean who, during the 18 months that we served together, was to become my closest friend.

Scotty was my age, born in the United States of Scottish immigrants. His mother died giving birth or soon thereafter. His widowed father, unable for whatever reason to care for him alone, took him to Paisley, Scotland, to be raised by his sister-in-law. He then returned to his home in Niagara Falls, New York, so during his childhood, Scotty saw very little of his father.

He and I had much in common, except for our schooling. His Dad could afford to send him to a private school in Paisley, so Scotty's formal education exceeded mine received in wartime London, both in quality and quantity. Nevertheless, we quickly became friends, and hit it off, right from the start.

The next day, we were each issued one Class A (dress) uniform, over-seas cap, khaki-socks and underwear, boots and leggings, poncho, helmet, field-jacket and fatigues. Our GI haircuts left us completely bald, and the mandated inoculations, put many under the weather, for more than 48 hours.

Eyes were examined, and those without 20-20 vision, were fitted with Army issue, steel-frame glasses. These were unattractive but utilitarian, guaranteed, so we were told, not to fly off our noses in combat. I remember finding that revelation comforting after being issued my M-1 rifle, and discovering that without my glasses, I couldn't line up the front and rear sights, which would have made my effectiveness as a rifleman, questionable.

I soon adapted to the long chow lines which wound around and through the mess-tent, and eventually to the dramatic impact of U.S. Army food on my digestive system. In the first 72 hours, the difference between my new diet and the British wartime rations to which I was accustomed, caused more visits than normal to the latrine, a facility which wasn't easy for me to get used to.

It was a large tent housing 40 rough-hewn wood commodes which had been erected over trenches, in two facing rows, with no dividers between the seats. Consequently, what had always been a very private and personal ritual, now had to be conducted in full view and just inches away from others likewise engaged. Frankly, where I was concerned, handling lethal weapons and explosives during basic training, was a helluva lot less stressful!

One of our days was devoted to Army protocol, the Articles of War and personal hygiene. The latter presentation featured a movie which included graphic close-ups of male and female genitalia ravaged by venereal disease. This was a real "downer" for those in the audience like me who had yet to experience their first intimate liaison with a member of the fairer sex.

We also completed beneficiary forms relative to the $10,000 life insurance policy we all received, compliments of Uncle Sam. That amount of insurance would be insignificant today, but having grown up in the Depression, it seemed like a fortune to me.

Finally, the few married guys in our group, and those who wanted to regularly send part of their pay to their families, completed the required GI Allotment forms. I'd shared my earnings with my parents starting with my first pay, so I didn't think twice about signing up to do this, even though I no longer lived at home.

I believe as GI recruits already serving "overseas," we were paid about $25 a month, which was increased after we finished basic training and received our first stripes. Not much, but still about five times what British "Tommies" were paid.

On May 7, just five days after I entered the Army, the German High Command, represented by General Alfred Jodl, surrendered unconditionally to Supreme Allied Commander General Dwight Eisenhower, at SHAEF Headquarters in Rheims, France. The war with Nazi Germany, which had begun 68 months earlier with the invasion of Poland, was declared over, and May 8, was proclaimed "VE Day" by President Truman and Prime Minister Churchill.

That momentous day in history, was cause for highly emotional celebrations in the United States, Britain and throughout the free world, particularly in the newly liberated countries of Europe. Unfortunately, as temporary guests of the soon to be infamous Colonel Kilian, our revelry was decidedly low-key.

In fact, we celebrated by packing our gear and getting ready for an inspection, having been told that we were scheduled to leave the 10th Depot on May 9, for a U.S. Army infantry basic training facility located somewhere in France.

My memory of the journey from Lichfield to our destination in France, has always been hazy, due in large part to the fact that as we shipped out of the 10th Depot, I was running a fever and should have been resting, not embarking on a 30 hour marathon.

We rode in open trucks part of the way, took a train from Birmingham to London and another from there to Southampton. There we boarded an aging transport which rocked and heaved its way across the English Channel to Le Havre, where it edged into a harbor dotted with the protruding hulls of many sunken vessels. And, in accordance with Army custom, at various points along the way we stood, or sat on our helmets, in the hot sun, and waited.

It turned out that my fever was vaccine related, and others in the group had been similarly afflicted. However, not knowing that at the time, I remember as I marched off the boat feeling weak and lightheaded, being pretty despondent and wondering whether I had what it would take, to get through basic training.

We stayed overnight at a tent-camp on the outskirts of Le Havre, before boarding a train which slowly chugged its way to Paris, stopping frequently due to the chaotic state of the French rail system, which had been practically destroyed by Allied aircraft. Trucks were waiting in Paris to take us to the U.S. Army 2941 Reinforcement Camp, located about 50 miles north-east of Paris, on the banks of the River Aisne, between Compiegne and Soissons.

The 2941 RC was established in the summer of 1944, after Nazi troops had been driven out of France. It was a facility with access to hundreds of acres of forested land, where troops newly arrived from the States, could be given a quick refresher course on infantry tactics and the firing of weapons, before being assigned as replacements to the Army's various combat divisions.

During The Battle of the Bulge, the camp was used to hurriedly make riflemen out of non-combatant troops, such as clerks and cooks, who were then dispatched to the front lines, to help halt and turn back the massive German offensive into Belgium.

As a basic-training camp, the 2941 RC, was not what I expected. The "barracks" where we were to spend the next 4 months, was a row of abandoned French cottages. Each tiny room, home to 4 men, came with 2 double bunk-beds equipped with straw mattresses. There were no chairs or tables, and without closets, we kept our clothes and personal items, in our respective duffel bags.

The kitchen and mess-hall were located in a large tent, outside of which hung a row of large, leather "Lister-bags" which contained our only source of potable water. This was laced with purifying chemicals and tasted pretty awful, but we were assured by the Army that it was safe to drink.

In another tent was a long rack of cold water sinks, and a ten-commode latrine. There was no permanent shower facility, but a portable system was trucked in every two weeks, and stayed long enough for us to occasionally enjoy the luxury of hot water. Fortunately, the River Aisne flowed past our cottages, its banks just yards away, and it was in its serene waters, armed with GI soap, that we bathed and washed our clothes, as best we could.

The Post Exchange (PX) and Dispensary were situated a mile from our quarters. Recruits were only permitted to visit the PX once a week, so its location was no hardship, and as we soon learned, the return trip, loaded down with our candy and free carton of "smokes," could be a unique and interesting experience!

The narrow road back to our quarters, was usually frequented by local "ladies of the night" working their daytime shifts, who'd offer a variety of sexual favors, in exchange for candy or cigarettes. One could either stop and partake of their services, or hand over a candy-bar or pack of cigarettes, and keep moving.

I confess, while I still looked forward to my first intimate encounter with the opposite sex, these roadside opportunities weren't exactly what I had in mind, so I'd beat the gauntlet by giving out cigarettes and "Zagnut" bars, my least favorite candy, which all too often, was the only one carried on the PX shelves.

I had hoped to bunk with Scotty, but was assigned to a room with three recruits I knew only by sight. One was a pleasant, quiet guy who was older than the rest of us, whose last name was Reid. The name of the character who took the bunk over Reid escapes me, but he had some very strange personal habits, which one day caused me to lose my temper, and the two of us to exchange blows.

My overhead bunk-mate's name was Omar Pound. He was an easy guy to live with, but rather secretive about where he'd been living, and where he'd gone to school. Though he always denied it, rumor had it he was related to Ezra Pound the American poet, who while living as an expatriate somewhere in Europe, had allegedly voiced sympathy for certain aspects of the Axis cause, comments which hadn't been well received in the States.

Omar had a severe allergy problem, no doubt exacerbated by his straw mattress, and he'd wrap an undershirt around his face before going to sleep. Many times, as I looked at his "mummy-like" shrouded head, and listened to his labored breathing, I'd wonder how he ever made it through the night, and given his condition why he hadn't been rejected for military service.

The morning after arriving at the 2941 RC, a sergeant rousted us out of our sleep before daylight, and marched us to the mess-tent for breakfast, after which he escorted us back to our quarters where we were ordered to make up our bunks and stand-by. About that time, we heard the tramp of marching feet and loud voices, heading in our direction.

Down the road, came a column of soldiers in fatigues and helmets with field-packs and rifles, marching in perfect unison and keeping the pace by shouting a crude rhyming ditty, the traditional Army way of "counting cadence" when marching.

Two sergeants led the column and a 2nd Lieutenant brought up the rear, and everyone marched by without a sideways glance except for the officer who smiled in our direction, before coming to a halt immediately in front of me. Still smiling, he said "I'm Lt. Connelly, how long have you been in the Army soldier?"

Smiling right back, I said "A week sir" and as if by magic, that friendly smile vanished and he roared, "Then you should know soldier, you're required to come to attention and salute every officer who approaches or passes you." Turning to the others around me, he said, "All of you, remember what you just heard, because the next infraction will carry a penalty."

With that, Lt. Connelly turned on his heels and headed down the road, to rejoin his now distant column, which we learned later was an earlier group of recruits, then in their 5th week of training, returning from a night-time field exercise.

Soon after my first "brass" encounter, we were marched by another sergeant to an open area used by the 2941 RC as a parade-ground, where every evening, all troops under its command, assembled for "Retreat" the military flag-lowering ceremony. Waiting for us to arrive, were the officers and NCOs who would instruct and guide us through 14 weeks of infantry basic training. We were ordered to be "at ease" and to sit down on our helmets. This Army way of sitting, had painful consequences for that part of the body making contact, but when we were in the field, it was the only option we were given, to take the weight off our aching feet.

We were officially welcomed as Company B, by it's Commander, Captain Sexmith who then introduced his other cadre members, 1st. Lt. McCardle, 2nd. Lt. Gilbert, 2nd. Lt. Connelly, who I'd already met, Staff-Sergeant Stiritz and five "buck" sergeants, Steinberg, Fagan, LeBlanc, Slusher and Tuckett.

The Captain indicated that with the war in Europe now over, the camp's days were probably numbered, but for the time being, it would continue to provide training to enlistees and draftees who entered the Army in Europe, in lieu of shipping these men to a Stateside facility.

He speculated that absent a massive airborne and amphibious invasion of their homeland, the Japanese would never surrender, and said that after our training, we'd likely be sent to the States and assigned to one of the many divisions that would be required in a full-scale assault. He urged us to take our training seriously, and learn as much as we could from our sergeant instructors, all of whom were recent combat veterans.

Captain Sexmith concluded his remarks by telling us that our training would begin at 08.00 the following day, and turned us over to one of the sergeants who marched us to the Supply Tent, where we were issued the basic weapons of the infantry, the Garand M-1 rifle and bayonet.

After chow that evening, a bunch of us sat outside watching the Aisne barge traffic, and talking about the unfinished war in the Pacific, which, if Captain Sexmith's speculation materialized, we'd be a part of, before Japan's defeat was final.

Having been blessed by fate to emerge unscathed through all the Nazi assaults on London by aircraft, flying-bombs and rockets, the probability that my life would again be at risk, this time at the hands of the Japanese, had me wondering how long I could expect my good fortune to continue. From that day on, I followed the Pacific war coverage as reported in the "Stars & Stripes" with as much interest as I'd previously given BBC broadcasts during the long war with Germany.

How difficult and costly the invasion of Japan would be, had already been brought into sharp focus a month before the war in Europe ended. On April 1, two U.S. Army divisions and two Marine divisions, a force of 60,000 men, were put ashore on the beaches of Okinawa, an island 360 miles south of the Japanese homeland.

The island's defense force of 120,000 troops, fought with fanatical tenacity for 81 days, before its commanding General committed suicide and 90% of the force had been killed and over 7,000 taken prisoner. Additionally, the Japanese lost 3, 800 planes and 180 naval vessels, including the "Yamato," which at that time, was the world's largest battleship.

American losses were also severe. Over 17,400 soldiers, sailors and marines were killed and 36,600 wounded, and 800 Allied planes were lost along with 36 U.S. Navy ships. This battle was over a 454 square-mile island, which the Japanese considered part of their homeland. When it ended on June 21, it was the bloodiest amphibious operation of the Pacific war, and a grim harbinger of the unprecedented losses which could be anticipated, if a massive invasion of Japan was necessary to her unconditional surrender.

Chapter 19

The Making Of An Infantryman, American Style

I doubt that many ex-GIs who went through infantry basic training in World War II, recall that experience with favor or nostalgia. Immediately after Pearl Harbor, as our nation rushed to build a wartime Army, recruits faced a mere 8 weeks of training and given the shortage of equipment and modern weapons at that time, the training that many received, lacked real "hands-on" experience.

Later, the training time was extended to 14 weeks, which is what I received at the camp in France. In all candor, my memories of that period are positive except for the living conditions, which were certainly not like those enjoyed by Stateside recruits. However, given that we were being prepared for the hardships and misery of combat, the primitive and sub-standard conditions at the 2941 RC, probably added to the training's overall realism.

Additionally, there were two major "plus" factors which in my opinion, contributed greatly to its quality. One, the war in Europe was over, so the camp had unlimited access to a huge cache of U.S. weapons and ammunition, and two, our instructors were able to teach us, not so much from the Army manual, but from their unique and invaluable, individual combat experiences.

On the first training day, we "expatriates" were divided into 12 man rifle squads. In a regular Army division, 3 squads would constitute a platoon, and 3 rifle platoons, plus a weapons platoon, would make up a company of about 187 men. However, while we were designated Company B, we numbered less than 50 men, so we actually operated throughout our training, as a single platoon of 48 men, composed of 3 rifle squads and a 12 man weapons-team.

For two weeks, to get us into better physical shape, hours were spent doing push-ups, sit-ups and other exercises, close-order drill and "double time" marching, and many sessions breaking down and reassembling our primary infantry weapon, the M-1 rifle, until we could do this with our eyes closed.

General "Blood and Guts" Patton purportedly once referred to the semi-automatic M-1 Garand, as "the greatest battle implement ever devised." That exaggeration aside, it was considered to be the finest military rifle available at that time. It weighed 10lbs and was top-loaded with an 8-round clip, which had to be pushed down into the bolt-action chamber in one quick motion, to avoid the painful consequences of an injury known as the "M-1 thumb!"

Reaching an acceptable level of proficiency with the rifle, also required instruction and practice with two companion weapons, the bayonet and the rifle-grenade. The Garand could be adapted to fire a grenade by clamping a launch attachment to the muzzle, and using a special blank cartridge, instead of a regular round.

When firing an anti-personnel or smoke-grenade, the butt of the M-1 was usually braced against the ground, which launched the grenade onto its target, in an arc. However, anti-tank grenades were armed with a contact fuse and needed to be launched in a straight trajectory. This required the grenade to be fired from the shoulder, and as I remember all too well, when used in that fashion, the M-1's recoil was like a kick from a mule!

We also learned how to throw smoke, concussion and fragmentation grenades by hand. All had a 4 second fuse and the fragmentation grenade was the most lethal. We were reminded often to get rid of any grenade quickly and carefully, after the pin was pulled and the "safety" released.

On our second visit to the grenade range, and just as we were starting to feel comfortable handling these dangerous objects, an instructor played a trick on us that I suspect every recruit has faced, in training. While showing us the correct throwing stance, he "accidentally" dropped a fragmentation-grenade after releasing the safety, about 10 feet from where we were all assembled.

Obviously, it was a "dud" from which the explosive charge had been removed, or I wouldn't have survived to tell this story. The idea was to see how we'd react if the grenade and the circumstances had been real, and I guess our collective response was just what the instructor anticipated. We all froze in our tracks, 48 unsuspecting and innocent would-be casualties!

Our bayonet instructor was S/Sgt. "Bayonet" Stiritz, who ·had earned his nickname serving with the U.S. 3rd Division in North Africa, by dispatching a German soldier with his bayonet, in a hand-to-hand encounter. Though I successfully "killed" a straw-filled dummy to Stiritz's satisfaction, it was difficult to picture myself thrusting 10 inches of cold steel into a human being, but in combat if my life depended upon it, who knows?

Our training also introduced us to the M-1 carbine, which was originally intended as a more effective substitute for the pistol carried by officers, and for use by supply troops and military police, who were not expected to routinely get involved in fire-fights. It weighed only 6lbs and lacked the Garand's accuracy and stopping-power, but its 15-round capacity gave it an advantage in sudden close encounters with the enemy, and consequently, it was commonly used in combat, particularly by paratroopers.

As previously indicated, all the infantry weapons of that time, were in ample supply, so many days and frequent nights were spent on the various ranges, using the BAR (Browning Automatic Rifle), the .30 machine-gun, the 60mm mortar and the 2.36 bazooka, in live-fire exercises.

A platoon's BARs and machine-guns gave it much needed rapid fire power, while mortars and bazookas provided it with on-the-spot artillery support and anti-tank protection. The BAR and the bazooka weighed 18lbs, while the light machine-gun and the mortar (which for carrying purposes, were broken down into two parts), weighed about 32lbs and 42lbs respectively, when fully assembled.

I enjoyed firing all these weapons, but for a guy like me with narrow shoulders and no meat on his bones to provide even a modicum of padding, carrying them any distance was sheer torture.

Another hefty weapon, rarely seen in Europe but used extensively in the Pacific war, was the M-2 flame-thrower, which weighed 70lbs. After firing this weapon, I concluded that if I ever did see combat, I'd never volunteer to be a flame-thrower operator, who was required to stand up under enemy fire, knowing that he had 5 gallons of jellied-gasoline strapped to his back!

One day, we watched our instructors demonstrate how to clear a path through barbed-wire entanglements and other defensive obstacles, using a "Bangalore-torpedo." Of British design, the Bangalore was a 5ft. long, 2in.diameter pipe containing 8 lbs of explosive. It was usually placed on the ground and pushed into the obstacle or area to be cleared, before being detonated by remote control. Additional explosive filled sections could be fitted together to increase its range and effectiveness.

A week later, while reconnoitering in a wooded area, our progress was suddenly halted by a barbed-wire entanglement. It was then we learned from our instructors, how to go over such an obstacle, when a Bangalore wasn't available to blast a path through it.

Our three biggest guys were ordered to run forward and throw themselves face down, on the wire. This done, the rest of us were told to run and leap over the wire, using their backs as spring-boards. Maybe this wasn't as hard on the poor souls spread-eagled on the wire as it sounds, but for the life of me, I can't recall how they extricated themselves and joined us on the other side.

During this exercise, I managed to validate my reputation as a certifiably-inept athlete. While my leap was OK, when I landed beyond the wire, I fell and rammed my M-1 into the ground, clogging the barrel with dirt and earning a reprimand from Sgt. Stiritz, that I'll always remember. With his face inches from mine, he yelled "You clumsy Limey bastard, I ought make you fire your g—dammed rifle and watch you blow your face away, but better than that, I'm gonna save you for the Japs!"

As is evident from this encounter, an Army drill-sergeant in 1945, was truly a master of his domain, and certainly not constrained by today's asinine rules of political correctness.

On evenings when we were not away from our quarters on a training exercise, we recruits participated in the camp's traditional "retreat" flag lowering. On one such occasion, after a long sweltering day in the field, and running way behind schedule, we were forced to double-time to the parade-ground, so as to be in formation when the ceremony began.

Standing there at attention, I suddenly felt weak and probably started to sway, as I heard someone yell "steady in the ranks," just before I blacked out and collapsed. Regaining consciousness, imagine my surprise to find Sgt. Stiritz, who several days earlier had called me a "clumsy Limey bastard," kneeling at my side with a look of concern on his face, asking "Are you O.K. son?"

I was quite mortified, although in retrospect, I realize I had no reason to feel that way. I'd been felled by heat-exhaustion and dehydration caused by well-meaning but wrongful advice imparted by our instructors, who would tell us to drink from our canteens as sparingly as possible, because in combat potable water would likely be in short supply, or unobtainable.

At the end of the day, they'd check to see how well we'd conserved our supply, and I was proud of the fact that I could usually present a full canteen of water for their inspection.

In today's military, the opposite advice is given and enforced. When my son-in-law a former Marine, went through boot-camp at Parris Island in 1990, he was ordered to drink at least 8 quarts a day, a regimen which obviously makes sense, given the known serious health consequences, associated with dehydration.

Our training also included several sessions on anti-personnel land-mines, using the German "S' and "Schu" mines, and a Japanese mine made of glass. Of the three, the "S' mine was the most lethal. When placed in the ground, only its signature 3 tiny prongs were exposed. When these were broken, they triggered a charge which launched the mine 4 ft. into the air, before it exploded, making the "Bouncing Betty" as it was called, a much feared hazard for troops entering areas once held by the enemy.

As a test following these sessions, a practice area was sowed with "Bouncing Betty" mines armed with smoke charges, which weren't expected to cause injury when they exploded. Our squads were required to work their way through the mined area on their knees, each man gently prodding the ground with his bayonet, while using his other hand, to feel for the tell-tale prongs.

When my turn came, I located a "BB" and was so intent on removing it safely from the ground, that I missed the prongs of its companion, unseen and buried a few feet away. As embarrassing as that experience was, I wasn't the only "casualty" that afternoon. Had we been dealing with the real thing, nine men or 20% of our group, would have been killed or seriously maimed!

Another exercise I well remember, involved digging a fox-hole, the ground soldier's traditional refuge from which he can stand and fire on attacking forces, or crouch in, to avoid return rounds or shrapnel. Depending on the terrain, constructing a hole 4ft. deep and 2ft. across, using an Army entrenching-tool, a small folding shovel with a short handle and a sharp pointed blade, was not an easy task.

After laboring away for hours in the hot June sun, an instructor informed us that on the following morning, our handiwork would be tested by having a Sherman tank run its steel treads directly over the holes, while we were crouching inside. Needless to say, upon hearing this, we all went into a frenzy of renewed digging, thoroughly convinced that our holes would collapse under the 30 ton Sherman, and we'd all be squashed, like so many bugs!

In truth, we recruits were once again the butt of an instructor's joke. When the Sherman rattled and growled towards us, instead of running its treads over each hole as was expected, it carefully straddled them, much to the relief of their nervous occupants.

While poison gas had not been used in the war with Germany, it was still a possible weapon of the Japanese if we invaded their homeland, so we went through the standard drill. Wearing gas-masks, we entered a shed filled with tear-gas, stood for several minutes, took a deep breath, removed our masks, which guaranteed that our eyes at least would temporarily feel the effects and discomfort of the gas, before exiting the chamber.

Thanks to the first-class instruction that we received before being allowed to handle any weapon, I can honestly say that I was comfortable and essentially unafraid of anything required of me as a recruit in training, with the exception of one particular night-time field assignment.

In full combat gear, we were loaded into small rubber boats, and ordered to paddle to a point about a quarter of a mile down the Aisne river, where we waded ashore and set-off on an extended hike which ended back at our quarters, just before daylight.

Because I'd never learned to swim, from the moment I boarded that flimsy craft, until I was back on solid ground, I remember being truly scared, knowing that if it sprung a leak or accidentally turned over, I would have gone to the bottom of that river like a rock! Fortunately, the only casualties from that overnight exercise, were 48 pairs of sore and very tired wet feet.

During our months at the 2941 RC, we trained rigorously five days a week. The weekends we usually had to ourselves, except that every Saturday night, five or six of us were assigned "KP" which meant working a 12 hour shift in the camp's kitchen. This was the usual punishment for any infractions during basic-training, when these were uncovered by Lt. McCardle and his accompanying NCO, during their Saturday morning inspections of our quarters.

Early on, we hung the nickname "Scrooge" on Lt. McCardle, and somehow this got back to him, but he never took offense. To the contrary, he seemed to relish its implication, occasionally referring to himself as "Scrooge," no doubt to remind us that where his inspections were concerned, he could be a mean S.O.B.

He'd check everything! Our rooms, rifles, uniforms, boots, foot-lockers, bunks and even our faces, for errant whiskers. Anything that didn't measure up to his standards, was noted by the NCO, and those with the most demerits, were always candidates for KP. I was put on KP five times, which wasn't bad, considering how hard it was to please the Lieutenant, something I learned on his first inspection, five days after our training began.

I thought I was home free, until McCardle peered into my face and frowned, saying, "Did you shave today, soldier?" I replied, "No sir, I don't need to shave every day." This was true, because it took me three days to grow enough whiskers to warrant the effort. Lt. "Scrooge" gave his best imitation of a smile and said, "You're wrong soldier, while you're here, you'll shave every day whether you need it or not! Sergeant, put this man down for KP tonight."

In my mind, more than 58 years later, KP and chickens are synonymous, because almost every Sunday at the 2941 RC, chicken was on the menu. On Saturdays, boxes of frozen chicken packed in dry-ice, were trucked into the camp mess-hall, to await those recruits whose misfortune it was to win that day's KP lottery.

As I recall it took more than 200 chickens to feed the camp's population. For whatever reason, these were shipped from the States with their innards intact, so when we reported for duty at 7.00pm, our first assignment was to reach into each chicken through its "rear exit" and yank out its insides, before the cooks prepared them for the ovens.

Frozen chicken innards are not easy to remove, especially when doing this under the eagle-eye of a mess-sergeant threatening all sorts of dire consequences, if during the process we'd rupture any internal organ which might then render the chicken unfit for human consumption.

When all the chickens and their insides had parted company, there was always a mound of potatoes waiting to be peeled, as well as umpteen dirty pots and pans that needed scrubbing. If we were lucky, sometime before the sun came up we'd get everything done, and if "Sarge" was in a good mood, he'd authorize Spam sandwiches all around. Sometimes, he'd even reach into his private pantry, and share cake or some other treat, items which were not likely to ever show up on his regular mess-hall menu.

Also on weekends, all recruits at regular intervals, were required to report to the 2941 RC guard-house for a 24 hour stint of guard-duty. We were posted at various points around the camp's perimeter, sometimes in pairs, but more often standing guard or walking the post, alone. After each two hour on-duty shift, we had four hours off, time in which we were free to nap, eat or play cards, just as long as we didn't leave the guard-house.

Because the bulk of our training time was spent away from our quarters, firing weapons on the various ranges or practicing small unit tactics in the camp's vast wooded areas, many of our meals were "K-Rations" which were designed for field consumption.

Three K-ration meal variations were available. Each featured a small can of a processed meat, either veal, spam or sausage, together with cheese and crackers, coffee and lemonade mixes, a chocolate bar, chewing gum, cigarettes, condiments and toilet-paper. The rations were packed in a waxed box, which would burn easily and long enough, to heat water to make instant coffee.

These meals may not sound very appetizing, but after living on British wartime rations for over five years, I personally had no complaints. Each guy had a favorite entrée, and we'd swap items from the boxes we were issued, until we all had what we wanted. Almost everyone except Scotty and I smoked, so we'd barter away our cigarettes for chocolate bars and cheese crackers.

One item carried by GIs in their field-packs, was the "shelter-half." This was a piece of canvas which, when mated to another shelter-half and then lashed to a couple of small poles, formed a "pup-tent." The end product, although open at one end, still afforded its two occupants, some protection from the elements.

I recall one very unusual pup-tent sharing experience while at the 2941 RC. One day, after a full morning of training, Company B set out on a 10 mile hike into the French countryside. It was late afternoon when we arrived at the remote area selected as our overnight camp-site. We were paired off and erected our pup-tents, after which we were turned loose until chow-time.

My tent-mate was Kilburn, another 18 year old who had also grown up in London. After we had erected our tent, he took off and I went and spent some time shooting the breeze with Scotty. Upon returning to the tent, I found Kilburn sitting outside looking highly excited and very pleased with himself, and when I crawled inside, I became pretty excited, too. In the rear of our tent, were three very old rusty, small-caliber artillery shells!

These had obviously been fired but had not detonated. My tent-mate had discovered them while exploring the woods around our site, but instead of giving them wide berth, he'd picked them up and carried them back into the camp. What he planned to do with these lethal souvenirs, was way beyond my comprehension.

Kilburn's thoughtless escapade had placed over 50 men at risk of death or serious injury, so there was only one responsible thing to do. I reported the incident to Sgt. Stiritz, and when he peered into our tent and saw Kilburn's collection, I thought he was going to lose it, a reaction that was understandable. He'd survived three years of combat, and thanks to a recruit's stupidity, his life had again been placed in jeopardy.

Stiriz reported his findings to Lt. McCardle and in minutes, everyone except Kilburn, was evacuated to safe distance and told to hit the deck and stay down. That done, my hapless tent-mate was ordered to carefully carry each unexploded shell out of the camp and back into the woods where they'd landed, months or years earlier, during the recently ended war in Europe.

Kilburn was lucky on two counts. Explosive compounds deteriorate over time and become unstable, so his odds at being a casualty while handling that ordnance, were high. And he could have been turned over to the Provost Marshall which would have meant some time in the stockade. Instead, Lt. McCardle let him finish his training, although I suspect that on all of his week-ends from then on, he belonged to the camp Mess-Sergeant, body and soul!

Soon after the Kilburn incident, I got into a fight with a room-mate (the one whose name I can't remember), over his habit of using shaving-cream to hold his hair in place after combing.

The cream would dry and he'd look ridiculous and of course, after a while, it made his scalp itch and he'd start scratching his head, and tiny white flakes would fly everywhere.

One evening, with both of us tired and edgy after 10 hours of training, I sounded off about his stupid hair, and he rebutted with something uncomplimentary about me. This led us to exchange several half-hearted punches before going outside, where we rolled around in the dirt, like a couple of very amateur wrestlers. I had his head locked under my right arm in a vice-like grip, when Reid, one of our room-mates, tried to separate us by yanking on my arm, and he pulled it out of its socket.

That brought the battle to an end! Out of the blue, Sgt. Slusher appeared, and fortunately he accepted my explanation that we'd just been horsing around, because admitting to the real scenario, could have put us both in trouble. He drove me to the Dispensary in his jeep, where a Medical Officer, after eye-balling my shoulder, handed me a face-cloth saying, "Put this in your mouth and bite down." With that, he gave my arm a pull and a twist, and popped it back into place.

With my arm in a sling and instructions from the MO to keep it immobilized for at least five days, I walked back to my quarters. Reid apologized for accidentally hurting me, and my erstwhile combatant sheepishly offered his hand in peace. I learned later from Omar, that while I was gone, Reid really chewed the guy out concerning his weird personal habit, and that apparently did the trick because from then on, his head remained shaving-cream free.

The next morning when we assembled for roll-call, my sling caught the eye of Lt. McCardle, and responding to his inquiry, I reported on my accident and the MO's recommendation. "Scrooge" frowned and said, "Soldier, if you're not out of that sling by the day after tomorrow, you'll be shipped out of this company to finish your training with the next batch of recruits, who come through."

At that point, I was half-way through basic training, so where I was concerned, being held back and assigned to another company, was the last thing I needed. Forty-eight hours later when I joined my fellow recruits at reveille, the sling was gone and my trusty M-1 was back on my shoulder. Little did I know however how much trouble I'd have with both of my shoulder joints, in the months and years that followed.

By July 2, victorious American troops on Okinawa had finished mopping-up isolated elements of Japanese resistance, and the campaign was officially declared over. For the next 30 days thousands of American and British aircraft pounded Japanese cities, ports, railways, airfields and military installations, while a fleet of warships, operating as an Allied task-force, steamed unchallenged into homeland waters, where their massive guns hurled tons of high-explosive shells onto coastal targets.

Japan was under day and night siege, and food shortages became so acute that civilians, acting on government orders, collected millions of bushels of acorns for processing into a substitute food product, to help relieve the widespread hunger. Despite these horrendous conditions and the obvious certainty that military defeat was inevitable, Japan's ruling junta voted on July 30 to reject the Allied ultimatum issued four days earlier, which again called for Japan's unconditional surrender.

By this time, after almost three months at the 2941 RC, Company B had progressed from a rag-tag bunch of raw recruits, to a well-honed infantry unit. We were anxious to finish our final weeks of training, after which we could count on week-end passes to Paris, before being assigned as rifleman-replacements to one of the many infantry divisions still in Europe, awaiting orders for rotation back to the States, and from there to the Pacific.

In fact, about 20 of us were so "gung-ho" that we approached Sgt. Stiritz to find out if and when we could volunteer as a group, to serve with the famed 82nd "All American" Airborne Division, which at that time was stationed in Berlin.

As I recall, the main motivation behind our desire to become paratroopers, was the extra "jmp-pay" we'd heard about and the signature, flashy "jump-boots" we'd seen and coveted, but Stiritz promptly dashed our hopes. He pointed out that replacements for airborne divisions in the ETO were required to have completed the basic paratrooper jump training, which definitely put us would-be volunteers, out of the running.

As a final exercise and culmination to what had been an extensive and broad-based infantry training experience, we were put through the camp's combat infiltration course, once during daylight hours and then again, under the cover of darkness.

The course was laid out over a wide area, and we were ordered to lie face down and crawl forward on our stomachs and elbows, following narrow, clearly marked trails for about 100 feet, with our rifles cradled across our arms, under barbed-wire strung 18 inches above the ground.

As we inched our way through, three machine-guns manned by instructors and battened down in fixed positions to prevent recoil-creep, were firing live ammunition including tracers, about 12 inches above the wire. Additionally, located throughout the course, at safe distances from the trails marked for our passage, hidden smoke charges were detonated by other NCOs, to simulate incoming mortar or artillery rounds.

With smoke-bombs detonating around me and hundreds of lethal machine-gun rounds snapping by 30 inches above my helmet, I stayed lower than a snake's belly, glad for once to be skinny.

At roll call on August 7, one of our instructors told us that on the previous day, something called an "atom-bomb" had been dropped by a B-29 on the Japanese city of Hiroshima. My limited formal education mirrored that of many in Company B, insofar as it lacked even a smattering of chemistry or nuclear-physics, so for us, the words "atom" and "nuclear" meant nothing.

Fortunately, Scotty and Omar with their grammar-school education, and another recruit named McCauley who'd graduated from college in Dublin, were able to provide a rudimentary "heads-up" on the significance of splitting the atom, and how the energy released could be harnessed into a bomb, with a destructive power greater than anything the world had previously created or witnessed.

Three days later, we learned that a second atom-bomb had been dropped on the city of Nagasaki, but absent any indication that this revolutionary weapon had caused the Japanese to throw in the towel, we remained unimpressed and continued with our training. Then on August 14, we heard the news we'd waited for. Japan's military leadership, on the orders of Emperor Hirohito, had surrendered unconditionally, and all hostilities came to an end.

On the following day, proclaimed and celebrated by the Allies as "V-J Day," the Japanese people heard the voice of their Emperor over the radio for the first time, announcing the surrender and ordering all citizens to lay down their arms. On September 2, on the United States battleship "Missouri" anchored in Tokyo Bay, a document of surrender was signed by the Japanese and witnessed by representatives of all the Allied nations, formally bringing the Second World War to an end, exactly six years after it began.

Since then, much has been said and written concerning the morality or necessity of using nuclear weapons against Japan, to secure its surrender. Every year, on the anniversaries of the Hiroshima and Nagasaki attacks, protests are heard here at home and around the world, usually from individuals who were born after the war ended, or whose own lives at that time were not at risk, had an invasion of Japan become necessary.

The facts are clear. On July 30, 1945 when Japan rejected the latest Allied ultimatum to surrender, it had 2.5 million troops on hand to repel an invasion, and millions of civilians who had been told repeatedly, that if the country was invaded, everyone including women and children, should resist and kill as many of the enemy as possible, even at the sacrifice of their own lives.

At that point, the leaders and top military advisors of the United States, Great Britain and the Soviet Union, unanimously agreed that Japan's fanatical leadership and armed forces had to be destroyed to secure its surrender, and that this could only be accomplished by a full scale invasion of Japan's home-islands.

Plans for this immense undertaking, called for two massive sea and air landings, the first on Kyushu (Operation Olympic), on November 1, 1945, and the second on the main island of Honshu (Operation Coronet), scheduled for April 1, 1946.

From what we and the British had learned from countless bloody encounters with the enemy since Pearl Harbor, it was clear that this final campaign would be the largest and most costly of the war. Conservative military estimates indicated that 1.5 million troops would be deployed in the initial landings, with another 4.5 million needed to provide the necessary reserves.

Based on American combat deaths and injuries suffered at Iwo Jima, Okinawa, Tarawa, Peleliu and on many other Japanese held Pacific Islands, estimated casualties from an invasion of the homeland, were staggering. For the British, as many as 500,000 and for the United States, two and a half times that number! Japanese military and civilian casualties, assuming the same level of fanatical and suicidal resistance that they had previously displayed, were expected to number in the millions.

Voluminous records support these facts and figures, so my position on the contentious atom-bomb issue, has never wavered. In August 1945, I was eighteen years old, a rifleman-replacement, about to be assigned to one of the 25 divisions deemed necessary to the success of a homeland invasion. Where I'm concerned, my chances of surviving that expected and unprecedented blood-bath, or escaping without serious injury, were slim indeed.

Thanks to President Harry Truman's courageous and morally correct decision to consider the lives of American troops more important than those of the enemy, I was one of thousands of young men who lived to witness the war's end, and return home unharmed. Every August 6th, I mix myself a high-ball and raise a toast to Harry, and remember his momentous decision, while counting my blessings again, always guilt free!

Chapter 20

From Compiegne, France to Marburg, Germany

We completed our 14 weeks of basic infantry training, 10 days after all hostilities ended, and learned that we'd been promoted one grade to Private First Class (Pfc). This made us eligible to sew one stripe on our uniform sleeves, and for an increase in pay of a few extra dollars a month.

We also got to exchange our despised leggings and "low" boots for regulation "combat-boots." As was the custom, rather than folding the ends of my pants legs and tucking them into the buckle-tops of my new boots, I bloused them, paratrooper style, and tucked them under condoms, which functioned as makeshift rubber-bands, and were guaranteed to hold one's pants, neatly in place.

Overnight, the circumstances of war had changed, and excitement for everyone at the camp, ran high. We newly-minted riflemen, no longer facing the hazards of combat, learned that we'd be going to Germany for a 12 month tour of duty in the Army of Occupation. Those veterans at the 2941 RC, including our instructors, who had earned the requisite discharge "points," anxiously awaited orders to be shipped back to the States, where they could expect to be promptly processed for discharge, and sent home.

However, before we all went our separate ways, Company B was treated to a "graduation" party which was attended by most of our officers and NCOs. I still have the mimeographed souvenir program received at that event. It's yellow and faded with age, but still legible are the autographs of Capt. Sexmith and the other cadre members in attendance. Lt. MCardle's signature, as if to remind me always, that very little we recruits said or did escaped his knowledge, reads as follows, "E. McCardle (Scrooge)."

Two days later, we received the promised 3 day passes to Paris. Scotty and I roomed together in an old hotel, walked the boulevards and the banks of the Seine and visited the Arc de Triomphe and other historical landmarks. After dark, we ran into the rest of our gang, first at the world famous "Folies Bergere" and again at the "Concert Mayo" a similar stage production.

These shows lived up to their artsy reputations, providing Scotty and I and Company B's few other remaining "innocents," with our first glimpse of the unclothed female form. Actually, both shows featured up to forty young ladies in various stages of nudity, all incredibly lovely and displayed rather elegantly, in a series of colorful and elaborately staged vignettes. Obviously, some events are more easily remembered and retained than others!

Despite the many erotic attractions and pursuits available in Paris, no member of Company B chose to go AWOL, and soon after we returned to the 2941 RC, our orders came through to leave France for an undisclosed destination, somewhere in the American Zone of occupied Germany. Having just traveled to and from Paris on an old but serviceable French passenger train, we assumed that would again be our mode of transportation, but no such luck.

Accompanied by three NCOs, we were loaded into 6x6 trucks and taken to the Compiegne railway station, where a steam-locomotive, that had clearly seen better days, sat hitched to three box-cars and a caboose, huffing and puffing awaiting our arrival.

The irony of the situation was not lost on anyone, and brought on a chorus of groans and expletives. Here we were, members of a great and victorious army, about to ride into the heartland of our recently defeated enemy in cattle-cars, the same kind of transportation used to take millions of Jews and others deemed undesirable by the Nazis, to concentration camp gas-chambers.

Nevertheless, orders were orders, and within the hour, the NCOs had assigned us 12 men to a car, and put their own gear into the caboose, which would serve as their travel quarters. It was then that we learned that our destination was Marburg, a city in central Germany about 50 miles north of Frankfort-am-Main.

As the crow flies, Marburg was only 300 miles away, but given the devastated condition of the French and German railway systems, our journey would take 36 hours, following a circuitous course through northern France into Belgium, continuing north to Liege, finally crossing into Germany at Aachen.

At that point, we were 150 air miles from our destination, but again, due to the horrendous state of the tracks, we were forced to continue on a northerly course into the Ruhr Valley, before finally heading in a southwesterly direction, and into Marburg.

Spending 36 hours in a box-car with eleven other guys, sleeping fully clothed on straw, with a back-pack as a pillow, forced to eat K-rations three times a day, and with no on-board latrine or bathing facilities, could have qualified the event as a rail-trip from Hell, but for me, an eighteen year old kid at the time, the experience probably seemed more like high adventure.

The late summer days were sunny and warm, the nights cool and comfortable. We rode with the car doors open, sitting with our legs dangling in the slip-stream, and took turns riding outside, perched on the rungs of the ladders at the end of each car.

This wasn't as hazardous as it sounds, because most of the time, the battered state of the road-bed and tracks, held down the speed of the train, to about 20 miles an hour. At dusk, we were shunted off the main track onto a siding, where we languished until daybreak, when once again, we got underway.

With many unscheduled stops for one thing or another, we had plenty of opportunities to change riding positions, stretch our legs and take care of our normal bodily functions, which out of necessity, were usually performed alongside the tracks. If this sounds inappropriate, remember that we were being transported without latrine facililties, through war-torn countryside in which much of the civil infrastructure had been destroyed, an area now teeming with thousands of destitute transients trying to locate their original homes, or at least find a temporary place to live.

My most vivid memories of that trip, relate to scenes I witnessed after the train crossed the Belgian border and slowly chugged into the Ruhr Valley, Germany's once proud industrial heartland. We went through one devastated town after another, in which every building had been leveled or was badly damaged, probably more as a result of continuous bombing by the RAF and USAAF, than from the ground battles fought there, as the German forces retreated.

Every station-platform was jammed with civilians, most of whom I assumed were German refugees, waiting for trains which, given the state of the system might never arrive as scheduled, if at all. Their faces essentially mirrored the same fixed expressions, sad, sullen or hostile. We stared at each other exchanging no words, the victors and the vanquished of a war that had ended four months earlier. For Germany's citizens, the consequences of it's defeat and unconditional surrender, had yet to be determined, and I guess the only thing these people had going for them, was the fact that the Ruhr Valley, despite being in ruins, was occupied by British armed forces, and not Stalin's vengeful Red Army.

Finally, our train pulled into Marburg, where a Quartermaster Corps Lieutenant and several trucks and drivers, were on hand for our arrival. The officer was clearly not happy with our "Sad Sack" appearance. We were all unwashed and unshaven, and those of us who'd chosen to ride on the outside of the box-cars, also wore a layer of soot, courtesy of the ancient steam-locomotive.

Marburg, a city situated on the River Lahn north of Frankfurt, was the site of a large U.S. Army Reinforcement Depot. It was our expectation that we'd stay there just long enough to be processed out to one of the Army's regular divisions charged with policing, patrolling and all other law-and-order enforcement activities, associated with a military occupation.

Having just been trained in the art of soldiering, that was the duty I'd hoped for, but unfortunately, the Depot itself was looking for new blood to replace its veteran cadre members, who'd recently been shipped back to the States, so most of us who arrived that day on the "box-car express," spent the next 12 months on permanent assignment at the Depot.

Scotty went to a Finance Unit in downtown Marburg. "Jock" White another Scottish-American and I, along with our basic-training comrade from Luxemburg, were trucked out to the Depot's 178th Reinforcement Company, part of the 69th Reinforcement Battalion, located on the outskirts of town.

The 69th and the 178th were both quartered in a complex which prior to the war's end had been a German military convalescent hospital. Those buildings not used by battalion and company regulars, served as temporary housing for the thousands of GIs eligible for discharge, who passed through on their way to the French port of Le Havre, where they boarded ships for home.

The 178th had bath and toilet facilities, luxuries I hadn't enjoyed for months, plus enough space to provide its permanent NCOs, with their own rooms. I shared space with four other guys for two months, before being promoted to Corporal (Technician 5th Grade), whereupon I inherited a room of my own.

I should hasten to explain, that by the end of 1945, so many troops had left the ETO, that the Tables of Organization of most units, had ample NCO openings. As a result, for those like me who were a year away from being discharged, promotion in rank came quickly, and certainly more easily than usual.

My first day at the 178th, I was assigned to assist the Company Mail Clerk, Sergeant Jesus Nunez, a naturalized Mexican-American who already had the magic number of "points" for discharge. Not having met anyone of Hispanic origin while growing up in England, I got a blast from the Sergeant when I used the English rather than the Spanish pronunciation of his first name, a mistake which everyone within earshot, greeted with laughter.

Actually, given my still noticeable English accent, every time I opened my mouth during those first few months at the 178th, I'd draw a laugh or two from the guys who knew me, and when around other GIs, I could always count on hearing someone in the crowd, after hearing me speak, ask the question, "Who's the g-damned Limey?"

Despite my initial "Jesus" faux pas, Sergeant Nunez and I got along fine and worked well as a team until his orders came through, and he left the 178th. I recall that our work-days were hectic, not from the negligible volume of mail we handled, but from the issuing and processing of individual Postal Money Orders for the hundreds of transient troops housed in our sector, who crowded into our Mail Room each day, seeking this service.

All over war-torn Europe, American products could be sold on the civilian black-market, for many times their original cost. Sgt. Nunez and I didn't know it at the time, but in carrying out our Post-Office duties, we were participating in a monetary process which was costing the U.S. government, millions of dollars.

For example, an 82nd Airborne trooper stationed in Berlin, could easily get the equivalent of $100 in German marks, for a carton of American cigarettes. The mark at that time was worth 10 cents, so that transaction put 1,000 marks into his pocket, which he could then use to legitimately purchase a $100 PMO made payable to a relative or friend in the States.

Simply put, German "funny money" was being converted into real American currency, and with thousands of such transactions taking place each day, many more millions of dollars were being sent back to the States, than had actually been issued in the ETO by the U.S. government, as military payroll. In December, 1945, when the 82nd Airborne Division left Berlin for the States and passed through Marburg, I can recall working over-time for several days, processing scores of individual PMOs worth hundreds of dollars, for troopers whose average pay was only about $50 a month!

Sometime in early 1946, the U.S. government finally put a stop to this monetary fiasco, by instigating a "Military Script" system, the compulsory use of which, pretty much guaranteed that PMOs sent to anyone in the States, were being purchased with U.S. military payroll dollars, backed by the U.S. Treasury.

With Sergeant Nunez's departure for home, I was made Company Mail Clerk, and when I needed assistance processing PMOs, someone else from the cadre would lend a hand. For a change of pace, I was also placed on special duty several times, serving as guard and overseer of the German prisoners-of-war who were being used to build fences and improve the roads, within the Battalion complex.

The POWs were housed nearby in a barbed-wire complex of tents, and were trucked into the 178th, early each morning. It was my responsibility to give them their work orders for the day, and make sure everything got done as planned. I spoke no German which wasn't a problem, because there was always at least one POW who could speak enough English for us to communicate, and get the men working. All I had to do then was to stay alert and see that no one goofed-off. As the guard, I was required to carry an M-1 rifle with a fully loaded clip, but with no round in the chamber.

Most of the POW's were over fifty, who'd probably served in World War I and had been conscripted again during the final months of Hitler's last-ditch, failed effort to halt the Allied advance into the Fatherland. They reminded me of my Dad, and having been raised to defer to, and respect my elders, I was uncomfortable giving orders to these "old" men, and embarrassed by their exaggerated air of servility, when in my youthful presence.

That any of them would try to escape, was not considered likely. The war was over, Germany was in ruins, the whereabouts and condition of their families unknown, and their ultimate release, just a matter of time. Accordingly, most were content that first post-war winter, to accept their POW status, knowing that unlike their less fortunate brothers in Soviet camps, they could count on three meals a day and reasonable treatment, including medical care, at the hands of their American captors.

In any event, my discomfort was soon remedied by my buddy from Luxemburg, who went to our CO and volunteered for POW duty, on a full-time basis. He was a big, tough-looking individual who in his early teens, had been forced to work as a slave-laborer, during the Nazi occupation of his country. He spoke fluent German and was plainly anxious to be in a position where members of the Wehrmacht, would be answerable to him for a change.

On the day he took over the POW detail, I stood back and watched. As soon as he began addressing the group in German, I saw all of their expressions change. By the time he'd finished, most were standing rigidly at attention, and when he gave the order to start work, they went about their tasks with considerable more speed and energy, than I had ever witnessed.

Later that day, I learned from "Lux" that he'd told the POWs where he was from, that he'd been a slave-laborer for almost five years, and that he wouldn't hesitate to shoot any German bastard who didn't promptly follow his orders! While I felt a bit sorry for the old men in his charge, given my friend's recent history, I could well understand and appreciate his attitude.

"Lux" continued to work the POW detail, until he was offered and accepted a transfer to a Military Police Unit, where his command of the German language would be more useful and productive.

Soon after arriving at the 178th, I heard about possible Nazi "Werewolf" activity in the Marburg area. I was told that soon after the war's end, a GI out alone, walking back to his unit after dark, was attacked, castrated and left to die.

The "Werewolf" organization had been formed in 1944, the brain-child of Hitler's right-hand man, Heinrich Himmler, to operate under the leadership of Himmler's Schutzstaffel (SS), for the purpose of conducting sabotage and other guerrilla activities against the Allies, if Germany was invaded and occupied.

Most "Werewolf" members were teen-agers, recruited from the ranks of the Hitler Youth and fanatically loyal to Hitler. When ordered, they could be counted upon to continue the war against the Allied occupying forces, even after Germany had surrendered.

A post-war book titled "The Last Nazis" by Perry Biddiscombe, Associate Professor of History at the University of Victoria, BC, Canada, tabulates 1944 to 1947 "Werewolf" activities in Europe. It contains a U.S. Army map of the "Civil and Internal Security Incidents" in the American Zone, from November, 1945 to January 1946, including "69 attacks on personnel," but the alleged Marburg castration incident, as it was told to me, was not mentioned in Biddiscombe's book, and quite possibly didn't occur.

Scotty and many of my other friends from basic training, were stationed in town several miles away, and I'd spend much of my off-duty time in their company. Usually, I'd get a ride on a 6x6 into Marburg, and between 9.00 and 10.00pm, trucks from the 69th Battalion cruised the center-city area picking up those of us who needed return transportation, so I rarely traveled alone.

Nevertheless, I still felt vulnerable at the possibility of meeting up with a crazy, unreconstructed Nazi with a knife, bent on separating me from my yet to be utilized "manhood," so when a transient GI passing through the 178[th,] offered to sell me a hand-gun, I made the purchase. It was a .38 Spanish-made revolver (probably a relic from

Spain's Civil War), and came with a dozen live rounds and several blank cartridges.

For the next couple of months, whenever I went into town off-duty, I carried my trusty six-shooter in my over-coat pocket. I took a chance doing this, because carrying a concealed weapon without specific authority, was contrary to U.S. Army regulations. It was always loaded in such a way, that in the event I was forced to use it, the first shot I fired would be a blank and the remaining five rounds, the real thing. I probably reasoned at the time, that it would be preferable to prevent an assault by scaring off my attacker, rather than shooting him!

One evening, while visiting with Scotty and some other guys, I made the mistake of showing off my "piece," and while it was being passed around, someone accidentally squeezed the trigger and fired the blank. Luck was certainly with me and everyone else in Scotty's room that night. Thanks to my unusual loading method, no one got hurt, and the Sergeant who charged in after hearing the gun-shot, after chewing me out, confiscated my gun, but in choosing not to report the incident, he saved me a lot of grief.

In November, 1945, I celebrated my first Thanksgiving Day, since claiming my American citizenship 8 months earlier. As I recall, we at the 178th were treated to a full-course meal, but it wasn't the traditional "turkey with all the trimmings" I'd heard about. Apparently, a friend of our Mess-Sergeant had used his M1 to bag a deer, so instead of getting turkey, we ended up with venison. To top off our feast, we each received a cigar, and despite being a non-smoker, in the spirit of Thanksgiving, I puffed away, all the time wondering how anyone could ever get hooked on cigars, given how awful I thought the darn things smelled and tasted!

Two days later, the 1st.Sergeant informed me that I'd earned a 10 day pass to either England or Switzerland. When the other men in my Company got leave, most chose to visit Switzerland, because as a result of that country's neutrality during the war, conditions there were so much better than anywhere else in Europe. However, with my family and friends located in England, it made sense for me to go there as often as I could before my service in Germany ended, and I was shipped back to the States.

So, together with scores of other GIs on leave, I rode a train from Marburg to Frankfurt. There I transferred to another train going to Paris, and then onto one heading for Le Havre. On each, I enjoyed the comfort of riding in a regular passenger coach, quite a different experience from my earlier box-car odyssey.

An Le Havre, those of us going to the UK, were required to stay overnight at "Camp Lucky Strike," a U.S. Army tent-city, through which troops passed on their way to the States for discharge. It was during that stop-over, that I had my first sexual adventure, an event that I'd not consider mentioning, much less describing, if the entire experience had not been so ludicrous.

It began innocently enough, at the Marburg station, where I ran into a couple of guys that I knew by sight only, from the 69th Battalion. They were also on their way to England, so we ended up traveling together, and at "Lucky Strike," we were assigned cots in the same tent. It was late afternoon when we arrived, and typical for a coastal town in late November, everything was shrouded in a cold, raw mist. While I was content to stay put in my tent, my traveling companions went off to explore the town, and didn't' return until early evening, after chow-time.

I learned that they'd taken a local bus up the coast a few miles to the village of Etretat. There they found a café that served them a meal of sorts, and where they'd met a friendly French girl they were adamant I should meet, and who, according to them, was anxious to meet me. From their breath, I could tell they had already consumed a fair amount of the region's cheap red-wine!

Anyway, they hammered away at me, until I finally agreed to go back to their bistro, meet their new friend and have a drink or two, provided that public transportation could be counted on to get us back to camp, before the "lights-out" bugle. With that assurance, I followed them out into the cold, miserable night.

We caught a bus to Etretat, and soon were enjoying the warmth of the café, where I'd been led to believe, a comely young French maid was breathlessly awaiting my arrival. When I asked where she was, I was told she was working, and when I inquired as to her employment, my new friends grinned and told me that she was a prostitute, and that they had arranged for us all to get laid!

With that, they both headed for the door and I followed, pretty much in a state of shock, a condition not helped when I saw standing under the nearest street-light, a little wisp of a woman who age-wise, appeared to be well past her 35th birthday.

The big guy in our threesome announced "I'm first" and headed in her direction, and they both disappeared into the darkness. He wasn't gone long, and upon his return, his buddy, without debating the order or sequence of things, took off for his beach liaison. When he got back, both guys retired to the café for a night-cap, leaving me outside to ponder my predicament.

It's amazing how much time a healthy, heterosexual teen-age male spends thinking and fantasizing when, how and where his first sexual encounter will occur, and with whom, and at age eighteen, I was no exception to the norm. However, not in my wildest dreams (or worst nightmares), did I ever imagine that the event I'd long awaited, would take place outdoors on a windswept beach, on a cold November night, with me third in line for the services of a prostitute old enough to be my mother!

I didn't know it at the time, and at the risk of sounding irreverent, I believe a guardian-angel of sorts, intervened on my behalf. When I failed to join the "lady of the night" on the beach, she came looking for me, and when I pretended not to hear her calling to get my attention, she walked up grumbling away in her native tongue, and shined her flash-light in my face.

Maybe it was the desperation in my eyes, but one look was all she needed. Shaking her head emphatically, she said, "I don't f—k babies," after which life-saving pronouncement, she walked off into the night! For once, I was glad that I looked younger than my years. While this fact had often annoyed me in the past, as a full-time employed teen-ager anxious to be accepted as an adult, at that particular moment, it turned out to be a blessing.

Needless to say, having survived that harrowing experience with my manhood, if not my dignity, intact, I was much relieved next morning to board a cross-Channel steamer for Southhampton. There I caught a train to London, where mercifully, my new acquaintances went their separate ways, never to cross my path again. I took a Tube train to Finsbury Park, and walked the last mile to my home, arriving just as my parents and sisters were preparing for bed. They still had no telephone, so I wasn't able to prepare them for my coming, but when I showed up after an eight month absence, while mightily surprised, they were clearly pleased to see me.

I spent the next few days, visiting friends in the neighborhood and at the CMC, where I'd once worked. Cliff Sparkes treated me to a dinner and I went with my Dad to visit my Aunt Nan. I also had dinner in the West End with a young lady I'd known for several years, but as a perpetually impoverished civilian, I'd never before invited out on a date.

Too soon, my leave was over, and I was back tracing in reverse, the long journey that had begun in Marburg. This again consumed two days of travel time, including an overnight stay at Camp Lucky Strike, where this time I hunkered down in my tent, with no plans for another trip to Etretat.

Unfortunately, what happened, or rather what didn't happen in that obscure coastal town, was relayed to someone at the 178th by one of the Battalion guys I'd traveled with. Soon my escapade was common knowledge, and instead of just being the Company "Limey," for at least a month, I was better known as the "Limey Baby!"

On the morning of December 9, 1945, on the outskirts of Manheim, a city about 100 miles south of Marburg, a large touring sedan bearing General George S. Patton and his aide, General "Hap" Gay, accidentally collided with a U.S. Army truck. Neither vehicle was badly damaged, and Patton's driver, Pfc. Horace Woodring, and Gen. Gay were only badly shaken, but Patton thrown forward in the collision, had struck his head so forcefully against the back of the front seat, that his neck had been broken, leaving him conscious, but paralyzed from his waist on down.

News of the accident, as reported in the "Stars and Stripes," swept like wild-fire through the Army of Occupation. Less than two months earlier, the 4-star General had been relieved as Commander of the Third Army, by Eisenhower, following a series of politically-incorrect comments about the Soviets, and his non-compliance with Ike's directives ordering the de-nazification of all post-war German municipal governments, in the American Zone. Since then, Patton had been Commander of the Fifteenth "paper" Army, charged with overseeing the compilation of a history of the many campaigns, in which he had played such a significant role.

The news that he'd been seriously injured, got mixed reviews. Most veterans of the Third Army, who had revered his leadership, despite his publicized personality flaws, had already left for home. Many in the Third Army who hadn't served under him in combat, saw the accident as the means to force old "Blood and Guts" out of Europe, and into retirement.

I don't think anyone was prepared however, for the news that on December 21, Patton, who had just celebrated his 60th birthday, had succumbed from his injury. Given his rank and illustrious military career, he could have been buried with much pomp and ceremony in Arlington Cemetery. Instead he was laid to rest in a simple grave in the American Cemetery in Luxemburg, beside some 7,000 GIs who had died in battle, under his command.

Patton had been one of my wartime heroes, so I was proud to learn upon arriving in Marburg, that the 178th was a part of his famed Third Army. I for one, mourned his passing, but in retrospect, like many others, I've concluded his death was timely and probably for the best. As the consummate warrior, Patton by temperament, was ill-suited to serve during a "peace" which at the time of his death, had already lapsed into the first stages of the so-called "Cold War," thanks to Stalin's paranoia where the Western Allies were concerned, and his plans to enslave Eastern Germany and the recently liberated countries of Eastern Europe, under Soviet communism and control.

In early 1946, the CO of the 178th, whose name I can't recall, shipped out, and was replaced by a 1st. Lieutenant newly arrived from the States, whose name I'll always remember but have chosen not to reveal, for reasons that will be obvious as I proceed.

He was a diminutive sandy-haired OCS graduate, who during his first week at the 178th, managed to alienate all of his NCOs including me, by his officious manner and obsession with establishing and enforcing new Company rules and regulations.

I was one of his first victims! A month before he arrived, I'd purchased a tiny bottle of Chanel #5 perfume in the Marburg PX. I figured that if I ever got another pass to London and finally met the girl of my dreams, this would make a great ice-breaker.

Unfortunately, clumsy me accidentally dropped and broke the bottle in my room, and despite frequent scrubbing efforts, the bare-boards refused to relinquish their heady and sexy aroma. This of course had not passed unnoticed by our previous CO during his routine inspections, but after questioning me and learning what had happened, he seemed amused, and let the matter drop.

Not so our new Commander. On his first inspection, he entered my room, wrinkled his nose in disgust and barked, "This room smells like a French whore-house," an observation that I wasn't yet able to confirm or deny. Then before I could respond, he turned to our 1st. Sergeant who was accompanying him, and said, "I don't know who authorized this Corporal to have his own room, but I want him out of here and bunking with another Corporal, today."

So it was, thanks to my new CO, Technician 5th Class Tommy Van Sciver and I became room-mates, beginning a friendship which would eventually influence where I'd choose to make my home, after my discharge. He was 23 years old, had been in Army 33 months, and his hometown was Reading, Pennsylvania. He had one sibling, a 17 year old sister named Emily. His natural mother had died from an illness some years earlier and his father had re-married, which gave Tommy and I, something in common.

He had a photo of Emily on his foot-locker, which caught my eye immediately. She was attractive and a senior at Reading High School and when Tommy suggested she and I become pen-pals, I jumped at the opportunity to make contact with an American girl. Soon we were corresponding regularly, and I looked forward to her letters, which always came with a lipstick impression of her lips and the letters "SWAK" on the back of the envelope. This I was told, meant that the letter had been "sealed with a kiss" which in those days, was a typical teen-age girl thing to do.

About a month after my run-in with our new CO, it was my room-mate's turn to feel his wrath. One day, Tommy apparently failed to salute the Lieutenant smartly enough, and was ordered to practice his salute in front of mirror, for 15 minutes a day for week, with me as an observer. He'd been in the Army longer than our CO, and was almost eligible for discharge, so this was a ridiculous and demeaning punishment, and unless the CO planned to personally act as a witness, it wasn't enforceable. As it was, Tommy and I enjoyed a 15 minute break each day, relaxing in our room with our feet up, while he supposedly practiced his salute!

CHAPTER 21

Demotion, Promotion And A Furlough to England

Soon after assuming command, my new CO decided that one important thing lacking at the 178th Reinforcement Company, was a place where transient officers passing through Marburg, could relax and enjoy a few "cold ones" during their evening lay-overs.

To this end, he decided that a small building on our complex, with a few renovations, would ideally serve that purpose. The renovating, which included building a make-shift bar and shelves, was done by German POWs, who might have also been willing to serve as bartenders, except that each evening, they had to be returned to their camp. For our CO, that was not a problem.

On the day that the 178th opened its Transient Officers Club, we enlisted men were suddenly saddled with extra duty one or two evenings a week, working as bar-tenders. Those who usually spent their evenings socializing over a beer, didn't seem to mind, but I rarely imbibed and frankly resented spending my off-duty hours watching others see how much booze they could put away, and still make it out of the door without my assistance.

After several weeks of that, I went to the Lieutenant and asked to be relieved of this duty, or transferred out of the 178th. When he asked why, I told him that I didn't like having to serve as a bartender, when I was supposed to be off-duty. He got red in the face and said he wouldn't relieve me of the duty, nor would he approve a transfer for any man, based on his not liking the duties assigned to him.

With that, my evening work at the TOC continued, along with my usual duties as Company Mail Clerk. One of my tasks was to make a daily run to the Army Postal Unit 872 in Marburg, to deliver the money I'd collected earlier that day, from Postal Order sales.

I'd make the trip in the Company jeep with another guy at the wheel, while I rode "shot-gun" with a .45 pistol strapped to my side. The firearm was deemed a necessity, because most days I'd be holding in my lap, a mail-bag containing thousands of dollars in cash. All my runs were incident free, which was fortunate, because the .45 pistol was one of the few weapons that I didn't get to fire, during my recruit training.

Over time, I got to know the APU personnel including its CO, an affable Lieutenant, who one day out of the blue, asked if I'd be interested in joining his unit. He was having staffing problems, as many of his regulars headed back to the States, for discharge.

Moving to the APU, sounded like the perfect solution to my problems at the 178th, so I responded in the affirmative and the Lieutenant indicated he'd contact my CO, and arrange for the transfer. Two days later, my 1st. Sergeant poked his head into the Mail Room, and asked what the hell I'd done now to piss-off the CO, who'd sent him in person to get "Smither's ass" over to his office, on the double!

I took from the Lieutenant's expression and demeanor, that he had no plans to act favorably on the transfer request he'd received on my behalf. I'm sure that my leaving wouldn't have bothered him had it been his idea, but the fact that I wanted out from under his command, probably offended his ego. To top it off, he accused me of going behind his back to the APU Lieutenant, after he'd refused my earlier transfer request.

I denied that was the case, but he made it clear he didn't believe me, and further indicated that if I did get a transfer, it would be without my Corporal stripes! I responded to that implied threat by saying, "Sir, I have a sister who's been in the British Army for three years, and she's still a private, so my being a private again, wouldn't bother me!"

Unfortunately, that statement really set him off, and he accused me of insubordination, at which point, I invoked my right as an enlisted-man, to request a meeting with the Inspector General. The local IG turned out to be an elderly Colonel, who listened with some apparent empathy to my version of what had transpired, while seemingly displeased that a simple transfer request from one officer to another, had led to his involvement.

Nevertheless, he reminded me that as an enlisted-man, it was my duty to carry out without question, the orders of an officer, and that if I had talked back to my CO in the manner and tone he alleged I had used, that would be insubordination, and demotion in rank would be appropriate and not unreasonable. Having said that, he advised me to live with my demotion, indicating that he in turn would order my CO to process my transfer without delay.

Within 72 hours, the 178th Reinforcement Company was history, except for the following amusing postscript. In the U.S. Army, "chicken-shit" was the term commonly used by enlisted personnel to describe an officer who acted like a martinet. While I was waiting on my transfer, my room-mate Tommy Van Sciver, got his orders to ship home, but before leaving, he vowed that following his discharge, he planned to send our CO a "surprise" package.

Tommy's step-mother worked at the W.T. Grant Store in downtown Reading, which had a department that sold canaries, parakeets and parrots. Through her, he arranged to pick up a day's supply of droppings removed from the bird-cages, which he then packed into a small Hershey's Cocoa can. After wrapping and addressing the package, he drove to Allentown, PA, a 60 mile round-trip to avoid it being mailed with a Reading, PA postmark.

I wasn't at the 178th when the package arrived, but a friend who was on hand, told me that the Lieutenant's explosive reaction to its contents, made it a banner day for everyone in the Company!

When I reported to duty at the APU, minus my Corporal's stripes, my new CO questioned me on the circumstances which had led to this. Without commenting pro or con, he indicated that if I performed to his satisfaction, I could expect to get one stripe back in 30 days, and regain my Corporal rank 30 days later, and I'm happy to report, the Lieutenant delivered on his promise.

My new quarters were located in a two-story house, where most of the APU 872 permanent staff were housed. I shared a room on the second floor with Pfc. Elwyn Olson, a guy my own age from St. Paul, Minnesota, who had just arrived from the States, after finishing his recruit training.

"Ollie" as he liked to be called, was my idea of the perfect room-mate. He was quiet spoken and civilized, unlike certain of our comrades, whose off-duty week-end antics sometimes turned our quarters into a fraternity house, which made me nostalgic at times, for the disciplined environment I'd known during basic training. Alcohol was usually the problem. Those who drank tended to drink too much, and then behaved accordingly.

One of the guys owned a Boxer puppy called Jack, and whenever the beer would start to flow, someone would pour a saucerful for the dog, and he'd lap it up, down to the last drop. One night, semi-inebriated I guess, he fell head-over-paws down the stairs, where he landed apparently uninjured, and slept away the night.

I don't know how long the dog lived enduring that kind of abuse, as his owner was transferred out soon after I arrived, but given how toxic alcohol is to most animals, I suspect that poor Jack's life's span, was destined to be on the short side.

In April, 1946, I celebrated my nineteenth birthday. By then, most ETO veterans had gone home, and their replacements were eighteen year olds, fresh from basic training. When I hit Marburg eight months earlier, I was the youngest member of the 178th Company, and had the least amount of service time, whereas at the APU, this was no longer the case.

I still spent many off-duty hours socializing with Scotty and others from my basic-training days, and occasionally "Ollie" would tag along. None of us were into heavy drinking, unless the number of cups of coffee we consumed at the Red Cross Club, put us in that category. As any GI who recalls the flavor and texture of RC donuts knows, coffee was the key to making them edible!

On one of my downtown jaunts, while indulging in a little friendly horse-play, I dislocated my left shoulder, an injury that I'd suffered to my right shoulder during basic training. An Army ambulance took me to the 280th Station Hospital, where I was examined by a Medical Officer, who tried unsuccessfully to get my shoulder back into place, a process made more difficult by my reaction and resistance to the pain caused by his manipulations.

Somewhat exasperated, he finally had the medic assisting him, place an ether-soaked gauze-pad over my nose, and out I went, thus enabling the Doc to do what had to be done. Nevertheless, his administering an anesthetic within an hour or so of my eating a meal, put me at considerable risk of choking to death, had I aspirated the contents of my stomach, while unconscious.

Luckily, that didn't happen, but I remember coming out from under the ether, violently vomiting over myself and everyone else within range. Perhaps my guardian angel was on hand, once again!

The 280th Station Hospital where I spent the next few days, sat high on a hill outside Marburg, from which vantage point, one could enjoy a panoramic view of the city and the River Lahn which meandered through its center.

While recuperating, I had a steady stream of visitors, including "Jock" White, who was still at the 178th RC. For some reason he gave me a cigar, which I proceeded to smoke, no doubt to prove I was well on the way to recovery. I remember this because I have a photo of me with my arm bandaged, wearing my sling on my head for some reason, clutching the cigar in my right hand!

Six weeks after my release from the hospital, I was pleasantly surprised to learn that I'd been promoted to Sergeant (Technician 4th Grade), which rank I held for the rest of my Army service.

My pen-pal Emily Van Sciver and I still corresponded regularly, and that summer, she asked me where in the States was I going to live, after my discharge. In response, I admitted that while I had no firm plans, I was toying with returning to my place of birth, Cleveland, Ohio, even though I had no relatives or friends located in that city.

Emily's next letter was truly a godsend! Apparently, her brother Tommy, my ex-room-mate, had often talked about my unusual English background and circumstances. When her parents heard that I was returning to the States without any specific location in mind, they had Emily write and invite me to come to Reading, PA, and live with them, until such time as I was sufficiently acclimated and comfortable enough, to strike out on my own.

That kind and unexpected invitation, to become part of their family, sight unseen, ranked right up there with that moment in London, when I claimed my American birthright and was accepted into the U.S. Army. Knowing that I now had a "home-town" that I could call my own, gave my spirits an incredible lift, and from that point on, I began counting off the days to my discharge.

In July, I became eligible for a two-week furlough. I expected my tour of duty in Germany to be over in three or four months, so this was probably my last opportunity to see family and friends in England, before I left for the States. After that, there was no telling when I'd be able to afford to visit them again.

My itinerary was similar to that I followed on my November, 1945 leave. I took a train from Marburg to Frankfurt, where I changed to one going to Paris, but this time, instead of heading to Le Havre, I caught a train to Dieppe. There, I boarded a British Channel ferry to Brighton, where I hopped a train to London, once again surprising my family by showing up unexpectedly.

My older sister Peg had been discharged from the WATS a month earlier, and already had a job. One amusing thing I remember about her, occurred the morning after I arrived home. I was still in bed, and she was leaving for work, she looked in on me, and was surprised to see knotted condoms on my combat boots. When I explained that these functioned as rubber-bands and enabled me to "blouse" my pants-legs, she commented somewhat wryly, that I might be better off if I always used "those things" on my boots, rather than for the purpose they were intended!

On this leave, I knew that I had a lot of final visits to make, and one of my first was to the plant in Chingford, where I'd worked before enlisting. I made the rounds and received a warm welcome everywhere, my approach often heralded by the person who saw me first, yelling, "Here comes our bloody Yank!"

At the Production Office, where I'd put in most of my working days, I was urged to come back for a second visit, to meet a girl who wasn't in that day, who everyone thought I should meet. Her name was June Willard, she was seventeen and described as slim and shapely, with gray-green eyes and dark-blonde hair, which she wore "Veronica Lake" style. Intrigued, I promised to return.

It was good to see my Uncle Bert again. He'd been recently discharged from the British Army, and was back at his old job in Sales. He took me to a local pub where he insisted on introducing me to everyone in sight, then treated me to lunch, while telling me stories about his service in Italy.

My dear old Dad, was anxious to show off his American son to the people he worked with, so I took a day to accompany him to his office. We went to lunch at a nearby restaurant, where to my surprise, his brother Sam was waiting. I appreciated my Dad arranging for this, because I hadn't seen my Uncle Sam in years.

On another day, my sister Mary skipped work, and we took a train to Mill Hill, to visit my Aunt Hett, with whom I'd spent many happy days during my childhood. Little did I know as I kissed her goodbye, that within the year, she would die from medical complications, following a long and painful bout with shingles.

Dad, not to be left out of the family visitations, took a day's leave from his job, so that he could accompany me to Walthamstow, where we spent time with my Aunt Nan and cousin Ivy, who by then was married and recently discharged from the WAAFs.

With all these jaunts, I hadn't spent much time with my step-Mom, so when she hinted that she'd like a day in the West End, I was happy to oblige, never anticipating that our being seen together in public, would trigger the reaction it did.

We started out early one morning, Mom in her Sunday best and me in my spotless uniform. We walked to Finsbury Park Station, found a seat on the crowded commuter train, and began chatting away, just like old times. It was then that I became aware of all the nasty looks we were getting from the other passengers, especially the women, and I quickly figured out the reason for this.

Mom was 53 years old and I was 19, but I looked younger. What everyone in the coach thought they were seeing, was an American GI consorting with an English woman old enough to be his mother, and their disapproval was obvious and universally shared.

Fortunately, I don't think Mom noticed the way people looked at us, and if she had, I suspect she wouldn't have known why, so we went on to have a great day. We walked up and down Bond Street, looking in the fancy shop windows, lunched at a restaurant she selected, and browsed for a while in Harrod's Department Store.

On the ride home, I witnessed the same hostile glances that I'd endured that morning on the way in. Before we got off the train, I almost jumped up and yelled at all those scowling blue-noses, 'Damn it, she IS my Mother," but for her sake, I held my tongue!

The next day, Mom and I and my step-sister Madeline, who was briefly living at home awaiting her husband Ken's discharge from the RAF, enjoyed a pleasant afternoon together chatting and walking around Hampstead Heath. This time, I saw no disapproving glances, perhaps because Madeline, who was 28 years old at the time, was assumed to be my "date," rather than dear old Mom.

I also had lunch with Cliff Sparkes and Ray Marshall. Cliff, probably for medical reasons, had escaped military conscription, but Ray was drafted into the British Army in 1944, and had only recently been discharged. We spent a couple of hours together, reminiscing over some of our more memorable boyhood escapades.

There was a reason that I often ate out. Although the war in Europe had been over for more than a year, conditions in Britain, including food rationing, were much the same. Visitors who stayed for extended period were issued temporary food ration books. My leave was too short to qualify, however, so whatever I ate at home, came out of my family's limited food resources.

As much as I enjoyed all these reunions, after months as a GI bachelor, I was anxious for female company, and was pleased when my sister Peg arranged a date for me with Terry, a girl a year or so older than I, who'd served with her in the WATS.

Terry lived some distance away, so we agreed by telephone to meet on a Saturday afternoon, at the Leicester Square Tube ticket office, and from there, go to a movie. Terry had seen a photo of me, and as there weren't that many Yanks in London anymore, she figured I'd be easy to spot. Peg described her as dark-haired, attractive and tiny, maybe 5'5" if she wore her spiked heels.

We both arrived on time, recognized each other, and walked out of the station to stand in line outside one of the cinemas in the Square, waiting for the matinee opening. We were chatting away, doing pretty well as blind dates go, when suddenly a U.S. Navy jeep pulled up alongside, and two white-helmeted members of the Shore Patrol jumped out, and asked me what I was doing in London.

It was unusual for Navy MPs to hassle an Army guy, but I let them see my travel orders, and just as I thought I was home free, they pronounced me "out of uniform" and indicated that they'd have to take me in to their Duty Officer. The charge was based on my having one button on my jacket unbuttoned!

I tried reasoning with them, pointing out that I was on a date, and even introducing Terry, but to no avail. Under the curious eyes of scores of spectators, they put me in the jeep, leaving Terry confused and wondering what she'd gotten into. As we took off, I called to her to wait, saying that I'd be back soon, although at the time I wasn't at all sure that I would be.

To make a long story short, earlier that day in Surrey, a GI in custody on a serious charge, had escaped from the MPs, and was presumed to have fled to London. As a result, all U.S. Army men in London were being picked up for questioning. After 20 minutes at the Navy brig in Russell Square, I was released to find my own way back to Leicester Square, where to my surprise, a sad-faced Terry was still waiting for me, outside the cinema.

By then, the movie we'd hoped to see, had already started, so we walked around for a while, and when we found a restaurant that looked promising, we stopped and had dinner. Despite the trauma of seeing her date "arrested" and hauled away, I think Terry enjoyed our time together as much as I did, but given my limited time in London, and the visitations I had yet to make, we parted with no plans to see each other again.

Since entering the Army, I'd continued my correspondence with Jim and Florrie Grenfell, my surrogate parents during my days as a school-boy evacuee. It had been two years since my last visit to their farm, so one morning, I caught a train out of Paddington to Truro, Cornwall. From there, I rode a bus to a point about a mile from the Grenfell's farm, and walked the rest of the way.

Jim and Florrie were surprised and happy to see me, but the next morning after we'd eaten breakfast, they had to leave to finish getting their second harvest of newly-mown hay, raked up and stacked. So as to spend time with them, I pitched in and helped. With no change of clothes, the best I could do was to take off my shirt and jacket, and worked stripped to the waist.

The others on the hay-rick were all farmers, whose waking hours were spent outside in all kinds of weather, and they had the tanned leathery skin to prove it. My decision to join them for five hours under the July sun, without applying any sun-tan or screening lotion, was a big mistake. I returned to London that night, sun-burned to a lobster-red, a condition first painful and then unbearably itchy, that bugged me for the rest of my leave.

Back in London, I followed through on my promise to pay a second visit to the CMC plant in Chingford, so as to meet the girl with the 'Veronica Lake" hairdo. June was indeed as attractive as I'd been told, and after we started to talk, I realized that I knew her Dad, who also worked at CMC, as a truck driver.

She was somewhat shy and reserved at first, perhaps because I was the first American serviceman she's actually met, but the fact that I'd once slaved away in her office, helped break the ice. With very little leave time remaining, I had to work fast, so I made a date with her, for the last Sunday of my leave.

Naturally, we had to rely on public transportation, and to save time, she agreed to take a bus from Chingford to Finsbury Park. There we met, and together rode the Tube to the West End, where we ate lunch, before heading to a movie matinee. While I can't recall the restaurant, I'll always remember the movie, "The Best Years of Our Lives," which remains one of my all-time favorites.

There was enough time after the movie, to escort June to her home in Chingford, and get a late bus back to Finsbury Park. I was surprised by how much I wanted to see her again, but all I could do under the circumstances, was to promise I'd write, and she in turn, vowed to answer my every letter. With that, we parted.

The next day, I again said goodbye to my family, and started back to Germany. If my various transportation needs had all fallen perfectly into place, it would have been a two-day trip. However, rather than risk arriving late and being declared AWOL due to an unexpected delay or missed connection, I budgeted three leave days as travel time. Little did I know, that fourteen rather unpleasant days would pass, before I arrived back in Marburg.

The Brighton train from London left on time, and when I arrived, the cross-Channel steamer was waiting and taking on passengers.

Once aboard, I went below to the ship's café, and ate a hearty lunch, which turned out to be a big mistake!

I'd already crossed the Channel four times without suffering anything more than occasional nausea. Given the nasty reputation of that narrow strip of ocean, that almost qualified me as a certified old salt, but my luck was about to run out. The day was overcast and blustery, elements which when combined with the usual Channel choppiness, had the ferry prancing at its moorings, a fair warning that lunch should have been avoided, altogether.

From the moment that we left the shelter of the breakwater, the ship assumed the characteristics of an out of control roller-coaster, and thirty minutes out, I was being violently sea-sick with most of the other hearty-lunch crowd, in the below-deck restroom. Soon the place was a disgusting mess, which in and of itself, was not conducive to calming and settling an upset stomach. As those who've suffered from the agonies of sea-sickness know, there are two stages associated with the malady. First you think you're going to die, and after a while, you hope you do!

As I staggered off the ship at Dieppe, I couldn't help thinking about the poor souls who two years earlier on D-Day, landed on the beaches of Normandy, while under fire. They had circled for hours, standing shoulder to shoulder in their heaving and rolling LCIs. How they were able to do battle, nauseated and dehydrated from bouts of sea-sickness, is beyond my comprehension.

The bumpy, rocking motion of the train out of Dieppe, did little to calm my tortured insides. When I learned in Paris that my train connection to Frankfurt was a "red eye," I was actually relieved, because the eight-hour delay gave my system a chance to recover. By the time I boarded the train that evening, except for a massive headache, I was feeling pretty much my old self.

I shared the train compartment with seven other GIs, who when I joined them, were already boisterous from having passed around a bottle of cognac, waiting for the train to get underway. I'd never tasted cognac, so when the bottle got to me, I declined, saying that I didn't drink "straight booze."

Unfortunately, that excuse didn't fly. One of the guys produced a canteen-cup and a can of grape-fruit juice. He filled the cup two thirds of the way with juice, topped it off with a gigantic shot of cognac, handed me the concoction, and invited me to drink. I knew then, it was going to be a long night, and outnumbered seven to one, I caved in to peer-pressure, and began to chug-a-lug.

That was my second big mistake of the day! Within minutes, the cognac kicked in and for the first time in my life, I was drunk. It was a sensation that initially I didn't much care for, and then soon learned to hate, when my long suffering stomach reacting to the alcohol, signaled that a repeat of its morning performance was imminent. However, this time I was on a train without the convenience or availability of a rest-room facility.

I lunged for the compartment door, pulled on the strap that lowered the window, and stuck my head outside, just before my stomach erupted. Unfortunately, in my drunken stupor, I faced in the wrong direction and threw-up into the wind, and much of what I'd expelled, blew back into the compartment, a situation not well-received by my travel companions, several of whom discussed tossing me off the speeding train, before cooler heads prevailed.

I can't remember ever being more miserable or embarrassed, but on the positive side, the experience was so memorably unpleasant, that over the past 57 years, I've never again imbibed to excess, and I thank my lucky stars that the one time that I let alcohol make an ass of me, I was miles away from friends and family.

Dawn was breaking as we pulled into Frankfurt, and my connection to Marburg, wasn't scheduled to depart for several hours. I'd been on my feet for 24 hours, and while my stomach was on the mend, I still nursed a stubborn headache. I needed a place to lie down, and an elderly German porter, who spoke some English, led me to a nearby passenger-coach, and suggested that I use one of its seats as a bed. I told him I had to be on the next train to Marburg, and he promised to return and wake me, for which courtesy I gave him two packs of Camels, and he walked away happy.

With my duffel-bag serving as a pillow, I fell into a deep sleep. At some time during my slumber I apparently put my arms up and rested my head on my hands, and while in that position, I dislocated my right arm. I recall waking up, but not being able to move, without causing excruciating pain to my shoulder.

I definitely needed assistance, so I began yelling for help, but no one heard me. Not until my porter friend appeared to make his promised wake-up call, was my predicament discovered. He rushed off and came back with an MP, and together they got me on my feet, and I walked to the main platform, where I sat for almost an hour, before an ambulance arrived to take me to the U.S. Army 297th General Hospital in Frankfurt.

By then, my arm had been out of its socket for more than two hours, and was really hurting. I hoped that a doctor would treat me without delay, but that didn't happen. Instead, I laid on an operating table for another 30 minutes, while five very young doctors, accompanied by an older hospital attendee, offered their various opinions on the best way to relieve my condition.

I figured the young Docs were recently inducted residents, who had arrived at the hospital at the same time as I did, because instead of wearing "scrubs" or white coats, they were still in their dress uniforms. This was probably their first "rounds" at their new hospital, and I happened to be the unlucky patient!

Finally, when each had examined me and been heard from, my errant humerus was popped back into place, this time with no adverse reactions to the ether, because thanks to the English Channel and the French cognac, my stomach was mercifully 100% empty.

I spent a week at the 297th before being released to return to my unit in Marburg, where I was relieved to learn that my CO had been notified of my whereabouts. The entire time I was in the hospital, I'd worried about being falsely classified as AWOL.

However, someone at my unit had inexplicably concluded that I would be hospitalized for an extended period, so they had my foot-locker shipped to the 297th. Unfortunately, it must have arrived after I left the hospital, and no one there apparently saw fit to return it to me, as I never saw it again. Everything I owned was in that locker, including my extra GI clothes, but the most important item lost, was my "Soldiers Deposits" book.

This book was a record of how much of my Army pay I'd saved since entering the service, which amount I'd counted on receiving as a lump-sum, at the time of my discharge. When I reported the loss to my CO, he was sympathetic, but warned that without the book, I might have to wait until after my discharge, and then make a claim to the Army Finance Office, to get whatever savings the Army's records showed were due to me.

But any despondency stemming from the loss of my foot-locker, was quickly dispelled by the news that I could expect to be shipped back to the States in late September. There I'd be given a 30 day leave, before being discharged in early November, and I was determined not to let anything interfere with my life-long dream, an event which then was only 60 days away. That meant staying 100% in step with whatever duties were assigned to me, and being extra careful where my unpredictable shoulders were concerned.

Over a period of twelve months, I'd dislocated my right shoulder twice, and my left shoulder once, and been advised by the doctor who treated me at the 297th, to submit to an operation on my twice injured shoulder, which he said would prevent this from happening again. He pointed out that having the surgery in an Army hospital, wouldn't cost me anything and I'd be eligible for lifetime service-connected, partial-disability compensation.

Somehow, being deemed "partially disabled for life" at age nineteen, didn't appeal to me regardless of what the compensation might have been, so I declined the operation. For the record, I dislocated my left shoulder for the second time in 1959, and in 1970, dislocated my right shoulder for the third time!

During those last two months in Germany, June and I were writing to each other at least twice a week, and these were not the "pen-pal" letters I was exchanging with Emily. We shared thoughts and feelings for one another that were unusually warm and personal, considering how little time we'd actually spent together.

I guess this was a case of "absence making the heart grow fonder" except that it made no real sense, given that we both knew that there was no possible way we'd see each other again, before I left for the States. Nevertheless, in my youthful ardor, I promised June I'd return to London to see her sometime after my discharge, despite having no idea how or when I could do that.

Once I knew when I'd be leaving Germany, I let the Van Sciver family know, and their response was to assure me again, that I'd be welcome in their home at any time. Emily wrote to say that her brother Tommy had gotten married and moved out of the house, and his vacant room was ready for my arrival. That sounded pretty terrific, because at no time during the seventeen years that I'd lived in England, did I ever have a room of my own.

I was often needled by a guy at the APU that I never liked, about my plans to settle in Reading, Pennsylvania. He kept asking me why a "Limey" would want to live in "Kraut-town," his pet name for Reading, because of its large ethnic German population.

He'd been stationed at Fort Indiantown Gap about 40 miles away from Reading, before being shipped overseas, and must have spent time exploring the town's seamier enclaves. Despite my obvious disinterest, he insisted on telling me time and again, that most of Reading's brothels were located on Cherry Street, and that "Dutch Mary" was the town's premier Madam!

My friend Scotty, and those stationed in Marburg who'd enlisted when I did, while living in Europe, were also scheduled to leave Germany sometime in September. Most wanted to be discharged in the States, but there were two brothers from Lancashire who were both married with children, who wanted to return to England, and I'm not sure where the Army processed them, for discharge.

On one of my visits downtown, I ran into McCauley, a buddy from basic-training I hadn't seen in ages, and was surprised to note that he was now a 2nd Lieutenant. I guess my jaw dropped when I saw his gold-bars, but I quickly recovered and gave him a perfect salute, which he returned with a somewhat embarrassed grin.

McCauley was born in the States of Irish parents, and had grown up in Eire. At the time of his enlistment, he was attending or had just graduated from a university in Dublin. While stationed in Marburg, he accepted an opportunity to be commissioned, and had just returned from OCS training. He and I had always gotten along, and when he saw my three stripes, he tried hard to sell me on signing up to also become a "90 day wonder."

I reminded him that I lacked his level of education, but apparently at that time, the officer ranks had been so depleted by the post-war demobilization, that the Army had lowered its OCS requirements, particularly for NCOs willing to sign up for a five year hitch. As much as this unexpected opportunity to earn a commission appealed to me, I was two months away from returning to the States, and nothing could top that. So, McCauley and I shook hands, I snapped him another perfect salute, and we went our separate ways.

I've often wondered about the choice I made that day. What if I'd decided to go to OCS, gotten my first choice of assignments, an infantry outfit, and in time earned a silver bar or two? Four years into my hitch, the Korean War began, and at age 23, I'd have been involved in my second war, but this time as a combatant, not as a passive civilian. Would I have survived that bloody conflict, unscathed as before, or been one of its tens of thousands of casualties? Perhaps my guardian-angel was there for me again, when I made that fateful decision.

CHAPTER 22

Farewell Marburg, Hello Reading, Pennsylvania

Finally, the great moment arrived! I was the lone guy shipping out that day from the 872nd APU, and just about everyone turned out to give the "Limey" a royal send-off. At the Marburg station, it was like a 2941 RC reunion, so many familiar faces were in the crowd, waiting to board the train.

Our destination was Bremerhaven, a German port on the North Sea, about 200 miles to the north-west. When we arrived later that day, the U.S. Army processing facility was jammed with military personnel of both genders, all heading back to the States.

During the war, the site had been an important German naval base. It boasted a huge cavernous hangar, originally built to house the Third Reich's Zeppelins, when those famous dirigibles were still operational. The U.S. Army now used it as a make-shift theater, where pre-discharge orientation meetings were held during the day, and movies were shown to the transient troops, after dark.

Two hangar stories are worth telling. On our first day, 500 of us assembled there to receive the "F-word" lecture, the Army's good faith effort to prepare our GI mouths for civilized ears back in the States, awaiting our home-coming.

I don't know how it was in the Womens Army Corps (WACs), or for that matter, whether wholesale cussing was a habit practiced by "officers and gentlemen," but during my time in the enlisted ranks, the "F-word" tended to be part of every GI"s vocabulary, as a pre-fix to nouns and verbs alike!

Clearly, the lecture was something everyone needed, but there was a least one exception in our midst. As the Marburg contingent left the hangar, joking about the foul-mouthed characters we'd apparently morphed into, Scotty quietly asked whether anyone had ever heard him swear. Amazingly, we had to admit, that in the many months we'd known and enjoyed his company, no one could remember ever hearing Scotty cuss, which had to be some kind of unprecedented record, in the annals of the U.S. Army.

The other hangar event which sticks in my mind, occurred on our last evening in Bremerhaven. A movie was scheduled and the hangar was filled to capacity with GIs and WACs, all wound-up about going home. As we waited for the show to begin, someone inflated a condom and tossed into the air.

Others followed suit and within minutes, hundreds of condoms had been launched, and were being batted around the hangar. These flying objects were soon joined by scores of inflated surgical gloves, no doubt provided by the medics in the audience. When the movie started, and the airborne rubber-goods fell back to earth and were popped, their collective demise sounded like the rattle of a pint-size machine-pistol, on automatic!

We were two days at the camp, before being trucked to the docks, where we boarded the "Lehigh Victory," a one-stack vessel that looked too small to accommodate the troops passing up its gang-plank, or large enough to comfortably master the mighty seas that lay between us and New York, more than 3,500 nautical miles away.

The "Lehigh" was a so-called "Victory" ship, designed towards the end of World War II, to replace the "Liberty" ships, the more famous product of Henry J. Kaiser, one of America's industrial geniuses of that period. Kaiser pioneered assembly-line, mass-production methods then unheard of in the ship-building trade, and during the war, he produced 30% of the USA's much needed cargo ships, and 50% of its small aircraft carriers.

The "Liberty" ship was a copy of the venerable British tramp-steamer, except that its hull was welded rather than riveted. This made it less expensive and greatly speeded its production, so that by the war's end, Kaiser could turn out one ship a day! The vessel was 441 feet long, 57 feet wide, weighed 14,000 tons and carried up to 10,000 tons of cargo.

The Victory ships came later and were essentially improved models of the Liberty class, with a greater speed and cargo capacity, and longer life expectancy. I'm not sure how many troops were aboard the "Lehigh Victory" when it left Bremerhaven and steamed slowly down the River Weser estuary and into the North Sea, but I'm certain it was filled to capacity.

Each hold had been converted to carry troops instead of cargo, by simply adding racks of narrow canvas cots, stacked on top of one another, four bunks high. There was barely room to move in the aisles between the racks, and we far outnumbered the latrine and salt-water wash-facilities, a real problem during the first few days, when most of the troops were afflicted with sea-sickness.

Three times a day at chow-time, we stood in line for hours. The procession snaked its way from our bunk area, up two flights of steps, out onto the open deck, traversing its length before heading down the steps at the other end, to the mess area. From there, we'd carry our full mess-kits to our bunks, or weather permitting, we'd go back on deck, and eat in the fresh air.

From the North Sea, the "Lehigh" steamed into the English Channel, where we saw an unusual sight, two halves of a ship similar to our own, floating some distance apart. One of our ship's crew told us these were the remains of a Liberty ship that had broken in two during a severe Channel storm.

He never explained how the two sections, rather than sinking, had continued to float, informing us instead that breaking apart was not uncommon for ships with welded rather than riveted hulls, which really made me feel good about the long voyage which lay ahead!

It took 24 hours for the "Lehigh" to bounce its slow way through the always choppy Channel. Having spent most of my life under the Union Jack, I was on deck to watch the coast of England fade into the distance. Once off Land's End, the long Atlantic swells took over, making a noticeable difference to the ship's motion, a change which triggered a new bout of sea-sickness, just as I thought the worst had passed. Fortunately, 24 hours later, my sea-legs returned, and I was able to rejoin the endless chow-line, with some degree of intestinal confidence.

In some respects, the fact that we were forced to spend so many hours a day lining up for food, was probably a blessing of sorts. We were transient troops with no duties to perform, on a ship with absolutely no facilities to help us pass the time.

Crap-games, card-games and shooting-the-bull on the crowded deck, were our only forms of entertainment. Anyone who had thought to bring aboard a bunch of used paper-backs, could have made a small fortune peddling them to book-starved guys like me. For baseball fans, the 1946 World Series was in full swing, and broadcasts of the game were picked up on the ship's radio-receiver, and piped over its PA system, for those who were interested.

Normally, a cargo-ship like ours, bound from Bremerhaven to the Port of New York, would cross the North Atlantic on a direct south-westerly course, a trip that would take nine or ten days. However, on the third day out, our ship's Captain got on the PA system and announced that to avoid a "disturbance" that lay directly in our path, we'd be heading due south for several hundred miles to a point on latitude with the Azores, before turning onto a north-west course directly into New York.

That decision while probably appropriate, added many tiresome days to the voyage. According to my Army separation papers, I was at sea a total of 20 days.

Finally, on the morning of October 2nd, I caught my first glimpse of the Statue of Liberty, and saw the huge sign on the New York coastline, which read, "Welcome Home-Well Done." After an absence of more than eighteen years, I was home at last!

After disembarking, we marched off the pier to a railway-siding, where a string of passenger coaches hitched to a Jersey Central locomotive waited to take us to Fort Dix, New Jersey, the last leg of our journey. I suspect that most GIs who passed through Dix, were not as impressed with its accommodations as I was, but compared to the Army facilities I'd been used to in England, France and Germany, they seemed almost luxurious.

As I remember it, the separation process took three or four days. We were given physicals and asked about any service-related injuries or medical problems. My records of course, documented the treatments and hospitalizations associated with my various shoulder dislocations, and a Medical Officer asked whether I wished to seek any corrective surgery, before being discharged.

He indicated that surgery in an Army hospital was a necessary "pre-condition" if I ever wanted to claim service-connected disability compensation, and I again declined, as I had when previously faced with that decision at the Army hospital in Frankfurt. I viewed my shoulder injuries as accidental, non-life threatening events, and I wasn't comfortable with the idea of accepting compensation, as if I'd been injured by enemy action.

With respect to my finances, I was relieved to learn that despite not being able to produce my Soldiers Deposits book, the Army's records reflected the balance as I remembered it, which meant that I'd receive the full lump-sum, at the time of my discharge.

While the final paper-work was being processed, we were given 24 hour passes, and Scotty and I took a train into New York City for some sightseeing. While there, we rode the subway to Brooklyn and visited with Irving Erdman, a guy who'd been stationed with me at the 178th RC. Since his return home, Irv had gotten engaged and insisted on driving us to his fiancee's house, after which he took us on a "Cook's tour" of his favorite Brooklyn haunts.

Finally the day came when Scotty and I left Fort Dix and parted company, he going north to Niagara Falls, New York, and I heading west to Reading, Pennsylvania. We'd been close friends for almost eighteen months, and were now about to begin entirely new lives in towns located some 400 miles apart. We promised to stay in touch, and went our separate ways.

It was a short bus ride from Fort Dix to Philadelphia. There I made my way to the Reading Railroad Terminal at 12th and Market Streets, and bought a ticket on the Pottsville train, which I'd been told would make two stops in Reading. Hearing for the first time, the mournful wail of the locomotive as it raced through the Pennsylvania countryside, that distinctive, uniquely American sound that I remembered from Hollywood movies, I got goose-bumps!

It was early evening on a clear crisp day in October, when I got off the train at Reading's Outer Station, dropped a nickel into the public telephone, and called Emily to announce my arrival. Within minutes, her Dad picked me up in his big 1936 Buick, and drove me to 604 North 2nd Street, where Emily and her step-mom greeted me warmly, as if I were family. From that moment, until the day that I moved on, they always made me feel at home.

The Van Scivers were a typical working-class family, not unlike my own. Tom the father, was my Dad's age, and like Dad, was a veteran of the First World War. He was employed as a steel-worker, at the Parish Steel plant in Reading.

His wife Bebe, was the sister of his deceased first wife. When their Dad remarried, Emily and her brother Tommy continued to call Bebe "Aunt," even though she was then their step-mom. Bebe worked at the W.T. Grant department store located in Reading's Penn Square. Emily, who'd graduated from Reading High School that summer, was not yet gainfully employed.

The family lived in a three-storey row-home which at that time, was probably close to 40 years old. In the winter, it was heated by a coal-furnace, and in the summer, open windows and electric fans were relied upon to cool the inside. Like every other house on the block, it boasted a front porch on which family members would congregate each evening to pass the time, while socializing with the next door neighbors, and others on the block.

Directly across the street, was a dairy operation managed by my ex-Army buddy Tommy. This guaranteed that I'd see him often, even though he was married and no longer living at home.

Within walking distance, were a number of "Mom and Pop" stores, which carried on their shelves and on their meat, fish and dairy cases and produce counters, a full range of homemaker needs, and if one wanted to shop at home, delivery trucks carrying the same items, plied their wares daily, on a door-to-door basis.

A trolley from downtown ran past our house, up North 2nd Street through Reading's north-west section, a "loop" route which eventually took it back to Penn Square. This made getting to and from the business, shopping and movie district, quick and easy. Above all, my new neighborhood was a safe and civilized place, where I could walk after dark, without fear or apprehension.

One piece of Americana that took some getting used to, was the sound of police-car and ambulance sirens. In wartime England, such vehicles signaled their approach with a clanging bell, while sirens warned that an air-raid was imminent. After I arrived in Reading, whenever I was awakened at night by the sound of a police or ambulance siren, my heart would race and my hands and legs would tremble, just as they had during the Luftwaffe and V-1 attacks that I'd endured in London.

Today, such a reaction would be viewed as classic "post-traumatic stress disorder" syndrome. Fortunately for me, the problem was short-lived. Within six months, the sound of a siren, day or night, no longer triggered any unpleasant wartime memories.

I arrived in Reading with no civilian clothes, so on the second day, accompanied by Emily and Aunt Bebe, I went downtown for the first time, and purchased a basic wardrobe; underwear, socks, shirts and ties, shoes, two sports jackets and slacks to match. I was still in the Army, so for a couple of weeks, I alternated between my civvies and my uniform, until November 3, 1946, the date that my discharge from the U.S. Army, became effective.

As much as I appreciated being a civilian again, my time in the Army was a positive and valuable experience. As a boy, I was fascinated by anything and everything relating to the military. When I volunteered to serve at age seventeen, I believed then as I do now, in the sentiment voiced by General George S. Patton, that "The highest obligation and privilege of citizenship, is that of bearing arms for one's country."

When I departed Fort Dix, I had the grand sum of $527.95 to my name, consisting of $300 mustering-out pay, $224.00 Soldiers Deposits, and a travel allowance of $3.95, to get me from the base to Reading. I've long forgotten what my initial wardrobe cost, but Aunt Bebe insisted that I open a savings account at her bank, the Reading Trust Company and deposit the balance of my remaining funds. With very little cash in my pocket, I knew I had to get a job without delay!

The first order of business, was to sign up at the Unemployment Office. As an honorably discharged veteran, I was eligible to receive $20 a week for 52 weeks, under a federal government program commonly referred to as the "52-20 Club," and within three weeks, I had collected my first check.

At that point, I'd been a guest of the Van Scivers for more than a month, and while they had never broached the subject, I was anxious to begin making a contribution to the family income, as I had done when living at home in London. I offered to pay Aunt Bebe $10 a week, half of my unemployment check, which she accepted and clearly appreciated.

Aunt Bebe's work-day at Grant's Department Store ended at 5:00pm. Every evening around that time, Tom would drive into Penn Square, to pick her up and bring her home, and usually I'd ride along, as a way of getting myself better acquainted with my new hometown.

One day, we started out much earlier than usual, so that he could show me the Tower and Pagoda, two of Reading's famous landmarks. Both were located high above the city on Skyline Drive, from which lofty vantage point, I was amazed to see how much Reading and the Schuylkill River, resembled Marburg and the River Lahn.

While in Germany, I had often wondered whether the "SWAK" letters I'd received from Emily, were a precursor to a budding romance, one destined to flower when we finally met. However, it didn't take long to realize that the necessary chemistry wasn't there for either one of us. We always got along, but ours was a brother and sister relationship, never anything else.

In December, I was surprised to receive a phone call from Scotty, who at the time, was visiting a relative on Long Island. Before heading home, he took a bus into Reading and stayed for two days, as another welcome guest of the Van Scivers. After three months in the States, we both had opinions and reactions to share.

Scotty indicated that he and his father were getting along pretty well, considering they'd lived apart most of Scotty's life, and thanks to his Dad, a long time management employee at the Union Carbide plant in Niagara Falls, he had a job waiting for him at UC, when he returned.

Knowing that my best friend was poised to become a wage-earning, tax-paying citizen, increased the discomfort I felt each time I picked up my 52-20 check and confessed to the Unemployment Office clerk, that I still didn't have a job. While only nineteen years old, if I counted my Army service, I'd been employed full-time for five years, and I guess goofing off for two months, was troubling to my so-called "Protestant work-ethic" heritage.

Typically, the folks at the unemployment Office focused on my pre-service employment as a Factory Shop Clerk and my military occupation classification Mail Clerk at time of discharge, in their efforts to assist in my job search. However, I wasn't that anxious to get work in either of my previous job classifications.

Then during the last week of December, I saw a "Male Help Wanted" advertisement in the local newspaper for "Insurance Career Opportunities" at the American Casualty Company's Home Office, then located at 6th and Washington Streets in Reading.

The ad specifically targeted recently discharged veterans, by trumpeting the fact that under the company's trainee program, ex-servicemen could secure on-the-job financial assistance under the new Federal initiative known as the "GI Bill of Rights."

This sounded like a great opportunity to me, so off I went to ACCO's Home Office, to see whether I had the necessary qualifications. While hopeful, I was apprehensive, concerned that my formal schooling in wartime England that ended before I turned fifteen, would hurt my chances if all the other applicants had graduated from an American high school.

The company's interview process was conducted after its regular office hours, and the evening that I showed up, for some reason, William Deak, its Vice President of Claims, was doing the honors. Mr Deak was a rotund, ruddy-faced individual, somewhat gruff but quick to smile, who after perusing my application, appeared less concerned in my schooling and more interested in my background, quizzing me at length as to why I grew up in England, and what it was like to live in London, during the war.

In fact, his only comment after I'd confessed that I couldn't produce a high school diploma, was that anyone at age seventeen who could hold down a fulltime job that required him to supervise and direct the daily activities of two other teen-agers, was certainly qualified to be a trainee underwriter! With that, he approved my application, and asked when I could come aboard.

I started work at the American Casualty Company the first week of January, 1947, as an Underwriter-Trainee under the GI Bill job-training program. There was a simple economic reason why so many employers at that time, enthusiastically entered into this new partnership with the Feds. It saved them big bucks!

I don't know what ACCO would have paid a non-veteran trainee, but to compete in the insurance labor market, it certainly would have been more costly to the Company, than it was to hire a veteran.

My starting salary was $165.00 a month. Of that amount, the Company contributed $90.00, and the government $75.00. Over the next two years, ACCO was required to gradually raise its share of my monthly income, so that at the end of the two year training period, the government contribution was down to zero, and my salary from the Company, was $200.00 a month.

On the first day as I rode the trolley to work, I was excited about starting a new job in a reputable business, that could offer me a long-term career opportunity. Unfortunately, I soon concluded that ACCO's Vice President of Underwriting to whom I reported, was more interested in getting another warm body to do the "grunt" work, than making sure that I was properly introduced to the basics of insurance and the rudiments of underwriting.

While I've long forgotten the guy's name, I remember him well. He had been discharged from the Army as a Colonel, having served out the war in Washington, DC, in a highly placed administrative position in the War Department.

He was a short, balding man in his forties, with a "Humpty-Dumpty" figure. On occasion, he'd walk through the Underwriting Department, but rarely did he acknowledge with a word or a smile, those who worked there. With that persona, and because everyone knew he still liked to be called "Colonel," he was known as "old satchel-ass" by the younger rank and file employees!

I was given a desk and a chair, and an Automobile Rule and Rate Manual, and essentially left to my own devices. Insurance manuals are designed for reference purposes, not for one's reading pleasure. Without any education or background in insurance, the manual I pored over on that first day, might as well have been printed in a foreign language, for all the sense that it made.

My entire first week, was more of the same, endless hours of studying manuals, with the monotony sometimes relieved when I was assigned to work with another person, proof-reading printer's type-set proofs of various policies and endorsements, before these were run-off in ACCO's in-house print-shop.

As if those activities weren't tedious enough, the second week I functioned as a "rate-checker." Armed with a manual, I checked the accuracy of the math in the rate calculations made by the underwriters, before their draft Declarations Pages went to the Typing Department for final policy preparation.

Compared to the tasks and the supervisory level of responsibility that I'd handled in my London job before entering the Army, what I was doing at ACCO was boring, and offered no challenge. Most disappointing was the total absence of any Company organized insurance educational sessions. I had assumed that such would be the keystone of any bona-fide training program, particularly one operated in partnership with the U.S. government and partially subsidized by taxes.

On the other hand, with respect to my personal life, I only had one complaint. By then, I'd made the acquaintance of several young women who I was seeing casually on a regular basis, but in the dating game, being known as a guy without "wheels" was a definite disadvantage, and I knew it was time to purchase an automobile.

Based on my very limited capital resources, the car I decided I could afford, was a 1933 Plymouth "rumble-seat" Coupe which cost $125. Considering that it had already been on the road for 14 years, its exterior and interior condition was surprisingly good, but the engine always advertised its age, with an embarrassing plume of blue exhaust-smoke, that followed me everywhere I drove.

Despite my continued frustration with my daily routine at ACCO, my Underwriting Department associates were always ready to assist when asked, and fun to work with. It was during one of my proof-reading assignments that I became friends with Syd Reber, who worked in ACCO's print-shop. Syd, who was married, was seven years older than I and lived in Laureldale, a Reading suburb.

We became good friends, eating lunch together in a "greasy-spoon" cafe at 7th and Franklin Streets, memorable not for its cuisine but for Frank its proprietor, who must have tipped the scales at 300lbs, at a time when obesity was a rare affliction.

Often on a Saturday, I'd spend the afternoon with Syd, the two of us chatting away about this and that, while he washed, polished and tinkered with his mint-condition 1932 Chevy Coupe. He had served with the 80th Infantry Division in the ETO, so we had plenty of Army stories to share and laugh about. We definitely enjoyed each other's company, and after a while, I began to think of him as the brother I never had.

After enduring three months of reading manuals and checking the math calculations of others, without any educational effort being expended by the Company on my behalf as an Underwriter-Trainee, I began scanning the Help Wanted ads in the local newspaper, hoping to find something more to my liking.

In those days, newspapers listed employment opportunities by gender, in separate Male and Female sections. One day, not having found any male jobs of interest, out of curiosity I went to the other section. There I spotted the following, "Young attractive woman wanted to run a photo studio. No experience necessary."

In Germany, after acquiring my first camera, I had enjoyed many hours of taking photos and experimenting with different lens settings, so a photo-studio position appealed to me. I decided on the spot to apply for the job, figuring I had nothing to lose.

Applicants were instructed to write to a designated P.O. Box. In my letter, in addition to my name, age, address and telephone number, I indicated I was a discharged Army veteran "with all the specified qualifications, except for the gender!"

I probably never expected to get a response, but two days later, I received a call from Mr. Tuck, manager of the Kay Jewelers store in Reading, one of a chain of stores throughout the States. The Kay company at that time, was in the process of expanding its retail jewelry operations, to include in-store photo-studios.

Tuck confessed up front that a man answering a Female Help Wanted advertisement, had piqued his curiosity, and although he still leaned towards hiring a woman, if I was serious about wanting the position, he was willing to give me an interview.

The Kay store was located on Penn Street, not far from ACCO's office, so the next day during my lunch hour, I met with Mr. Tuck, and to make a long story short, he offered me the job, provided that I'd be available to attend a three-day training course in Washington, DC, which the Kay Company had scheduled for newly-hired photo-studio operators.

The position paid only $30 a week, which was less than my combined ACCO salary and G.I. Bill subsidy. However, thanks to the unprofessional way the company was conducting its Underwriter-Trainee program, I'd pretty much lost interest in the insurance business, so I accepted Tuck's offer.

Upon returning to ACCO, I went to my supervisor Walter Stump and gave him a week's notice of my plans to leave. Walt was surprised and disappointed, and when he learned the nature of my new job, it was clear from his expression, that he thought I was crazy!

In response to his asking why I was leaving after only three months, I said that I was disappointed, having been hired under an Underwriter-Trainee program, only to find that ACCO had no such organized program, and that the rate-checking, proofreading and other clerical tasks that I performed during those three months, were in my opinion "women's work" and should have been assigned accordingly.

Voiced in today's society, such an opinion would be blatantly sexist, and I'd be the first to agree! In 1947 however, all work was rigidly categorized by gender, and most clerical duties were performed by women, and that was the point I was trying to make.

The truth is, growing up as I did, listening at the kitchen table to the the woman's point of view on every subject, as voiced over the years by two mothers and three sisters, I suspect that I was programmed to understand and sympathize with "women's equal rights," even before the cause and its issues got off the ground.

The first Monday after leaving the American Casualty Company, I reported to Mr. Tuck at Kay Jewelers and learned that he had already scheduled my attendance at the photo-studio training course in Washington, DC, from Wednesday to Friday of that week.

I assumed that the round-trip would be by bus, but Tuck surprised me with a bus ticket to DC, and an airline ticket for the return journey. Having never been on an airplane, I was thrilled at the prospect and left Reading suitably impressed with this unexpected "perk" associated with my newfound position.

I went into the training seminar concerned about my lack of experience in the field of photography, but it was soon clear that running a Kay studio wouldn't require technical expertise. The camera used was probably a Speed-Graphic, old but reliable. Mounted on a tripod, it came with a black "cloak" which I learned to drape over my head, while focusing the lens and positioning my subject on the back-plate, before taking the picture.

Each studio was equipped with two lights and an "umbrella" which made the lighting process relatively simple, and the developing process itself, was contracted out to an independent photo lab.

Actually, more time was devoted to salesmanship than photography, with great emphasis placed on the art of convincing customers to purchase more photos than they originally thought they wanted, and preferably in the more luxurious and expensive combinations. Unfortunately, earning a living as a salesman had never appealed to me, and before the seminar ended, I was having second thoughts and some misgivings, about my rather hasty career-path change.

Returning to Reading on a Capital Airlines DC-3, was exciting as most first flights into the wide blue yonder tend to be, but less pleasant than I'd expected. Severe turbulence turned the ride into one not unlike those that I'd endured on my various boat trips across the English Channel. In the years that followed, I flew thousands of passenger miles on all types of aircraft, from the Piper-Cub to 747s, but never again did I leave the ground without "Dramamine," always my stomach's best friend!

The Kay Jewelers store in Reading, kicked off its new photo-studio addition, with newspaper advertising and a mailing to its customers of record, inviting them in for a free photograph, and for about two months, I had all the business I could handle.

I enjoyed meeting new people on a daily basis, although I must confess that I much preferred working with adults than children. I tried hard to pose and photograph everyone to their satisfaction, and most of the time, I think I succeeded. When it came to that part of the job that I wasn't keen on, namely convincing customers that they wanted more than the "free" photo, I used a soft-sell approach, and based on my sales, I think I did pretty well, but unfortunately, not well enough for Mr. Tuck.

This was a guy, who when he knew I had customers in to see their proofs and make their selections, he'd barge into the studio and listen to my sales presentation, and if he thought I wasn't pushing hard enough, he'd butt-in and make a pitch of his own.

Quite a few customers were turned off by his intrusive hard-sell tactics and responded accordingly, then after they'd left, he would chew me out for not selling more aggressively. Given my somewhat combative personality, after several of those sessions, I knew instinctively that he and I were on a collision course.

What really soured me on Tuck, was an incident involving his wife, who would often stop by the store to see him, if she was shopping in the vicinity. On one of those visits, seeing that I wasn't busy, she asked whether I'd mind picking up her dry-cleaning from a nearby store. I was glad for a break in the monotony, and off I went.

When I returned with the dry-cleaning, Mrs. Tuck was talking with her husband. As she thanked me, she slipped a 50cent piece into my hand, but in a flash, Tuck grabbed it back and gave me a quarter instead, all the while berating his wife in front of me and the other store employees, for being overly generous!

I'd been only too happy to run the errand, and certainly wasn't expecting a gratuity, but his boorish behavior so ticked me off, that I slapped the quarter down onto the jewelry counter-top, and walked back to my studio, convinced that I didn't want to work for "Mr. Cheap" any longer.

CHAPTER 23

A Promise Kept, A Relationship Resolved

By September, four months after its opening, the Kay photo-studio business was down to a handful of customers a week. I was spending most of my time bored to tears, waiting for the next customer, so I decided to look for another job. This time however, I only focused on the Male Help Wanted advertisements!

Having burned my bridges at ACCO, I was hesitant to re-apply there. Another retail store position didn't interest me, and I couldn't find a job that called for the qualifications and experience, that I had gained while working in England. With no new career opportunities on the horizon, I concluded that it was probably an opportune moment to visit June Willard, the girl I'd met in London in July, 1946, while on my last Army furlough.

When we parted, I made a somewhat rash promise. I told June I'd visit England after my discharge, with the idea that we'd spend enough time together, to see if our initial mutual attraction was still alive, and worth pursuing, and in that context, we had faithfully corresponded with each other, for more than a year.

I decided to keep my job at the studio for another month, while making plans to leave for England in October. I had a friend who worked at a travel-bureau in Reading, and he filled me in on my travel options, and made the necessary arrangements.

In 1947, a round-trip by air between New York and London, cost close to $800, which was much more expensive than ocean travel. There were many great ocean-liners to choose from, and having crossed the mighty Atlantic a year earlier on a Victory ship, I was determined to make my next trip on a larger more sea-worthy vessel, and under less crowded conditions.

To this end, I booked passage from New York to Southampton on the 83,000 ton "Queen Elizabeth," and for the return voyage, on her sister ship the 80,000 ton "Queen Mary." The round-trip Tourist Class accommodations cost $300.00. While this entailed sharing a cabin with three other guys, that was a great improvement over the troopship's cargo-hold, where we were packed like sardines.

Both "Queens" had illustrious World War II records. Between them, they carried 24% of the total number of American troops that were transported to Europe. Given their high speed, they always traveled alone, never as a part of a convoy, and by the war's end, they had made a combined total of 37 Atlantic crossings.

In late September, I gave notice to Mr. Tuck, and was surprised that he seemed almost relieved that I was leaving. I found out later, that at the time I quit, the Kay Company was planning to close the studio anyway, because the revenue it was generating, did not measure up to their expectations.

On October 3, 1947, a year after my return to the States, the "Queen Elizabeth" steamed slowly out of New York's harbor and headed for Southampton. At her usual speed with ideal weather the crossing took less than five days, but like many passengers, I spent the first 36 hours in my cabin, once again suffering through the misery of sea-sickness.

Few of the great ocean-liners of that era, were fitted with stabilizers, and as the QE ploughed through the massive Atlantic swells, she simultaneously rolled from side to side and pitched up and down, a stomach-churning ride that few land-lubbers could tolerate, without predictably unpleasant consequences.

However, once I got my sea-legs, my appetite and will to live returned, and I began to enjoy the liner's first-class dining pleasures, its evening dances and other shipboard attractions.

We docked in Southampton on schedule, and within hours I was in London, and reunited with my parents and sisters. I'd shared with them my travel plans, so they were expecting me, but for some reason, I'd decided not to tell June and surprise her instead.

The next day, I took a bus to Chingford and showed up unannounced at June's house, much to the surprise of her mother who had never before laid eyes on me. She rose to the occasion though, and when June came home from work and walked into the kitchen, there was her American pen-pal chatting with her Mom, over a pot of tea!

Poor June was clearly unnerved by my unexpected appearance, and I felt really bad at having surprised her in that fashion, but after the initial shock had passed and we'd had chance to chat, I knew I'd been forgiven, and that she was glad to see me.

That evening, we took a bus out to a pub called the "Queen Elizabeth" which was located on the outskirts of Chingford, close to Epping Forest. It was one I wanted to visit again, because when I worked at the CMC plant, I'd spend many Saturday nights dancing in its adjacent ball-room. Unfortunately, that wartime mecca had long since closed, but the pub was as warm and inviting as ever, and we settled for a quiet drink and a long talk.

All too soon, I had to take June home, then rush to catch the first of two buses that would get me from Chingford to Finsbury Park, from where I walked the last mile home. Over the next four weeks, we saw each other at least twice a week, and each visit required that I ride four buses and walk two miles. Boy! how I missed my old Plymouth, blue exhaust-smoke, notwithstanding!

During one of my visits with June, I phoned Phyllis Greenleaf my friend from the CMC, who also lived in Chingford, and learned that she had been recently married to Eddie Gillam, her longtime boyfriend. She was anxious for me to meet her new husband, and invited June and I to join them that Saturday evening, along with several other young couples, at a neighborhood pub.

It was great to see Phyllis again and to meet Eddie, who told me about the shore-leave he'd spent in Boston, during his wartime Royal Navy service. I enjoyed the evening and assumed June did too, and when Phyllis and Eddie invited us to go dancing with them the following week, I accepted.

London's public dance-halls and orchestras with their big-band sound, were still very popular, and June and I went dancing with the Gillams several times, before I realized that she wasn't having as much fun as I was, on these evening get-togethers.

She finally confessed that dancing was not one of her favorite pastimes, nor was she fond of multiple couple dating, so from then on whatever we did, it was usually just the two of us. One advantage of this, was that it gave us more time to concentrate on each other, which after all, was the main reason for my trip.

It took about two months before we both realized and finally acknowledged the fact, that we just weren't meant to spend our lives together. Central to that conclusion was June's certainty that she didn't want to leave England, and my equally adamant conviction that I never again wanted to live outside of the USA.

Once we'd laid our cards on the table in this regard, it made sense to end the relationship, and in early December we stopped seeing each other. June shed some tears at the break-up, but we parted as friends with no recriminations, and as was mutually agreed, we never communicated or saw each other again.

I was twenty years old, had no job waiting for me in Reading, my limited savings were almost depleted by the cost of my trip, so I was actually relieved by the turn of events. On the down-side, I wasn't due to return home until the following month. Obviously, had I know June and I would part so soon, I would have planned for a shorter visit.

Over the next six weeks, I hung-out with Sparkes and other old friends from my school days, visited various relatives, had a date with Doreen, a friend of my sister Mary, and traveled to Chingford to see Phyllis and Eddie, several more times.

Even though the war had been over for two years, I was shocked to see that little had changed in England. Food rationing remained in effect, and many products and necessities were still in short supply or unobtainable. In an effort to rebuild Britain's war-shattered economy, the government had ordered companies to concentrate on manufacturing products for export only, thus enabling the country to earn much needed dollars.

As a visitor to England for an extended stay, I was issued a food ration book. This was a great help to my Mom, as was the parcel of canned food items that came in the mail just before Christmas, from my good friends in Reading, Syd and Jeanne Reber.

The week before I was scheduled to return home, my eighteen year old sister Mary was diagnosed with TB, which came as a big shock to the whole family. Fortunately, after four months of bed-rest and treatment, the disease was declared arrested and after another month's stay in a convalescent home, she was able to return home and begin work again, on a part-time basis.

Before she became ill, Mary was seeing a Canadian sailor she met in London, who was serving on an aircraft carrier, then based in Scotland. They were married in late 1948, and when her husband's ship returned to its home-port of Halifax, Nova Scotia, she followed and began a new life in Canada.

When it was time for me to leave for home, I'm sure I never thought that it would be sixteen years before I'd again see my Dad and step-Mom, or that six years would pass before I'd see Mary, when she drove to Reading for a brief visit.

Peg and I however, were soon re-united. After her wartime service in the British Army, she had re-claimed her American citizenship, and in April 1948, she returned to the States, to stay with me in Reading. In 1950, she moved to Philadelphia, and since then we've lived close enough to each other, to get together regularly.

At noon on January 28, 1948, the "Queen Mary" steamed slowly out of Southampton into the English Channel, where she picked up speed and headed on a westerly course into the Atlantic. It was a cold, windy and overcast day, and that evening, we were informed by the ship's captain, that some "unpleasant" weather lay ahead. What a typically British understatement that turned out to be!

I still have in my possession, a treasured, albeit faded copy of an abstract of the ship's log, which describes the weather that we encountered on that memorable voyage, as follows.

"Jan. 29, moderate gale, rough sea, heavy swell. Jan. 30 and 31, whole gale, very rough sea, precipitous swell. Feb 1, storm, very rough sea, precipitous confused swell. Feb. 2, gale moderating to light breeze, heavy swell. Feb. 3 and 4, moderate variable breeze, slight sea and swell."

The QM could travel at more than 30 knots, and in good weather cover the 2,132 nautical miles from Southampton to New York, in less than five days. We spent six days, seventeen hours and 43 minutes at sea, averaging 19 knots. On January 31, at the height of the storm, the ship progressed a mere 276 nautical miles!

Needless to say, during the first two days at sea, there were many empty tables in the dining rooms. When I finally felt well enough to sample my first breakfast, I'd no sooner taken my seat, when a woman at another table jumped up and vomited, and the sound of her stomach contents hitting the floor, sent me and a half-dozen other poor souls, high-tailing it back to our cabins!

Moving from one deck to another, was a real challenge. I'd be walking up a flight of stairs, when suddenly the ship would tilt so dramatically that gravity-wise, the "up" stairs would become "down" stairs, and without a firm grip on the hand-rail, I'd have ended up flat on my face.

Riding an elevator was a weird experience, too. When the ship heeled over, all fixed objects leaned in the same direction, but gravity kept an elevator's passengers standing at a different angle from that followed by the moving elevator, and the visual impact of this, would often trigger a bout of vertigo and nausea.

Additionally, at regular intervals throughout the storm, the ship's stern would lift out of a wave-trough, and its four huge propellers would "grab air" momentarily, causing the entire vessel to shudder and vibrate from one end to the other.

Despite all of this, dances were still held each evening in the ship's various ball-rooms. Ropes were set up around the dance-floor perimeters, so that those hardy couples who insisted on fox-trotting no matter what, had something to grab onto if they lost their balance. One moment a couple would be laboring to dance "up-hill," and the next moment they'd be heading helter-skelter "down-hill" instead, a very weird experience indeed.

Passengers were advised not to venture outside on the decks during the storm, but one day I went up to the top deck, and peered out the glassed-in entranceway. I've no idea how high the waves were at that time, but I remember that the ship ploughed into a trough so deep, that I actually caught a glimpse of the ocean, above and beyond its three massive smoke-stacks!

That sight was enough to convince me how lucky I was at that particular moment, not to be in the middle of the Atlantic Ocean, on a vessel smaller than the venerable "Queen Mary."

Finally, on the morning of February 4, 1948, we reached New York harbor where tug-boats greeted us, and eased our massive ship into her berth, without mishap. The weather was cooperating by then, and as I joined hundreds of other passengers on the open decks, I remember still, the emotional tug on my heart that I felt, at that first welcome glimpse of the New York skyline.

I'd spent my childhood in England and was privileged to live there during it's epochal moment in history, immortalized by Winston Churchill as Britain's "finest hour," and yet when I saw Lady Liberty, I knew without a doubt that my heart and soul belonged to the land of my birth, and that now I was truly home!

Fresh From Basic Training. Marburg, Germany
September 1945

"Scotty" McLean and me. Marburg, Germany.
February 1946

Newly Minted Sergeant. Marburg, Germany.
June 1946

With my sister Mary and Aunt Hett.
London, July 1946.

My sisters, Peg and Mary. London 1947.

My father and step-mother. London, 1950.

CHAPTER 24

Business Career Highlights, Community Activities And Major Personal Events, 1948 to 2003

Upon returning to Reading in February 1948, after four months in England visiting family and friends, I had no job and my modest savings were almost depleted. Fortunately, I remained a welcome guest in the Van Sciver home, and somehow I managed to continue to pay for my room and board. Despite my best efforts however, six weeks later, I was still unemployed.

While I was away, Tommy Van Sciver left his job at the local dairy, to work for the Reading Railroad, loading and unloading box-cars. Desperate for a pay-check, I actually considered joining Tommy on the loading-platform, when Fate intervened.

While downtown one day, I ran into Walter Stump, my supervisor during my earlier short-lived stint at the American Casualty Company. When Walter learned that I was unemployed, he urged me to re-apply to ACCO and give the insurance business another chance. He warned however, that having previously walked away from a GI bill sponsored program, my continued elegibility would hinge on the results of an exam administered by the Veterans Administration, aimed at evaluating and measuring my "suitability and educational qualifications" for the position.

I took the exam, and based on the VA's findings that my qualifications were equal to those of a college-freshman, ACCO accepted me into its insurance-trainee program, on April 1, 1948.

Unlike my earlier frustrating experience with the Company, I had no complaints this time around. On my first day, I was assigned as the trainee assistant to the Superintendent of the Rates and Forms Division. He was charged with administering ACCO's obligations under the laws regulating the business of insurance, in the 48 states where the Company was licensed to operate.

In the majority of states, insurance companies were required by statute, to file with the Insurance Departments, all policies and their related endorsements, rates and premiums, and secure their approval, prior to making these products available to the public.

The work was challenging, educational and interesting, and thanks to a boss who provided oversight while pretty much giving me a free hand, I began to learn that specialized end of the business.

In 1950, I married a young woman who'd started work at ACCO a year earlier. Married previously while still in her teens, she had a son David, who was eleven-months old when we met. David's biological father had waived his parental rights as a condition of the divorce, so I was the only Dad that David would ever know, and I proceeded as quickly as possible to legally adopt him, so that he'd have my name, before he started school.

Five years into the job, my boss was transferred to ACCO's Service Office in Springfield, Massachusetts, and I took over as Superintendent of the Division. Three year later, at age 29, I was elected an Assistant Secretary, the youngest person ever to be made an officer, at that point in the Company's history.

I was also appointed an Associate Editor of ACCO's employee magazine "The Tom-Tom." One of my early tasks was to write a series of articles on the Company's major operating departments. This gave me a firsthand, in-depth look at a number of specialized insurance functions, and provided me with knowledge and information that would prove invaluable, as my career progressed.

During this period, my family grew to include a daughter Nancy, born in 1954, and another son James, born in 1959.

In 1962, Republican Bill Scranton was elected Pennsylvania's Governor, and after he took office, scores of Democrat political appointees left the State Capital, to be replaced by Republicans. In this regard, I was approached by my county Republican leaders, to accept an Insurance Department appointment in Harrisburg, as a Deputy Insurance Commissioner. I'd been quite active in the GOP, serving as the Republican Committeeman for Reading's 15th Ward, Chairman of Berks County Young Republicans and as a member of the Berks County Republican Senior Committee.

This was a opportunity and a challenge that I couldn't resist! I knew that experience as a State regulator would enhance my insurance career, and Harold Evans, ACCO's President, who had also served as a Deputy Insurance Commissioner years earlier, called me to his office, and encouraged me to accept the post.

Regretfully, my marriage of 13 years had by then deteriorated to the point where our differences were irreconcilable, and we agreed to a divorce. However, I was adamant that this not occur before Jim our youngest child was 10 years old, so that I could continue to exert my paternal influence, during his formative years.

Living under the same roof as father and mother, but not as husband and wife was difficult, but for the most part, until the time that my wife instigated divorce proceedings and I moved out of the house, we accomplished that with few displays of acrimony in front of our children.

I left ACCO in November 1963, and each day for the next two years, I drove a round-trip of 124 miles between Reading and Harrisburg. It was a long and tiresome commute, but the job was well worth it. I gained a whole new perspective on the business of insurance, and enjoyed my duties as a regulator, except that working with my new boss, Insurance Commissioner Audrey Kelly, seemed at times, to be a cruel and unusual punishment!

Audrey is long deceased and deserves to rest in peace, so I'll not comment on some of the bizarre decisions I thought she made as Commissioner, which so often put us at odds professionally.

In the summer of 1965, Pennsylvania's Commonwealth Secretary Craig Truax, asked me to serve as the State Director of the Pennsylvania Teen-Age Republicans (TARS). The TAR clubs then active throughout Pennsylvania, needed some centralized adult direction, and I took on the task even though the requisite statewide visitations, took quite a bit of my personal time.

Nevertheless, I was glad that I'd accepted the assignment, because in that capacity, I was privileged to meet one of my wartime heroes and our 34th President, Dwight D. Eisenhower. Four years out of the White House, "Ike" was the featured speaker at the 1965 TAR Convention in State College, PA.

"Ike" and me. State College, PA
August 1965

Two years of Audrey Kelly's brand of leadership was enough, and when offered the job as Marketing Vice-President for the Volkswagen Insurance Company in St. Louis, Missouri, I resigned my Department position in November 1965, and headed west.

By then, my eldest son David was a senior at Reading High School, and given the state of my marriage, I made the decision to leave the family in Reading, at least until he graduated, and fly home as often as I could. Being away from my kids for weeks on end was tough, but I had permission to use VICO's long-distance line to call them every day, which was good for them and me.

Unfortunately, my career move to St. Louis, was one that I soon came to regret. VICO wrote automobile insurance only, and after my two years in Harrisburg, where I was routinely involved in top-level regulatory decisions and activities covering all lines of insurance, my new responsibilities were comparatively narrow in scope, and much less interesting or challenging.

Before long, having concluded that the VICO job, as the British would say, "wasn't my cup of tea," I started to look for an opportunity to return to Pennsylvania, and that presented itself in November 1966, when Bill Scranton was succeeded by Ray Shafer, another Republican governor.

In selecting his cabinet, Shafer replaced Audrey Kelly as Insurance Commissioner, with David Maxwell, a Philadelphia attorney. This action boded well for the Insurance Department, and when in January 1967, through the good graces and political clout of my friend Dan Huyett, Chairman of the Berks County Republican Party, I was offered the Department's second highest post, that of Chief Deputy Insurance Commissioner, I was elated.

David Maxwell, a Harvard Law School graduate, was a gentleman and a scholar, with a polished manner and a wry sense of humor not unlike my own, and from our first encounter, he and I got along famously. As Commissioner, he was charged by Governor Shafer with revitalizing the Insurance Department, and developing a package of consumer-friendly legislation, aimed at bringing some necessary reform to the insurance business in Pennsylvania.

To this end, he put together an enthusiastic team of young management level employees with whom I was privileged to serve, a team which over time, became known as "Maxwell's Army."

Additionally, as Chief Deputy, I was charged with most of the Department's everyday administrative responsibilities, including providing direction and oversight to the Commissioner's goal of upgrading the Department's career employee positions. Maxwell gave me pretty much a free rein in that regard, quite a different approach from the micro-managing I'd endured under Audrey Kelly.

From August 20 to November 6, 1968, Maxwell was granted leave to work in Washington, DC on behalf of Richard Nixon's campaign for the Office of President, and during his absence, I was appointed Acting Insurance Commissioner.

In May, 1969, Maxwell appointed me Chairman of a 16 man ad hoc committee of medical, legal and insurance representatives charged with finding a long-term solution to Pennsylvania's mounting medical malpractice insurance crisis. My Interim Report before leaving the Department on the Committee's activities, was widely circulated in medical, legal and insurance circles.

In August 1969, I married a beautiful young woman who, despite the eighteen year difference in our ages, was clearly meant to be my partner for life. We'd met a year earlier in Lebanon, PA, at a meeting of the Young Republicans of Pennsylvania organization. No longer an active YR member, I attended reluctantly, only because I knew that some other "oldtimers" would be there for a re-union.

Sally, my wife to be, was a Pittsburgh native who also attended that meeting with some reluctance, having worked an overnight nursing shift at Allegheny General Hospital, before being picked up by a friend and driven to Lebanon.

Clearly, Fate had a hand in dispatching us from opposite ends of the state, to a meeting in a Lebanon hotel, and then guiding us to the hospitality suite of Don Bair, a Republican member of the Pennsylvania House of Representatives from Pittsburgh, who I knew from my Chief Deputy activities. Don was also a friend of Sally's parents, and it was he who did the honors of introducing us.

The chemistry between Sally and I was instant and mutual, and after more than 33 years of marriage, we both agree it remains as strong as ever. In 1970 we were blessed with the birth of our only child, a daughter, Vivian Lee.

In the Fall of 1969, Commissioner Maxwell left Harrisburg to accept a political appointment in Washington, DC, and George Reed, the Department's General Counsel, was Governor Shafer's choice as his replacement. Reed, like Maxwell, was exceptionally qualified for the job, and an all-round great guy to work with.

In November, 1970, Democrat Milton Shapp was elected Governor of Pennsylvania. Like many other Republican appointees in Harrisburg who saw the political handwriting on the wall, I resigned my post as Chief Deputy, and began searching for employment elsewhere.

As a result of my medical malpractice insurance activities, I was hired in January 1971, by Parker and Company, a Philadelphia insurance brokerage, which several years later, was merged into the Frank B. Hall organization, a national insurance brokerage firm.

As a Senior Vice President, my role was that of Administrator of the professional liability insurance program sponsored by the Pennsylvania Medical Society (PMS), and underwritten by the Argonaut Insurance Company. While working in that capacity, I was recruited to serve with a number of different groups, all of which were involved at that time, in seeking a solution to the ongoing nationwide medical malpractice insurance crisis.

In December 1971, I was appointed to the U.S. Department of Health, Education and Welfare's 11-man Insurance Issues Advisory Panel, a part of HEW's Commission on Medical Malpractice, which had been created at the specific direction of President Nixon, to probe on a countrywide basis, the problems allegedly associated with medical malpractice claims.

From 1971 to 1975, I served on the National Association of Insurance Commissioners Industry Advisory Committee on Medical Malpractice, and also as the Insurance Consultant to the Joint Committee on Professional Liability of the Pennsylvania Medical Society and the Pennsylvania Bar Association.

In December 1975, the Pennsylvania Insurance Commissioner appointed me a member of the Ad Hoc Industry Committee on Medical Malpractice, charged with the formation of the Pennsylvania Joint Underwriting Association, a newly-legislated insurance entity.

By 1975, Argonaut no longer wanted to underwrite the PMS insurance program, forcing the Society, like other state medical associations at that time, to seriously consider forming and capitalizing a medical malpractice insurance company of its own.

As the Society's insurance consultant, I was charged with preparing a report on the feasibility of such action. At a July 1976, special meeting of the PMS House of Delegates, the report was accepted and approval given to the Society, to form and capitalize its own stock insurance company.

As author of the feasibility study, I guess it could be argued that I had been present at the new company's gestation, and as I followed its formation and capitalization, the more certain I became that I wanted to serve as its first President. In 1977, when the PMS engaged an

Executive Search firm to locate a suitable candidate, I threw my hat into the ring.

Twenty other guys applied for the position, all with impressive credentials and several with law degrees. My edge was my experience, a 30 year career uniquely diversified between the company, broker and regulatory sectors of the insurance industry, and in October, 1978, the PMS Board elected me to serve as the first President and Chief Operating Officer of the Pennsylvania Medical Society Liability Insurance Company (PMSLIC).

While my Insurance Department medical malpractice insurance related activities, and my years at Frank B. Hall as the Administrator of the PMS/Argonaut program, no doubt played an important part of the Society's choice, I'm sure it was also influenced by the fact that out of all the applicants they had to choose from, I was the "devil they knew!"

At the time that I was hired, I was PMSLIC's only employee. My marching orders were simple, put together a management team and support staff, and have the Company fully operational in six months. That I actually met that deadline, was due in part to the fact that for the previous six months, apparently imbued with unbounded optimism, I'd carried around a lined pad, in which I recorded my every thought, as to what I'd need to do to get an insurance company off the ground and running, from scratch.

Without a doubt, my role as a company President and COO, was the most challenging and personally satisfying experience of my insurance career, perhaps because it was always my passion, never just a job. While President, I was also privileged to serve on the Board of The Insurance Federation of Pennsylvania, including a term as its Chairman, and as a Trustee of the Physicians Insurers Association of America, a national association of physician-owned medical malpractice insurance companies.

When I retired in August 1991, PMSLIC was the premier provider of physicians professional liability insurance in Pennsylvania, and I left the Company confident that it would continue to prosper, thanks to a management team and support staff, second to none.

My introduction to volunteer civic and community activism, occurred in 1953 when a friend took me to a meeting of the Reading Junior Chamber of Commerce. The "Jaycees" at that time, was an international organization for men only, from ages 21 to 36. Its mission was to provide leadership opportunities and participation in civic affairs, during a man's early adult years, when such activities were generally considered to be the province of the community's older generation.

For as long as I can remember, I was always more keen on leading than following, and in the Reading Jaycees, there was always a new, untried project to be tackled, or an open leadership position to be filled, and I was soon hooked!

I remained an active Jaycee until required to leave at age 36, receiving numerous honors and commendations, including the "Key-Man" Award, the only member in Reading Jaycee history to twice receive that designation. I also served in all the officer slots, including President, and in that capacity I made club history again, as the only one to ever face impeachment proceedings!

The year was 1957, and like most Americans, I'd been shocked and saddened by the fact that it was necessary for President Eisenhower to send units of the 101st Airborne Division into Little Rock, Arkansas, to protect black children from white mobs, as the children attempted to enter previously all-white schools, under a Federal court-issued desegregation edict.

After that incident, I thought it appropriate for me to do something positive for the burgeoning civil rights movement, and on the night I was elected President, I announced that one of my goals was to open up the Reading Jaycees to African-American men. At the time, all the Club's members were white, and to the best of my knowledge, no other Reading civic club had black members.

This announcement brought a heated reaction from one member who said if I did this, he would introduce a resolution at the next meeting calling for my impeachment and removal from office. He followed through on his threat, but I'm glad to say that after considerable debate, a majority of those members present voted against my being impeached. It was a secret ballot, so I never did know whether I squeaked through, or won by a landslide!

At the following meeting, I introduced and proposed for membership, William Miller, an African-American self-employed barber, whose application the Board subsequently approved. I then asked Bill to serve as Chairman of the 1957 Jaycee Christmas Parade, in which most of Reading's churches participated.

The Parade's theme was "Let's Put Christ Back Into Christmas," and I gambled that the person charged with organizing and directing such a project, regardless of the color of his skin, would be given the respect and cooperation he deserved.

Bill did an excellent job as Parade Chairman, and during his time as a Jaycee, he proposed several acquaintances for membership, and some years later, one of those young men was elected as the first African-American President of the Reading Jaycees.

At the end of my year as President, I received the Pennsylvania Jaycees' "Outstanding Local Chapter President" Award in Reading's population division, which in 1957, I believe included the cities of Allentown, Erie and Harrisburg. In 1958, I was elected a Regional Vice President of the Pennsylvania Jaycees, and in that capacity I served for a year, as state liaison to the ten local Jaycee chapters then active in Berks County.

Looking back at my ten years as a Jaycee, I'm convinced that the business success that I later enjoyed, was due in no small part, to the leadership and personal development opportunities, then central to the Jaycee mission. As a member, I was able to accept the challenge of leadership, and prove myself worthy in a venue where success or failure carried no personal or business penalty, and participate in a hands-on learning and maturing experience, that ultimately proved to be valuable to my insurance career.

My Jaycee experience also introduced me to the personal satisfaction that comes from voluntary civic and community service, which over many years, has given me so much pleasure.

Some of my activities in addition to those that were related to my church affiliation, included serving on the Boards of the Berks County Children's Aid Society and Council of Social Agencies, as President of the Rotary Club of Harrisburg, President and Trustee of the Americans for the Competitive Enterprise System (ACES), President of the Hershey Ronald McDonald House, Director of the Capital

Health System Services (Harrisburg Hospital) and currently, as a Director of the Pinnacle Health Foundation.

I've been privileged over the years, to meet and work with an army of caring souls, whose generous and unselfish commitment to community needs, continues to be an inspiration to continue to serve, wherever my time and talents can make a positive contribution.

Proud father, with Vivian and future husband Christopher, and
David's wife Polly. Seated:Nancy, James with wife Rosemary and
David.
My PMSLIC Retirement Dinner, September 1991

Sally and me.
September 1991

A. John Smither

EPILOGUE

More than 56 years have passed since I returned to the United States after an 18 year absence. Thanks to the generosity and kindness of a Pennsylvania family who took me into their hearts, sight unseen, Reading, Pennsylvania became my adopted hometown.

Fresh out of the Army, I was 19 years old with $500 to my name, and an education received in England that had been seriously disrupted and shortened by wartime conditions, culminating in my so-called "graduation," four months before my fifteenth birthday.

Whatever I've been able to accomplish in my insurance career and community and civic activities, is certainly a testament to this great country of ours. Only in America would I have been afforded so many opportunities to prove my personal potential, and rise above the expected achievement level usually attributed to someone with a limited formal education.

As a grateful beneficiary of so many "only in America" opportunities, I owe much to those in business, politics and medicine, who managed to see beyond my education, and whose faith, trust and confidence in my talents and acquired abilities was so important to my personal life and business career.

Whenever I'd visit my father in London, up until his death in 1986, at age ninety, he still loved to talk about his life in Cleveland, Ohio from 1920 to 1928, and he'd always use the word "opportunity" to describe the major difference, in his opinion, between America and his native England.

He believed that in America, the opportunity to succeed (or fail) was available to everyone, as he put it, "even for working-class blokes like me," whereas in the England he knew, it usually came to only those from the "right" schools with the "proper" accents.

Major changes in American society have occurred since my Dad lived here, and for that matter, much has changed since 1946 when I returned, but America as the great land of opportunity remains unchanged and as enduring as ever, a beacon brighter and with more promise, than can be found anywhere else in the world.

People of every color and ethnic heritage, are still flocking to America, drawn by our unique promise of opportunity. Most of them, neither want nor expect anything more, and through faith, perseverance, hard work and a little luck, they too will prove the continued reality of the American dream, just as I did.

May God Bless America, my home sweet home, now and always.

A. John Smither
Mechanicsburg, PA
February, 2003

BIBLIOGRAPHY

Backs To The Wall...Leonard Mosely
Blitz Over Britain...Edwin Webb and John Duncan
Blood, Tears And Folly...Len Deighton
Bombers and Mash...Raynes Minns
Downfall...Richard B. Frank
Evacuees...Mike Brown
Five Days In London-May 1940...John Lukacs
Flags Of Our Fathers...James Bradley with Ron Powers
Flying Bomb...Peter G. Cooksley
Follow Me And Die...Cecil B. Currey
History of World War I...American Heritage Publishing Co.
Lichfield...Jack Gieck
No Time To Wave Goodbye...Ben Wicks
The Champagne Campaign...Robert H. Adleman and
        Colonel John Walton
The Eagles' War...Vern Haugland
The Home Front...Susan Briggs
The Last Nazis...Perry Biddescombe
The London Blitz...David Johnson
The US Army In World War II...Mark R. Henry
World War II Almanac...Robert Goralski

A. John Smither

About the Author

John Smither was educated in London, England. He entered the insurance business in 1948 as an Underwriter-Trainee, and retired in 1991 as a company President and Chief Operating Officer. He currently resides in Mechanicsburg, Pennsylvania with his wife Sally, a retired registered nurse, and their two cats.

Printed in the United States
35200LVS00005B/190-213

9 781410 742179